JUST GIVE ME THE ANSWER$

EXPERT ADVISORS ADDRESS YOUR MOST PRESSING FINANCIAL QUESTIONS

SHERYL GARRETT, CFP®

with Marie Swift and The Garrett Planning Network

Vice President and Publisher: Cynthia A. Zigmund
Acquisitions Editor: Mary B. Good
Senior Project Editor: Trey Thoelcke
Interior Design: Lucy Jenkins
Cover Design: Design Solutions
Typesetting: the dotted i
Photo Credit: T. Michael Stanley

Published by Dearborn Trade Publishing
A Kaplan Professional Company

Printed in the United States of America

04 05 06 10 9 8 7 6 5 4 3 2 1

Library of Congress Cataloging-in-Publication Data

Garrett, Sheryl.
Just give me the answer$: expert advisors address your most pressing financial questions / Sheryl Garrett with Marie Swift and The Garrett Planning Network.
p. cm.
Includes index.
ISBN 0-7931-8339-1
1. Finance, Personal. I. Swift, Marie. II. Garrett Planning Network. III. Title.
HG179.G37 2004
332.024—dc22

2004000083

Dearborn Trade books are available at special quantity discounts to use for sales promotions, employee premiums, or educational purposes. Please call our Special Sales Department to order or for more information at 800-245-2665, e-mail trade@dearborn.com, or write to Dearborn Trade Publishing, 30 South Wacker Drive, Suite 2500, Chicago, IL 60606-7481.

DEDICATION

To the countless individuals who have had a hard time finding competent, objective financial planning services and advice when they needed it and on their terms.

Contents

Today, honest, trustworthy, and hardworking Americans like yourself are in need of financial help. But where can you go? Whom can you trust?

I remember advising Janet and Jim on the *Oprah Winfrey Show.* Janet's eyes opened wide as I explained to her how small changes could make a big difference in her financial future. And Janet then took some actions based on that guidance. But what if that guidance wasn't trustworthy? What if I were telling Janet to buy some financial product solely because I was making money from it?

The mission of my organization, Family Financial Network (http://www.familyfn.com), is to help hard-working Americans fulfill their financial dreams. Objective, conflict-free financial planning and advice for working Americans is now within reach. When everyday Americans and do-it-yourselfers need assistance from a professional advisor, they can seek out an advisor who will work with them on their terms. And now, they can turn to *Just Give Me the Answer$.* By following simple tips, the reader can learn how to save hundreds to thousands of hard-earned dollars. Everyone should own his or her own copy of this invaluable resource.

Just Give Me the Answer$ is brought to you by someone folks can trust. Sheryl Garrett was named one of the 25 Most Influential People in the financial planning industry by *Investment Advisor* magazine in May of 2003, along other such notables as Alan Greenspan, Charles Schwab, John Bogle, and Noble Prize winner William Sharp, and for good reason. She has become a pioneer in the financial planning industry. She and her network of advisors share one very powerful core principal: that all people should have access to competent, objective financial advice when they need it. The advisor should have only the client's interests at heart and should not be receiving commissions or other payments for "selling" products that are not in the client's best interests. The Garrett Planning Network members seek to empower their clients to make smarter financial decisions through this book and via financial literacy programs, community education, and one-on-one financial coaching. These highly skilled financial advisors work with their clients on a fee-only, hourly, and as-needed basis to evaluate and implement the strategies outlined in this book. Family Financial Network will soon be aligning with the Garrett Planning Network to ensure that objective, conflict-free financial advice is available to all Americans.

Now, Sheryl Garrett, with Marie Swift and The Garrett Planning Network, have developed a breakthrough guide to financial matters. They have expertly compiled *Just Give Me the Answer$*, a reference guidebook of their most frequently heard questions, and they provide detailed responses, answers, and direction for each of the 134 tips contained within these pages. You now have a resource that you can rely on time and time again to get answers to your financial questions from more than 75 experts.

Most people are not interested in reading a whole book about personal finance to gain a few grains of wisdom that apply to their situation. After all, we're all too busy for that. Yet, money management decisions face every person in society, often on a daily basis. We want answers when we need them. *Just Give Me the Answer$* does just what it says.

Sheryl Garrett has delivered the quintessential personal finance reference guidebook. It's easy to use, straight to the point, and, most importantly, written by experts you can trust.

Jennifer Openshaw
CEO, Family Financial Network
Host of Public Television's, *What's Your Net Worth?*
http://www.familyfn.com

Preface

This book is your personal *money guide resource.* It answers, in plain English, your most pressing financial questions. The result of an eighteen-month-long collaborative effort, it reflects the expertise and insights of 75 of the nation's brightest financial planners. All the contributors are members of The Garrett Planning Network, the nation's premier group of independent, hourly as-needed, fee-only financial planning professionals.

Founded in 2000, The Garrett Planning Network and its members seek to empower their clients—and now you—to make smarter financial decisions. This book is designed to provide you with as much professional guidance as possible without knowing your personal circumstances.

Just Give Me the Answer$ not only offers valuable tips on how to manage your personal financial affairs better but also satisfies one of the primary aims of The Garrett Planning Network: to continually raise public awareness of the need for and the benefits of competent, objective financial advice.

HOW THIS BOOK BECAME A REALITY

This book began as a nexus of ideas. In the 1990s, two friends and colleagues, Randy Gardner and Julie Welch, both Certified Financial Planner™ professionals and Certified Public Accountants, began collaborating on a valuable money guide, *101 Tax Saving Ideas* (Wealth Builders Press, 2002). The book, now in its sixth edition, is so well done that we thought readers also would like a book containing 101 money management tips.

So, in summer 2002, more than 100 financial planners gathered at our national conference to brainstorm ideas for the content of *101 Money Management Tips.* Task forces and writing teams formed, and research began. As you read this book, you sometimes will see two or more people as contributors of a specific tip. These financial professionals teamed to produce the very best advice for you. Even if just one contributor is named, a team of peer reviewers (other financial planning professionals) also checked and rechecked facts.

This book is the culmination of our collective ideas and contributions, gathered and refined over more than a year and expertly blended and polished by

Marie Swift, our head editor and project leader. Sheryl Garrett, CFP®, who according to *Investment Advisor* magazine is one of the most influential people in financial planning today, is responsible for the initial concept, execution, and final review. This book—and The Garrett Planning Network—carries her name and seal of approval.

This *money resource guide* is in question-and-answer format because, as practicing financial planners, we hear many of the same questions time and time again from our clients and from people we come into contact with. If we can provide guidance in book format and offer additional resources for learning, we feel that we are providing something that's missing for many readers.

We intended originally to self-publish the book as *101 Money Management Tips,* but thanks to Dearborn Trade Publishing's interest and support, we now offer you *Just Give Me the Answer$.*

HOW TO USE THIS MONEY RESOURCE GUIDE

Most people don't have the time or interest to develop a thorough, current knowledge of all the issues in this book. To save you money and provide a sound resource, we have included answers to some of the most pressing financial questions we hear.

The flip side of saving you money is saving you time. You don't need to read this book cover to cover; instead, you can focus on what's important to you *now.* If you have a specific question like, "Should I refinance?" for example, or want an overview of a specific topic like asset allocation, or need a thorough understanding of a subject like retirement planning, turn to the Table of Contents or Index to find what you need. Consider this book your reference guide to personal finance. Below is a closer look at some sample questions you might have and how to find the answer in this book:

- *To find answers to a specific question.* I'm getting ready to buy a new car. Would I be better off taking the 0 percent financing or the $2,500 cashback offer? Turn to the index and locate a tip that addresses the issues involved. You will learn quickly how to calculate the financial ramifications. Making the right decision could save you hundreds of dollars.
- *To get answers to more involved decisions.* I'm getting ready to retire. What do I need to know to make the best decisions? There are dozens of issues to consider. Turn to Chapter 5 on retirement planning and quickly review all the tips. Many will apply to your situation, and some may refer you to another tip. For instance, if you have a question on how and when to take a retirement plan distribution, the answer is in the Retirement Planning

chapter, while the income tax implications of your decision are covered in the Tax Issues chapter.

- *When you need help on a topic but don't know where to start.* I want to send my kids to college. My children are ages 5, 9, and 16. What should I be doing now to prepare? Read all of Chapter 4 on education funding. It offers advice on the best ways to save for your younger children's education, as well as information on current tax credits available, how to maximize financial aid opportunities, and tips on managing your cash flow.
- *When you want a crash course on all the major issues affecting your personal financial life.* I'm midcareer but haven't paid much attention to my personal finances. I just turned 40, and a bell went off in my head. I need a comprehensive cram course on financial planning. Where should I begin?" Read the whole book cover to cover.

HOW TO LEARN MORE ABOUT THE CONTRIBUTORS

More information on each of the book's contributors is given at the back of the book. For additional help or clarification, or if you want to offer feedback, feel free to contact any of the contributors directly or through The Garrett Planning Network headquarters via http://www.GarrettPlanningNetwork.com.

This is your personal financial answer book. Use it, and you will become wiser and richer for your effort. Planning pays off.

ACKNOWLEDGMENTS

This book is the product of a collaborative effort of 75 financial planning professionals, all of whom are members of The Garrett Planning Network, Inc. From brainstorming the most pressing financial questions they hear repeatedly from their clients to researching information, contributing content, and proofing portions of the book, these dedicated professionals have given their time and insights in the hope that this book will directly benefit you.

I am especially grateful to those who went above and beyond the already high standard of participation. Randy Gardner provided thoughtful direction, leadership and insight; he also helped co-edit the book. Our *Chapter Champions,* as they were dubbed along the way, spent a considerable amount of time checking and rechecking facts and adding additional perspectives. Thank you Brad Bond, John Carrig, Rosie Danielson, Kathleen Dollard, and Colleen Miller.

Additional thanks go to the research and proofing team: Jim Blankenship, Bruce Brinkman, Eva Brodzik, Tim Brown, Deidra Fulton, Mary Gibson, Steven

Lyddon, Martin Mesecke, Glenda Moehlenpah, Jim Pasztor, Pauline Price, Bill Rodau, Todd Shepherd, Brenda Sherbine, William Swift, and Noreen Whalen. Please accept my heartfelt thanks if you helped with proofing the book galley or provided other assistance near the end of the project. (Your names may not appear in this acknowledgements section, but you know who you are.)

I also wish to thank my staff. Eva Brodzik, Jamie Breeden, Andrea Poisner, and Justin Nichols: It is because of your enthusiastic and steadfast support, that I am able to carry the torch. Thank you for embracing our Network's mission to the fullest extent possible. Truly, you are the best team I could hope for.

I also wish to thank Cynthia Zigmund, publisher, and Mary B. Good, acquisitions editor, at Dearborn Trade Publishing for their vision, guidance, and enthusiastic support of this project.

There is one other very special person to thank. Marie Swift has been my faithful writing partner, communications coach, publicist, friend, and ally since 1998. Her continued talent, energy, and vision have made an enormous difference in creating this book—and in countless other professional collaborations and undertakings over the years. The depth of knowledge and commitment she contributes to all we do is priceless.

As I look back at the eighteen months it took to write and produce this book, I feel truly blessed and humbled. What an honor it has been to work with each and every one of these dedicated professionals and to bring *Just Give Me the Answer$* to you.

Sheryl Garrett, CFP®

Chapter

1

FINANCIAL PLANNING FUNDAMENTALS

TIP 1 COMMON MONEY MANAGEMENT MISTAKES AND HOW TO AVOID THEM

Q. We are newlyweds, just starting our financial journey together. What advice do you have to help us avoid financial pitfalls?

A. It is great that you're already talking about money and how to make the most of your financial situation. Whether you are just starting out on your financial journey or well along the path, the following tips and professional insights should help you avoid the mistakes that people most commonly make.

Success is never an accident. It is always the result of high intention, sincere effort, intelligent direction, and skillful execution.

—ANONYMOUS

Top 12 Money Mistakes People Make

1. Not living within your means. We live in a consumer culture. Sometimes it seems as if everyone is buying new cars, taking expensive vacations, and dining out. If your credit card bills are painful, you already may know that you're living more lavishly than you should. Perhaps that's why you picked up this book. Or, even though things seem fine, you may have a hunch that you're not using your money as wisely as you could. This is a good time to ask yourself, "What are my long-term financial objectives?"

2. Failure to set goals. If you don't know where you're going, you may wind up somewhere unpleasant. That's as true on a road trip as on your financial journey. Whether you dream of long-term financial security, greater prosperity in the near future, sending the kids to Harvard, providing for elderly parents, or retiring to a tropical island, if you haven't identified and prioritized your goals, you haven't taken control of your financial future. Once those goals are established, you can make spending and investment decisions that will lead you in the right direction.

3. Not saving enough. Figuring out how much you need to save can be complicated, but chances are you need more than you think. Americans are living longer, so your retirement nest egg may need to last 25 to 35 years or more, providing an income adequate for your lifestyle while keeping up with inflation. Social Security benefits will be dismally inadequate for most people, so many professional financial planners don't even include them or reduce the estimated benefits drastically in retirement income projections.

Even if you're just starting out and have little discretionary income to set aside, getting into the habit of saving is important. Take advantage of 401(k)s with company matching or other tax-advantaged investment vehicles such as IRAs and Roth IRAs. The power of tax-deferred investment returns that compound over your entire working life is tremendous.

4. Failure to create and stick to a budget. Few people create a budget and stick to it. Nonetheless, after you've set your financial goals and developed a budget, you need the discipline to stick to your plan and achieve your long-term goals. Often, people find that once they've taken control of their finances through goal setting, planning, and budgeting, the resulting sense of well-being far outweighs any disappointment they feel from not spending as much.

5. Too much debt. Ideally, a home mortgage is all the debt most people would have. It's considered "good debt," because your home has appreciation potential and mortgage interest is deductible. For most people, however, having mortgage debt alone just is not realistic. They need to borrow to buy automobiles and to make other major purchases. Here are three guidelines to help determine your maximum level of debt.

1. Monthly housing expenses (rent or mortgage payment plus real estate taxes and insurance) should be less than 28 percent of pretax income.

2. Total monthly debt payments should be less than 36 percent of pretax income.
3. Consumer debt payments should be less than 20 percent of after-tax income.

You are wise to stay below these limits if possible. And do try to pay down consumer debt as quickly as possible. Carrying credit card balances month to month (just paying the minimum) is an absolute no-no. If you can't pay your monthly credit card bills in full each and every month, then you're living beyond your means—period.

6. Failure to maintain sufficient (or having too large) cash reserves. Most people should keep the equivalent of three to six months' worth of expenses in liquid, accessible accounts. The lower amount may be appropriate for two-career couples or singles with a second source of income; the higher amount is better for one wage earner families or if your income is volatile. Unless you have special circumstances that warrant greater liquidity, keeping excess cash in low or noninterest-bearing accounts is undesirable, because inflation eats away your money's purchasing power over time. For example, with 4 percent annual inflation, over 10 years, a dollar loses roughly one-third of its purchasing power. Yikes.

7. Insufficient disability insurance coverage. Many people purchase life insurance but don't realize the importance of disability coverage. You are more likely to suffer loss of income due to prolonged illness or injury than you are to die prematurely. In addition, the financial consequences to your family from a disability can be disastrous—not only does income stop, but expenses can rise due to the costs of treatment, rehabilitation, or long-term care. If you're self-employed, purchase your own disability policy. If an employer offers group disability coverage, be aware that it may have some big loopholes. Read the policy carefully and consider replacing or supplementing it with additional coverage.

8. Failure to keep an up-to-date Will. It's surprising how many people don't bother with a proper Will. They mistakenly believe that if they don't have a large estate, it's not necessary. But if you die intestate (without a Will), the state will determine how your assets are distributed. Estate planning is critical if your assets are more than $1 million, including life insurance and equity in your home. To avoid having your hard-earned assets eaten up by unnecessary taxes, you should explore tax minimization strategies with a qualified attorney.

Don't overlook the fact that, if parents die without a Will, minor children become wards of the state, with the state ultimately choosing their guardians. If you have children (or plan to in the future), your Will should identify guardians in the event of your death. Note also that if you move to a different state, you may need to get a new Will. Estate planning is not just for the wealthy. Don't put off to tomorrow what you could be doing today.

9. Failure to diversify. Simply stated, diversification means not putting all your eggs in one basket. Remember the Enron scandal and those employees and retirees with all their retirement assets invested in company stock? They lost everything when the company went bankrupt. Had they been properly diversified, the scandal might not have been as financially disastrous.

Diversification means spreading your assets among several different types of investments—like stocks, bonds, cash, and real assets. Diversification among different asset classes can lead to higher returns and lower risk over time. Asset allocation takes diversification one step further (see Chapter 7 on investing).

10. Too much focus on short-term investment results. Investors often think that they should try to time the market—buy stocks before the next big market rally or sell before the next downturn. That's just not possible over any meaningful period of time. Instead, your asset allocation and investing strategy should be based on your age, life circumstances, and when you need the money. For example, a 25-year-old might have a portfolio weighted heavily toward growth stocks, because a person just beginning their career can tolerate near-term volatility in exchange for the superior long-term growth that the stock market historically has delivered. On the flip side, a retiree who needs a stable cash flow should probably have a greater proportion of fixed-income investments.

11. Failure to get advice from an expert when needed. Most people never seek professional financial advice. Unfortunately, it is easy to understand why. The prevalence of financial advisors who sell products can be a real turnoff. Because their compensation is directly affected by the recommendations a client implements with them, their advice may not always be in their clients' best interests. Fortunately, though, a growing number of fee-only financial planners will address your concerns by working with you on an hourly, as-needed basis without account minimums, long-term contracts, or commission-based bias.

While a planner can help with virtually any aspect of personal financial management, at a minimum you should get professional help with certain issues.

- How much will you need for retirement?
- How much will you need for your children's education, and what are the best ways to fund it?
- How much should you save on a systematic basis to achieve those goals?
- How can you best allocate your portfolio between different asset classes?

- What are the best options when approaching a transition point in life such as a new job, marriage, home purchase, having children, or retirement?

The cost of professional financial advice is small compared with the potential costs of not getting professional help.

12. Not being an educated investor. Have you seen the bumper sticker, "Ignore your teeth and they will go away?" The same can be said for your money. If you don't take care of it, it may not last long. Managing your money is a lifetime project, so continue to work diligently and become better informed.

Reading this book as well as credible magazine and newspaper articles and listening to reliable experts are all great ways to get started. Just watch for hidden agendas and biases, and don't listen too closely to the daily news and stock market talk. Remember, financial news shows need to garner audiences, too, and because personal finance is not usually a racy, exciting topic, sometimes the "news" gets overly sensationalized or exaggerated.

Also, educating the client is a major objective of a good financial planner, so if you opt to work with a planner, make sure they are willing and able to explain things clearly. If you have a life partner, both of you should be involved. Too many people rely on their spouses or partners to make all the household financial decisions, ending up woefully unprepared to handle the finances when the unthinkable happens.

End Note$

You work hard for your money. By educating yourself on personal financial matters and becoming a better-informed consumer, you can make smarter decisions about money and enjoy greater peace of mind now, while building for a more secure financial future.

KAREN KEATLEY, MBA, CFA, CFP® (Charlotte, North Carolina)

TIP 2 HOW FINANCIAL PLANNERS WORK AND GET PAID

Q. A friend told us about a financial planner who has been around for a long time and seems to have an impressive resume. How can we be sure we are working with a planner who is right for us and will look out for our best interests?

A. Education and experience are important, but a financial planner who looks great on paper still may not be right for you. You need to ask specific questions and be prepared to understand the answers you receive. Several good advisor-interview questionnaires are available from the industry's leading professional organizations. Several sources are listed below in this Tip, under "Interviewing Financial Planners."

Amazingly, people are embarrassed to ask an advisor how and how much they get paid. Don't be. It's your money, so look for the best value in everything you buy, including financial advice.

Seek Out the Expertise You Need

Look for an advisor who maintains a thorough knowledge of the financial issues important to you. If you need an overview of your entire financial situation, consider working with an advisor who has earned the CFP® professional marks of distinction.

Also, look for someone experienced in working with people in your situation, and who truly wants to work with and help you. While many financial advisors focus on serving the wealthy, and impose minimum income levels, investment assets, or annual fees, a growing number of qualified advisors can and will work with you on an independent, commission-free basis.

Look at the Package of Services

One way financial planners differentiate themselves is in how they package and deliver services. Most veteran advisors prefer to work with clients on an ongoing basis. They target clients needing comprehensive financial planning advice and investment management services, meet with them two to four times per year, and may charge annual retainer fees (these fees can be substantial). Clients who opt for an ongoing retainer relationship are referred to as delegator-type individuals. Other planners have begun to work with their clients on an hourly, as-needed basis. Clients who want advice only when they request it, are known as validators or do-it-yourselfers. While the annual retainer-fee scenario may be effective for clients who need or want to turn over the management of their financial affairs to an advisor, many people cannot afford or justify the ongoing fees. To determine which type of working relationship is right for you, ask yourself if you want periodic input to or validation of your financial decisions or full-time financial management. The cost difference is significant, so don't pay for more service and advice than you need. Making mistakes with your personal finances is the most expensive lesson you will ever learn. When you need professional guidance, seek it out and be willing to pay for it.

Consider Compensation

Also important is how an advisor is compensated and by whom. It's imperative that you are aware of how that compensation may affect your relationship with the advisor and the recommendations you receive. Financial planners and consultants, investment advisors, registered representatives, insurance agents, stock brokers, and bank representatives may all be compensated via commissions and/or fees, and often both. Additional information and a series of charts that allow you to compare planners' compensation across various service models and portfolio amounts can be found at http://www.garrettplanning.com.

Commission-compensated advisors. The oldest and most common form of compensation is commissions earned on the sale of insurance and investment products. Though many honest, qualified advisors earn a majority of their income from commissions, conflicts of interest may arise. These people are paid for recommending and selling products from companies that, in turn, pay them commissions. Consciously or unconsciously, that may influence their recommendations.

It's also important to understand that commissions, fees, and loads generally are not charged as a separate line item, instead being hidden or absorbed into the investment. If you don't normally write a separate check to compensate the advisor, it may seem as if the advice you are getting is free. Of course, it's not, nor should it be. Note: The term *fee-based* is synonymous with *fee plus commission.*

Salaried financial advisors. If a planner is a salaried employee of a bank, financial firm, or discount broker, they have much less potential compensation conflict. Still, you should always ask about sales quotas, incentives (like bonuses or vacations), or if the advisor in any way is directed to recommend certain financial products over others.

Salaries often depend on an advisor's ability to meet sales quotas; and quotas, incentives, and directives can lead to divided loyalties.

Fee-only advisors. Fee-only financial advisors are compensated exclusively by fees paid directly by clients. They do not accept commissions or compensation from any source other than their clients. A client writes a check or receives an invoice for the amount to be withdrawn from their investment account to pay the fee. The costs of the advisor's services are very clear. Consequently, the vast majority of inherent conflicts of interest regarding compensation are removed from the equation.

Fee-only wealth managers. Comprehensive, fee-only advisors traditionally charge a flat fee for the initial comprehensive financial plan, then charge an annual retainer or a percentage of the assets for which they provide ongoing financial management services.

Fees for comprehensive financial planning and asset management typically range from 1 to 2 percent per year on a total investment portfolio. The management fee is debited from the investment account, usually on a quarterly basis. The bottom line is that these advisors attempt to set fee schedules and minimums to compensate them fairly for their time and expertise. Ask yourself, however, if you need all they provide on an ongoing basis. You may be paying for and receiving more than you really need.

Another consideration with asset management arrangements is that the planner may tell you that they are on your side because of the financial incentive to help your portfolio perform well. In theory this sounds good, but you need to make sure you are not taking on more risk than you want simply to make a higher short-term return on your investment portfolio.

For those with sizeable investment portfolios, or individuals in unique or complex financial situations that need lots of hands-on professional assistance, a fee-only advisor working for a percentage of assets or one who charges an annual retainer may be the way to go. These are typically comprehensive, ongoing financial planning relationships, where investment portfolio management, estate planning, and charitable giving all are considered and explored. This approach is most appealing to people who want an all-inclusive financial manager and can afford to delegate management of their financial affairs to that person. If you want this level of service, be sure to ask for both client and professional references. You're thinking about turning over management of your financial affairs to another person. You owe it to yourself to do your homework.

Hourly, fee-only advisors. When a client wants to maintain an active role in and more control over their financial affairs, or doesn't have the big portfolio required by some firms (the typical account minimum for fee-only asset management is $250,000 or more), hourly, fee-only advisors are a good option. Such advisors can provide competent, affordable advice.

Fortunately, many advisors offer their services for a flat amount by the project or the hour. This opens the door to one-time meetings, financial checkups, and the opportunity to get a second opinion before a big financial decision. It also works if you want to develop a long-term relationship, because all charges are on the table and can be contracted on an as-needed basis. The reality is that most people probably don't need or want a full-time financial advisor but would truly benefit from meeting with a planner from time to time. Being able to do so on an hourly, as-needed basis puts you in the driver's seat, letting you determine the scope of engagement.

Interviewing Financial Planners

A list of questions is available on the National Association of Personal Financial Advisors' Web site (http://www.napfa.org). Download their brochure, "How to Choose a Financial Planner," and their interview questionnaire, or use The Garrett Planning Network's "Advisor Interview Questionnaire" (see http://www.GarrettPlanningNetwork.com). Be sure to complete a questionnaire for every planner you interview.

Start your quest by visiting the advisor's Web site. Hopefully, the site will answer many of your questions. An independent advisor's site often won't be as flashy as that of a big company, but ask yourself how much of the big company's content directly applies to the advisor you're interviewing. Don't be fooled by glitzy, grand Web sites.

Also, be wary of advisors whose sites require you to divulge personal information and/or contact information as a prerequisite for access to the information pertinent to prospective clients.

When you find one or more advisors who appear to meet your primary requirements, call them. If you're comfortable in the initial few minutes of the call, ask to meet in person. Beware of the advisor who wants to meet right away unless you have indicated that it's an emergency. That advisor may be too new, too desperate, or too pushy.

Most financial planners and advisors will offer a free initial interview or get-acquainted session. Based on the complexity of your situation and scope of services needed, these meetings can last 45 to 90 minutes. In the meeting, be sure to address the issues that are most important to you first. This will save time for both of you.

The initial interview should provide the following:

- Answers to all the questions on your Interview Questionnaire
- A written proposal or contract that outlines the services the advisor recommends and how, when, and how much they will be compensated
- A list of financial documents and data needed to perform the analysis and provide advice
- A target time frame for when the services could be rendered
- An appreciation for the advisor's professional style and communication and listening skills

Under no circumstances should you start working with an advisor until you're satisfied with the interview process, the recommended services, and the method and amount of compensation. Don't let anyone pressure you, but understand that it's the advisor's responsibility to help you take actions they think are in your best interest.

You also may want to ask the planner how they define success with a client. If the response is "an expected rate of return on the investment portfolio," that tells you the advisor may focus primarily on investments and total return. It's an easily measured yardstick, but at what cost? Did they take unnecessary risks with your investments because the rate of return goal was not appropriate for you? On the other hand, if the advisor defines success "based on the client's achievement of his or her financial objectives," that tells you that they approach client relationships with a holistic or comprehensive view. Many of the benefits of financial planning are intangible. The holistic financial advisor may define success as achieving clients' peace of mind, securing their retirement, or helping them realize their dreams.

Consider asking the advisor for referrals from other clients or peer professionals, and interview those people as well. But keep in mind, advisors will select people who will say good things about them.

If you ask the right questions and hear the right answers, you are more likely to end up with the right planner for you.

Additional information and a series of charts that allow you to compare planners' compensation across various service models and portfolio amounts can be found at http://www.garrettplanning.com.

SHERYL GARRETT, CFP® (Shawnee Mission, Kansas)

TIP 3 IDENTIFY AND PRIORITIZE YOUR GOALS— THE FIRST STEP TOWARD FINANCIAL SUCCESS

Q. We would like to buy a larger, newer house, but we are concerned about how this purchase might impact our other goals. Can you provide some advice on setting and prioritizing our goals?

A. You are to be commended for your forethought. It's important to identify and document your most important life goals before making major decisions such as buying a larger home. While the immediate question is whether you can afford to buy that home, first ask yourself, "What are my financial objectives?"

The Big Picture

Consider this example. Say you're a young couple, and you both want to retire at age 66. You also want to send your children to private high schools, fund your children's college education, and take an annual family trip to Europe. Each of you should now ask yourself, "Would I have any additional goals if I knew I had only two years left to live?" Let's say that you would not change your goals, but your spouse would like to spend less time at work and more time with the family.

Though your spouse makes a good living, you quickly realize that your resources might not fund everything you want to do. So you now reconsider the goal that originally prompted your question, the bigger and newer home, within the context of *all* your goals. It is not enough just to identify your goals; you must prioritize them, too.

What Are Your Most Important Financial Goals or Concerns?

If you are working with a financial advisor, they first must understand your goals and priorities before developing a worthwhile plan or offering meaningful advice. If you're developing a financial plan on your own, realize that goal setting is the first and most important step in the financial planning process. There's no advantage to implementing a plan or taking advice that leads to the wrong goals.

Here is a process to help you identify and prioritize your goals.

1. *List all your financial goals.* Sit down with a piece of paper or at a computer and start listing your goals as fast as you think of them. Don't stop to evaluate; just identify and list them. Afterwards, ask yourself what else you would want to do if you knew you had only two years to live and add those things to your list.
2. *Prioritize your goals.* If you could achieve only one goal, which would it be? Put a *#1* next to that goal. If you could achieve only two goals, what's the second goal you would choose? Put a *#2* beside that, and continue the process until all the goals on your list are numbered. No two goals can have the same number.

   Sometimes it helps to segregate your goals into *critical* and *noncritical*, then prioritize them within each group.

   Still another technique is to group the items on your list by time frame. One group of goals, for example, must be accomplished within the next two years, another group within five years.

If you are a couple, consider doing this exercise separately, each completing your own list of prioritized goals. Then meet to discuss what you have in common and any differences. Create a third list that represents your jointly agreed-upon family goals and priorities. With this level of careful thought and discussion, you can then go forward in life with both a solid family plan and coordinated individual plans for achievement and success.

You'll miss 100 percent of the shots you don't take.

—**WAYNE GRETZKY,** ice hockey great

Benefits of the Goal-Setting Process

The goal-setting process outlined above benefits you in a number of ways. First, it will save you time and money. Armed with a prioritized list of goals, you and/or your financial planner will spend less time guessing and more time planning for successful outcomes. If you are working with an advisor who charges for services by the hour (like all members of The Garrett Planning Network), less time spent on the "maybe this or maybe that" scenarios means lower overall fees.

Second, thoughtful goal prioritizing leads to a deeper understanding of what's important to you, as a couple and as an individual. This can strengthen your relationship and help you resolve to make sacrifices for the sake of achieving a more important goal.

Third, setting goals can be fun. It is a chance to reach for those goals that everyday distractions have knocked off your radar screen or to reconsider goals you had lost hope of achieving. Goal setting can reenergize your sense of the possibilities for your life.

Finally, recommitting to your personal and family priorities allows you, your spouse, and your financial advisor if applicable to turn each goal into a project and work on the steps necessary to accomplish them all.

RICH CHAMBERS, CFP® (Menlo Park, California)

TIP 4 FINANCIAL PLANNING AND GOAL SETTING—MORE TECHNIQUES FOR SUCCESS

Q. I hear and read a lot about financial planning and goal setting. How do I get started?

A. The financial planning process is like fortune-telling. While financial planning is very sophisticated, mathematically based, and intricately complex, it's still forecasting the future.

What Financial Planning Is

The financial planning process helps you get from where you are today in life to where you want to be, and it provides a framework for making related financial decisions. Properly structured, the process helps you evaluate everyday choices and the interrelated financial implications so you can better allocate your resources—personal and financial—to meet your goals.

The resulting satisfaction with various aspects of your financial life can provide a basis for improving your financial literacy, enabling you to move forward with greater confidence.

Financial planning is about setting personal and financial goals, then figuring out how to achieve them. It's an ongoing process. A plan must be reviewed periodically and adjusted if necessary to ensure that it continues to direct you toward your goals.

Turn Simply Stated Goals into Specific, Personally Affected Statements

Establishing personal and financial goals is the first step. Typically, your goals will be general: "I want to retire comfortably," "I want to educate my children," or "I want to start my own business." You may express your retirement goals as, "I want to travel and play golf," or "I want to give back to the community by volunteering."

But these statements don't necessarily tell the full story. What exactly do these statements mean to you, and what will it take to achieve your goal? That's important, because everyone's answer is different. And, if you know the financial and personal resources needed to achieve something, you can make sure you're properly allocating and using those resources. After all, you don't want to fall short of realizing your goals later in life.

Let's look at a few common goals and how to turn them into measurable action plans that integrate into your financial future.

Retire comfortably. Comfort is the key. What will it take for you to be *comfortable?* How you answer that question determines how much money you need to set aside. Perhaps you want to own your home free and clear and equip it so that you can live there despite any physical challenges. That can require renovations that take financial resources. So for you, *comfortable* may mean setting aside a certain amount of money. But you also have to consider whether your lifestyle will allow you to leave money to your heirs, or whether inflation will require you to tap into those funds.

The key is to clearly define your comfort in personal and financial terms so you can model your projected use of money over time. You also need to understand how financial returns and accessibility needs can affect achieving your desires.

Educate your children. Does this mean providing every dime to get through college and perhaps graduate school, or just supporting them by cosigning student loans, matching income dollar-for-dollar, or some other way of helping out? Maybe your parents could not afford or chose not to help you with your education costs, and that experience influences how you will help your children. Again, the key is to explain clearly what this goal means to you in personal and financial terms so you can assess the financial impact on your resources.

Start your own business. This goal alone can fill many books. What you need to know, though, is whether you have the strengths, knowledge, skills, interest, and financial resources to achieve this goal. Because so many personal considerations enter into this kind of decision, financial considerations almost take a back seat. But the bottom line once again is to explain clearly what this goal means to you in personal and financial terms so it can be worked into your financial framework.

Play golf and travel. This statement is pretty broad. By *travel,* do you mean keeping your home as a base, or selling your house and moving elsewhere? Will you use an RV, and drive from place to place, staying with family and friends? If you're an RV enthusiast, what are the anticipated costs of operation, maintenance, campgrounds, and service centers? If you're a world traveler, will you be out of the United States for extended periods? Are you thinking about cruise ships or day trips? It's all travel, but each has a dramatically different effect on personal and financial resources.

By *play golf,* do you mean a friendly game pulling a handcart at the local municipal course? Or will it be a day at the country club with friends, meeting for lunch first then drinks and dinner later, hiring a caddy, renting a golf cart, and putting a little wager on the outcome? The costs for each level of personal involvement are very different. How often will your financial resources support a $200-plus golf day versus a $30 golf day?

Define your goals now so you don't wake up ten years into retirement and realize that you are on the path to financial distress.

Give back to the community by volunteering. This requires you to consider the same personal issues as starting your own business: your strengths, knowledge, skills, interest, and financial wherewithal. Then you can better match your personal attributes to causes that make you feel enriched and fulfilled.

Thinking beyond simply stated goals is the essence of establishing personal and financial goals. But how do you begin to articulate your goals and objectives in such deliberate and precise terms?

Future Change: Internally Generated and/or Externally Driven

To help articulate your goals, start by looking at your future based on two approaches.

1. *Internal.* Think about your current and future (desired) lifestyle. Both are related to how you currently spend your time and money. How do you visualize that changing in the future?
2. *External.* Think about the other people in your life or influences beyond your direct control. Things happen simply because of the way you structure your life. Business partners come and go, as do living companions. Children, if you have any, will have different financial needs as they age. Work transitions, legacy transitions, and financial transitions are other issues to consider. You know such transitions will eventually occur, but you do not know when. You also know that you need to plan for how to deal best with these circumstances, using your available personal and financial resources.

Reflecting on your satisfaction with various aspects of your financial life provides a basis for improving your financial literacy so you can move forward with greater confidence.

STEVEN S. SHAGRIN, JD, CFP®, CRPC, CRC®, CELP (Youngstown, Ohio)

TIP 5 ENHANCED LIFE PLANNING STRATEGIES BOOST PERSONAL SATISFACTION AND FINANCIAL SUCCESS

Q. What is *life planning,* and how does it differ from *financial planning?*

A. Life planning is an evolved approach to financial planning that takes into account financial issues from a personal perspective. When you're aware of the personal dynamics, you can more easily make the lifestyle changes necessary to realize your most important goals. With a better understanding of your personal goals, your financial planning will be better tailored to your personal needs, and you'll more likely adhere to your plan.

The Lifestyle Approach

The lifestyle approach helps you consider what you enjoy in your current work environment as well as in your personal life. For example, work may enable you to achieve financial security, make decisions, lead others, organize, socialize, be creative, learn, have a structure or routine, and more. Consider your key strengths. Perhaps you're enthusiastic, thoughtful, trusting, open-minded, optimistic, understanding, sharp, friendly, relaxed, alert, intuitive, patient, efficient, supportive, and more.

Life planning uses lists like these to stimulate your recognition of additional strengths that you may not have considered. It's a great feeling to see all your strengths listed in one place.

Next, look at your transferable skills and how you could use them in the future as a second career or perhaps as a volunteer. Transferable skills include your knowledge and abilities. Knowledge could be in music, carpentry, first aid, photography, mathematics, travel, the Internet, auto mechanics, animals, home repair, wine, and much, much more. Abilities could include communicating, supervising, editing, listening, painting, selling, negotiating, public speaking, and so on.

Now focus on possible alternative or second careers, or volunteer activities, that build on your strengths, knowledge, and abilities.

Other lifestyle issues include the following:

- Your residence (and secondary residence, if applicable), with respect to both the type of location or community as well as the type of dwelling and amenities
- Hobbies and interests
- Physical and exercise activities
- Travel

Each lifestyle concern generally involves financial and personal resources, although hobbies and interests also can be sources of income. For each, estimate the expenses involved and their approximate timing.

Armed with this information, you can begin to model your financial plan based on your lifestyle desires.

The Life Transitions Approach

As mentioned earlier, this part of your financial life often depends on other people or influences beyond your direct control—things happen simply because of the way you have structured your life. Examples include the following:

- *Family.* Changes in marital status; transitions with children as they mature; issues with aging parents and care-giving; health concerns with self, spouse, or parents; and empty nest issues.

- *Work.* New job; job loss; changes with business partners; buying, selling, or closing a business; changing career path; transition into retirement; simplifying work life; promotion, or job restructuring.
- *Financial.* Buying or selling home; buying vacation home or timeshare; debt concerns; investment gains or losses; relocation; or inheritance or windfall.
- *Legacy.* Developing or changing estate plan; developing end-of-life plan; increasing charitable giving; or special financial gifts to children or grandchildren.

Each transition requires you to reflect on personal considerations and related financial consequences, to understand the impact on your financial life, and to identify resources for finding additional information to help you navigate changes successfully.

With this in mind, you can formulate a financial plan based on the life transitions most likely to occur.

What Is Your Financial Satisfaction?

The process of planning and goal setting also involves recognizing the components that contribute to a sense of financial satisfaction. Some of the nation's leading life planners use the Financial Satisfaction Survey™ from Money Quotient, Inc., because it fosters an understanding of the practical and emotional factors that contribute to financial well-being.

Questions you should reflect on include the following:

- How satisfied are you with your ability to meet financial obligations?
- How satisfied are you with the income from your current job or career?
- How satisfied are you with your spending habits?
- How satisfied are you with your level of debt?
- How satisfied are you with the amount you save and invest regularly?
- How satisfied are you with your current investment choices?
- How satisfied are you that you're on track to building a sufficient retirement nest egg?
- How satisfied are you with your ability to provide financial help to family members?
- How satisfied are you with your level of financial education?
- How satisfied are you with your emotional response to your personal finance issues?
- How satisfied are you with your working relationships with your financial service providers (e.g., insurance agent, banker, broker, financial planner, and accountant)?

These and other questions help you focus on what you need to know to become more financially satisfied so you can better review, organize, and improve your financial life. If the life planning approach appeals to you, there are financial planners who have completed additional professional study in this area. If you are interested in learning more about the life planning movement, or in finding a class that will help you better understand your relationship to money and life goals, a great place to start is the Kinder Institute of Life Planning's Web site at http://www.kinderinstitute.com.

End Note$

Once you know the financial issues from your personal perspective, you can make small lifestyle changes as you become more aware of the life transitions you face at work, with family, with your legacy, and with your finances. Your planning will be better structured to your personal needs and therefore easier to follow.

STEVEN S. SHAGRIN, JD, CFP®, CRPC, CRC®, CELP (Youngstown, Ohio)

TIP 6 GETTING YOUR FINANCIAL HOUSE IN ORDER—TIPS TO GET AND STAY ON TRACK

Q. I could be doing more to organize my financial affairs, but I barely have time to pay bills and balance the checkbook, let alone take a more organized approach that would help in times of emergency or personal disruption. What first steps should I take?

A. There are times every year (at the new year and tax time, for instance) when it seems logical to pull together essential financial and personal information for your family and heirs. The horrific events of September 11 increased most Americans' sense of vulnerability. The silver lining is that people now are more willing to address financial planning and estate planning issues, to obtain or increase their life insurance coverage, and generally to put their financial affairs in order.

Get Organized

A first step to get on track is to organize your routine and day-to-day financial tasks. The second—and perhaps most important step—is to organize your essential financial information so that your loved ones will be able to function without additional or needless burdens in the event that something happens to you.

While organizing your financial affairs may sound like a daunting task, it really isn't, and it actually saves time and expense in the long run. Here are a few tips to make the process easier.

Start a basic home filing system. Gather all the piles of papers and sort them by the following categories:

- Bills due
- Important/Keep
- Toss/Shred

Then buy colorful file folders and label them for each household expense or activity. If you do not have a file cabinet, buy a plastic file bin or an accordion file. Create one or two files for unpaid bills. As the bills come in, open them, clip the statement to the return envelope, and place them in the Bills Due file. Some families create two Bills Due files: one for the first pay period of the month and one for the second pay period.

Create other files for the Important/Keep stack of essential household information such as receipts and warranties. Empty your wallet and photocopy all your credit cards, health cards, and any other cards with information that would be handy to have if you lost your wallet. Do this once, then update the file any time there is a change. If you have important papers and do not want to rent a safety deposit box, at least keep your valuable papers, insurance policies, and passports in a fireproof lockbox.

When you bring mail or paperwork into your home, immediately open, review, and sort these items into the three primary categories so that you handle your papers only once. It's said that we spend, on average, six weeks a year looking for misplaced stuff. Imagine how much time you would save if you had a good system in place—not to mention the unnecessary expense of late charges.

Are you one of those people who rationalize that the reason you're so disorganized is that you don't have the time to get and stay organized? Consider for a moment that you actually have less time, more frustration, and potentially more expense because you are disorganized. Invest one or two days in setting up a system, and you will thank yourself every time you pay bills, pull your tax information together, or need to get your hands on an important document quickly.

Create a family financial binder. The easiest way to organize the most critical information that your family would need in event of your death or incapacity is to put your documents into a single binder. Many important documents and records should be kept in a safe deposit or fireproof lockbox, including original or certified copies of birth certificates; Social Security cards; passports; records of adoptions, marriages, and deaths; citizenship and veteran's papers; stock or bond certificates; and insurance policies.

While you can compile the binder anytime, it's sometimes easier to do it in the first quarter of the year when much of the data arrives for tax preparation purposes. If updated regularly, the binder simplifies tasks like preparing taxes, obtaining or refinancing loans, and completing many other ongoing financial activities. More importantly, updating the binder allows you to take stock of your financial situation.

You can create the organizer yourself or buy premade ones. A couple of sources include HOMEFILE® Publishing, Inc., 800-695-3453 (http://www.organizerkits.com) or Prosperity for Life, 888-698-0815 (http://www.prosperityforlife.org).

If you do it yourself, you will need a large three-ring binder, a three-hole punch, some plastic page protector sheets, and 12 tabbed section dividers. Make a label and/or cover sheet so your binder is clearly identifiable. Create separator pages with index tabs for the following sections: essential personal papers; sources of income; financial assets; deeds and titles; insurance policies personally held; employer-provided benefits; mortgages, loans and other liabilities; Wills, Trusts, and other legal documents; advisors/contractors; executor instructions; letters to loved ones; and other.

Once you have the organizer

- *decide who will create and maintain the binder.* That's invaluable for spouses and/or adult children who must suddenly take over because of death or incapacity. It especially makes sense for the spouse who normally does not handle these affairs to be the one to compile the contents of the binder.
- *watch your mail.* As each comes in, copy the year-end statements from all your financial institutions (banks, mutual fund companies, mortgage lenders, credit cards, insurance companies, etc.). Include year-end pay and benefit statements from employers, pension plans, retirement plans, and the Social Security Administration (your Social Security Benefits Statement will arrive a couple of months prior to your birthday). The original will go into your tax return preparation file and/or safe deposit box. The copy will be inserted into your binder. Make a note of all current beneficiary and transfer-on-death designations in force for any of these accounts and policies.
- *copy all the important documents in your safe deposit box.* Make sure to return the originals to the box promptly. Insert the copy into the binder, under the proper tab, with a notation as to the location of the original document.
- *look through your wallet.* Copy the front and back of your credit cards, health insurance cards, Social Security cards, and any other cards with essential

information. The idea is to create a paper trail of essential information in case your wallet is lost or stolen.

- *tell appropriate family members about the existence and location of the binder.* If you like, create a duplicate binder for safe keeping at the office or a loved one's home.
- *update the binder as information changes.*

The binder's tabs.

- *Essential personal papers.* Personal and family documents like marriage licenses, divorce papers, birth certificates, adoption papers, and Social Security information
- *Sources of income.* Employment or business revenue information
- *Financial assets.* Investment and related information
- *Deeds and titles.* Copies of your home, automobiles, or other deeded assets
- *Insurance policies, personally held.* Copies of key pages from your personal life insurance, disability, long-term care, and automobile insurance policies
- *Employer-provided benefits.* Copies of health insurance cards, flex spending plan, company disability plan, life insurance policy, etc.
- *Mortgages, loans, and other liabilities.* Information on your mortgage and other substantial loans such as automobile and student loans
- *Wills, trusts, and other legal documents*
- *Advisors/contractors.* Your attorney, stockbroker, financial planner, insurance broker, accountant, physician, religious leader, banker, trust officer, and so forth. Staple a business card for each advisor to the sheet. This section also may include contractors that provide ongoing home maintenance, pest control, or security (include copies of contracts).
- *Executor instructions.* Specific funeral and obituary information, as well as any other instructions, to your executor. You might include a list of people to notify in the event of death or emergency and a letter to your loved ones that conveys your values and thoughts on life.
- *Other.* Miscellaneous catchall section

Start Now

Taking the time to organize your papers now ensures a more manageable situation if you die or become incapacitated. You will leave a legacy of love and communicate your wishes through your letters and organized plan. You will simplify routine financial tasks and streamline the process for yourself at tax preparation time. The new year and tax season are excellent times to compile and organize your essential financial information, but *today* is always the best time to get started. Don't let another day go by without starting this important project. Planning pays off.

SHERYL GARRETT, CFP® (Shawnee Mission, Kansas)

TIP 7 LIVING RESPONSIBLY—WITH OR WITHOUT A BUDGET

Q. I know I should floss my teeth every day . . . and have a budget. But what if I hate budgets and can't stick to one?

A. Most people fall into this category. If your credit card debt is mounting and/or you're not saving more than 10 percent of your gross income for future needs, you probably should make some tough spending decisions, put together a budget, and follow it. On the other hand, if you pay all your credit cards in full each month and are saving what you need to, then you might not need a full-blown budget. You may, however, still run into occasional cash flow problems, so the following recommendations can be of help.

Managing Cash Flow

Keep in mind that 10 percent of your gross income probably is the minimum you need to save each month. You will be much better off if you calculate what it will take for your retirement, college for the kids, a vacation home, etc. and then set that aside first, each and every month.

Once you're routinely saving the 10 percent or more, it's time to build up an emergency fund. That's usually the equivalent of three to six months' basic living expenses set aside in a savings account or money market account. Calculate how much you should have, then decide how much to set aside regularly. Consider regular contributions to your emergency fund as a bill that must be paid. If you receive a tax refund, annual bonus, or other windfall, add that to your savings account, instead of spending it.

Next, list the big expenditures that happen on an irregular basis and estimate their annual cost. Include property taxes and homeowner's insurance premiums (if not escrowed by your mortgage company), auto and life insurance premiums (it is often cheaper to pay annually), anticipated medical and dental bills not covered by insurance, anticipated home maintenance/renovation projects, appliance replacements; vacations, camp for the kids, estimated quarterly income taxes, additional taxes due in April, gifts and holiday spending, etc. Add the total and divide by the number of times you pay bills in a year. For example, if you're paid every two weeks, divide by 26. Add this "escrow amount" for covering irregular expenses to the amount you have decided to set aside in your emergency fund every pay period.

Every time you pay bills, write a check or transfer this "escrow amount" into your savings account or money market account. Better yet, set up an automatic transfer. What you do not see, you will not spend. When it comes time to pay the auto insurance bill, the money will be available, and you will be able to pay it easily.

After you have set this money aside and paid all the bills, you'll know how much you have to live on until the next paycheck arrives. This approach may take some getting used to, especially if what's left doesn't seem like enough. You may need to stop using credit cards until you get a handle on how much you have to spend between paychecks. However, once you make the necessary spending adjustments, you'll know that you're living within your means, saving for a rainy day, and saving for your future. You will be in control of your finances.

KATHLEEN R. DOLLARD, CFP®, MBA (Boxborough, Massachusetts)

TIP 8 EMERGENCY FUNDS CREATE A NEEDED SAFETY NET

Q. How much should I keep in an emergency fund, and where should I keep it?

A. Establishing an emergency fund should be one of your first financial planning goals. Its purpose is to have cash available when the unexpected happens, such as the furnace breaking down or an unexpectedly high medical or dental bill not covered by insurance. It's generally much better to use your emergency monies than to build up debt on your credit card or borrow money in some other way.

A Top Priority

Setting up an emergency fund should be a top priority. But if you have credit card debt or personal loans—you should pay that off first. It does not make sense to carry a credit card balance and pay interest of 9.9 to 21 percent (or more) while you have cash sitting in a savings account earning 1 percent. Paying off the credit card debt is the best return you can get on your money.

Once the credit cards are paid off, use those monthly payments to build up your emergency fund.

How much should be in my emergency fund? The amount depends on how well you've covered your other financial liabilities, how many dependents you have, the amount of your monthly fixed expenses, the stability of your income, your access to low-cost loans, the state of the economy, and the job market.

As mentioned earlier, a general guideline is that at least three to six months' worth of living expenses should be set aside for an emergency. For example, if you suffered a serious illness or disability and there was a gap between when your sick pay ended (usually one to two weeks) and your long-term disability payments began (generally after six months), presuming you have long-term disability insurance, you would need cash to live on for several months.

Three to six months' worth of living expenses may be appropriate when your income is secure and the economy and job market are in good shape. But when the economy is uncertain, six months' to a year's worth of living expenses is more appropriate. If you get laid off in a poor economy, it could easily take that long (or longer) to find a new job with comparable income. Unemployment compensation may help for a little while but, at the most, it is typically no more than 50 percent of your former income, much less if you were highly paid. For example, the maximum unemployment benefit in Massachusetts is about $507 per week (before taxes), which is only about one-quarter of the weekly pretax income of someone who makes $100,000 a year.

Direct and indirect methods of calculation. There are two ways to estimate how much money should be in your emergency fund. With the direct method, add all the payments you would need to make in a year even if you lost your job. That could include mortgage payment(s), property taxes, insurance, car payments, credit card payments, utilities, groceries, basic clothing expenses, etc. Divide the total by 12 months for a monthly average and then multiply the result by 3, 6, or 9 depending on how many months of expenses you want to have covered. A problem with this approach is that it's easy to overlook some expenses.

The indirect method leaves less to chance. Most people spend all that they bring in. So take your annual income and subtract payroll and income taxes, as well as regular contributions to retirement plans, college savings, and any other savings programs you contribute to. Multiply the result by the number of months you wish to cover. This is the safest way to estimate your actual spending needs.

Whatever size cushion you decide on, the important thing is to start saving now and do it on a regular basis. Consider having a set amount withdrawn automatically from your checking account every month or every pay period. What you don't see, you'll be less likely to spend.

Where should I keep this money? When starting to build an emergency fund, the best place for it is probably in a savings account where it's FDIC insured, and earns a little interest. As you accumulate a few thousand dollars, shop around for higher rates in a money market account. Bankrate.com (http://www.bankrate.com) is a good place to start.

You may want to consider certificates of deposit (CDs), too. If you need the money before the CD matures, you will pay a penalty—typically three to six months' interest—but it might make sense to use a CD for a portion of your emergency fund. Shop for the best rates at Bankrate.com.

What if I need to spend this money? If it's truly an emergency, that's what the money is for. But replenish it as soon as possible. If it's not really an emergency and you need the money, you need to plan your cash flow better or cut back on expenses before spending the money.

KATHY DOLLARD, CFP®, MBA (Boxborough, Massachusetts) and
ERIC RABBANIAN, JD, CFP®, MBA (Austin, Texas)

TIP 9 UNDERSTANDING YOUR CREDIT SCORE

Q. While recently applying for a loan, the lender mentioned my credit score. What is a credit score, and what does it tell the lender about me?

A. A credit score is a number calculated by credit bureaus to quantify your credit history. Lenders use it to assess credit risk, and it serves as an independent measure of your trustworthiness to repay a loan. It's a snapshot of your credit history that changes over time. The number ranges from 300 to 850 but is typically between 500 and 800. A higher score is associated with a lower probability that you will default on a loan: the higher your score, the better.

What's a FICO Score?

The terms *credit score* and *FICO score* are interchangeable. A company called Fair, Isaac, and Co. created the credit scoring system. A credit score, in essence, quantifies qualitative information—not an easy task. Qualitative information regarding outstanding loans, history and timeliness of payments, pursuit of credit, length of credit history, and types of credit used are fed into an algorithm that generates a credit score.

Who Uses Credit Scores?

Many businesses deem the scores as vital to the lending process, and their use is expanding. Claiming a logical connection between credit risk and other insurable risks, homeowners and auto insurance providers also use credit scores to determine insurance ratings and premiums.

Before 2001, lending institutions were not permitted to tell you your credit score. But in April 2001, an improvement to the Fair Credit Reporting Act (FCRA) obligated credit bureaus to disseminate credit information to consumers.

Collecting Credit Information

The United States has more than 1,000 credit bureaus or credit reporting agencies (CRAs). Every 90 days, a data furnisher (bank, credit card company, court clerk, or mortgage lender) typically updates credit bureau(s) on your accounts, reporting things like timely or late payments, deferred payments, current loan balance, current payments due, and account closings. Credit bureaus are responsible for keeping and maintaining an accurate, current credit file for each consumer. All data furnishers do not supply information to each credit bureau.

Most lenders request information from one of the three largest bureaus: Equifax, Experian, or TransUnion. The data kept on file includes the following:

- Names and account information for past and current creditors, including the date each account was opened, the credit limit, and the highest dollar amount ever charged
- Payment history including late payments (by 30, 60, 90, or 120 or more days)
- Employer's name and employment history
- Home ownership status and previous addresses
- Public record information (such as foreclosures, bankruptcies, and tax liens)
- Overdue account referrals to collection agencies
- Inquiries made within the last six months for additional credit

Reporting Credit Information

A credit bureau reports information to credit grantors and lending institutions in addition to its credit-storage function. The reporting function is regulated by the FCRA to protect your rights as a consumer. Some states have additional laws to protect consumers.

Some of your basic credit rights, according to the federal government, include the following:

- The right to receive a copy of your complete credit report. It's free within 60 days of receiving a denial of credit based on a CRA report, and the laws will expand in 2004 so that everyone can get a free credit report at least once a year.

- The right to know who received your credit report in the last year for most purposes or in the last two years for employment purposes.
- The right to know why you are denied credit.
- Any company that denies your application must supply the name and address of the CRA contacted, provided the denial was based on information given by the CRA.
- The right to dispute any information found in your credit file.
- You cannot be denied credit based on your race, sex, marital status, religion, age, national origin, or receipt of public assistance.

BRYAN CLINTSMAN, CFP® (Southlake, Texas) and **TIMOTHY A. VAUGHN,** MBA (Bel Air, Maryland)

TIP 10 HOW TO IMPROVE A CREDIT SCORE

Q. My credit score is not as high as I would like. How is my credit score calculated, and how can I improve it?

A. Fortunately, boosting your credit score is relatively simple, but it takes time.

Five Factors Used in FICO Scores

Despite the efforts of the Fair Credit Reporting Act to lift some of the secrecy surrounding credit reporting and scoring, many calculation details are still unknown.

As discussed in the previous tip, the most widely used computer-scoring model is FICO. It uses five, variously weighted factors to calculate the total score. The approximate weights of each of the following factors are in parentheses.

1. *History of payments (35 percent).* Includes the timeliness of payments and date of the most recent problem.
2. *Outstanding debt (30 percent).* Includes the total amount of debt owed relative to the consumer's credit limit.
3. *Length of credit history (15 percent).* The longer an account is open, the higher a consumer's score.
4. *Pursuit of credit (10 percent).* Applying for new credit accounts negatively affects this component.
5. *Types of credit (10 percent).* Opening an account with a utility company is scored more favorably than opening one with a finance company.

Other scoring methods may use different factors and weights, and your credit score may vary 30 to 100 points depending on the scoring algorithm used. Race, gender, age, income level, national origin, sources of income, religion, and marital status may not be used in calculating your credit score. As a result, it is possible for you to have a high income but a low credit score.

How to Obtain a Credit Report and Credit Score

The first step in improving your credit score is to obtain a current credit report. The major credit bureaus allow you to do this on their Web sites.

- Equifax (PO Box 740241, Atlanta, GA 30374; 800-685-1111; http://www.equifax.com) provides a credit report with a BEACON® score calculated by the Fair, Isaac model.
- Experian (National Consumer Assistance Center, PO Box 2002, Allen, TX 75013; 888-397-3748; http://www.experian.com/consumer)
- TransUnion (Consumer Disclosure Center, PO Box 1000, Chester, PA 19022; 800-888-4213; http://www.transunion.com) also offers credit reports with credit scores. The scores they use are EMPIRICA® and Experian/Fair, Isaac Risk (FICO) scores, respectively calculated using models similar to the Fair-Isaac algorithm.

All three reporting agencies charge similar fees (around $20). However, in 2004 the laws will change so that everyone can receive a free credit report at least once a year.

Under the current laws, if you live in Colorado, Georgia, Maryland, Massachusetts, New Jersey, or Vermont, you are entitled to a free credit report and score once a year from each bureau. Until the new laws go into effect, almost all states allow you to receive a free credit report if you fall into one of the following situations:

- You were denied credit based on your credit report within the past 60 days.
- You were denied employment based on your credit report within the past 60 days.
- You are unemployed and plan to seek employment within the next 60 days.
- You receive welfare.
- You believe you are a victim of fraud.

You can also obtain a free report and credit score based on the CreditXpert™ algorithm by visiting http://www.eloan.com.

Best Way to View Credit History

The best way to view your credit history is through a three-in-one consolidated report that combines information from each of the three major credit reporting agencies into one report. It takes all three reports to get a full picture of your credit history. All three agencies offer the consolidated reports for approximately $40 per person. Because credit information is compiled for each individual, couples need to purchase one for each spouse.

How to Improve Your Credit Score

A few simple steps can help you improve your credit score or maintain an existing excellent rating.

1. Review your credit report thoroughly. In general, they're prone to errors. If you find one, contact the credit bureau in writing and send documentation that verifies your claim.
2. Pay your bills on time. Timely remittance is especially critical for ongoing, routine payments such as mortgage or rent.
3. Reduce your number of outstanding credit cards; close unused credit accounts and get confirmation of their closing in writing.
4. Maintain reasonable debt ratios for your asset and income level.
5. Avoid maxing out credit accounts. Spread charges over a few accounts.
6. Only apply for credit you need. Remember, aggressive pursuit of credit negatively affects a credit score.
7. Establish and maintain credit accounts for a long time.
8. If adverse financial circumstances prevent you from paying bills in full, contact the companies or creditors to arrange to pay a smaller amount. Be proactive and keep communicating with your creditors.

Beware of services that claim they can fix a bad credit history or inaccuracies. Nothing but time and diligence can repair your credit history.

End Note$

While all this may seem like a lot of work to review and improve your credit history, few things can help you as significantly in your financial life. You will enjoy the rewards for many years to come.

BRYAN CLINTSMAN, CFP® (Southlake, Texas) and **TIMOTHY A. VAUGHN,** MBA (Bel Air, Maryland)

TIP 11 THE BENEFIT OF MAKING SUBTLE CREDIT SCORE IMPROVEMENTS

Q. My credit score has never prevented me from getting a loan. So what's the advantage of improving my score by just a few points?

A. Although your credit score may not prevent you from getting a loan, it may cause you to pay more to borrow money. As credit scores increase, the interest rates to borrow money tend to decrease. So you may have missed out on the most competitive interest rate the last time you borrowed money. With mortgages, for example, a slight decrease in interest rate from an improved credit score can mean significant savings over the life of the loan.

How to Obtain the Best Interest Rates on Loans and Mortgages

Having the best credit score possible improves your odds of getting the best rates on loans and mortgages. You can see how a higher credit score helps by visiting http://www.myFICO.com, a Web site from Fair, Issac, and Co., that each day correlates rates on mortgages, home equity, and auto loans with a borrower's credit scores.

This correlation is the net effect of two lending practices. First, some lending institutions will lend only to people who meet certain stringent criteria, including a high credit score. All consumers who meet the criteria get the same low interest rate. Other lenders use a tiered pricing structure, so that two consumers with vastly different credit scores may be offered financing, but the person with a higher credit score gets a lower interest rate.

Data from sources like http://www.myFICO.com can help you shop around for an appropriate interest rate for your credit score. The potential savings warrant a close look at your credit report before taking out your next loan. Increasing your credit score now may lead to a significant savings next time you borrow money.

BRYAN CLINTSMAN, CFP® (Southlake, Texas) and **TIMOTHY A. VAUGHN,** MBA (Bel Air, Maryland)

TIP 12 HOW TO RESOLVE CREDIT PROBLEMS

Q. Recently I was turned down for a loan because my credit rating is too low. What would cause my credit rating to be low, and how can I fix it?

A. As mentioned earlier, good credit makes an enormous difference to your financial health and your ability to borrow money at reasonable interest rates. A credit history is the record of how well you have handled your financial obligations over a period of time.

To help correct a poor credit report

- know where you stand with the credit bureaus right now.
- understand what causes a credit score to be low.
- dispute negative credit information.
- add positive credit information.
- keep your credit rating healthy.

Credit Card Balances

The best way to improve your credit score when you have credit cards with high account balances is to pay off the debt, then keep balances low enough to pay the cards off each month. If a card's limit is $2,000, and you have a balance of $1,800, the account's debt-to-credit ratio is 90 percent. A guideline is to have no more than 40 percent debt-to-credit per account. Pay down your credit cards with high interest rates first. Always remember: if you only pay the minimum payment each month, you'll never get out of debt.

Negative Public Records

Negative public records, collections, or bankruptcy will lower your credit scores. Most bankruptcy information will remain on your credit report for ten years from the date of filing. Unpaid tax liens generally will be reported for an indefinite period of time depending on your state of residence. Paid tax liens may be reported for seven years from the date of payment. All other public record information, including discharged Chapter 13 Bankruptcy and any accounts containing unfavorable information, generally remains for seven years, depending on your state of residence.

More Steps to Improving What's Already on Your Credit Report

You have the right to challenge or dispute any incorrect items. Your credit report comes with a Dispute Form that you can use to write a letter disputing any discrepancies. Your dispute letter should always include your name, address, and Social Security number. List the name and number of the account you are disputing along with a brief explanation of why you are disputing the information. Only correct two or three accounts at one time, so you do not give the wrong impression and your request is taken seriously.

You should receive a response in approximately four weeks along with a new credit report allowing you to check the results. If you have more credit challenges, send a new dispute letter for the next two or three accounts, and continue this process until all of your inquiries have been addressed. Persistence and patience with this process are key.

If you don't receive a response to your original letter, send another stating the following:

- The date you sent the first letter
- That they have not lived up to their responsibility to investigate this account
- That they are in violation of the Fair Credit Reporting Act
- That the disputed account must now be removed from your credit report
- That you may file a complaint with the Office of the Attorney General and the Federal Trade Commission if they do not comply
- That you may pursue with an attorney your right to recover damages under the Federal Credit Reporting Act

Adding Positive Credit

One way to build positive credit is to open a secured credit card. The card company requires you to deposit an amount of money (say $500), then allows you to use your credit card up to that balance limit. Paying off your secured card monthly reestablishes a good payment record and rebuilds your credit. It's also a great way to build new credit. Parents may want to consider opening a secured credit card for their teenagers to show them how to build good credit. Lenders consider the following items to be positives when checking your credit:

- Four to six active, paid-as-agreed credit card accounts
- High credit limits on all your credit lines ($2,000 or more)
- Low outstanding balances
- A large purchase paid off in a timely manner (on a credit card)
- Good payment histories for 12 to 24 months (the longer the better)

SHERRY HINRICHS (Santa Rosa, California)

TIP 13 STEPS TO PREVENT IDENTITY THEFT—DON'T LET IT HAPPEN TO YOU

Q. Identity theft is in the news. How common is it, and what can I do to prevent this from happening to me?

A. Identity theft—stealing someone's personal identifying information, then fraudulently using it to establish credit or to take over existing accounts—is the #1 white-collar crime in America today. MasterCard® and Visa® losses due to identity theft approach $1 billion a year, according to the General Accounting Office. Some 250,000 to 750,000 Americans are victims of identity theft each year, and this number is growing rapidly.

Could It Happen to You?

Many people naively believe that identity fraud occurs only when a wallet is stolen or private information is given to unscrupulous parties over the Internet. But a confidential statement in the trash, stolen mail, or a photocopied ID card is a first step to identity theft and a point of vulnerability for almost all of us. With this information, an identity thief could open the door to your bank and investment accounts, order new credit cards, and maybe even get a mortgage in your name.

If you think it can't happen to you, think again. Consider one identity theft victim's all-too-common story.

> I was alerted to more than $35,000 in credit card transactions when a collections agency called my house. This involved nine different companies in less than a 60-day period. Interestingly enough, no driver's license, Social Security card, or mother's maiden name had ever left my possession. However, when I saw the applications at several department stores, it was all there—but with a different lady's picture. It took many months and much effort to resolve the matter properly.

Using the most basic personal information, almost anyone can put their picture on a counterfeit driver's license and pretend to be you to open credit card accounts. Only when you apply for credit or you need a current copy of your credit report, do you find out your record is filled with late payments, collections, and delinquencies.

While phony credit cards are frightening, identity theft can get worse. Once a crook has a counterfeit driver's license with your name on it, they can visit any branch of your bank and clean out your accounts.

How to Protect Yourself

Caution and protection are key, and so is a healthy paranoia. Beyond the obvious recommendations such as shredding your sensitive trash and guarding your Social Security number, be aware of your exposure through corporations and organizations. For starters, identity fraud rings can exist at your bank, department store, or financial institution or in the back office of an Internet service provider. Too many employees, not all of whom may be ethical, have access to your records. Be wary of ever disclosing more private information than necessary, avoid any unnecessary credit lines, and deal only with well-known providers.

Other preventive measures include the following:

- *Watch the incoming mail for your regular bills.* If one is missing, track it down immediately. Filled-out checks can be acid-washed and filled back in with new payees or amounts due.
- *Shred your documents.* How much information can be found in your trash? Experian, the credit reporting agency, went dumpster diving in 400 household garbage bins. It found that 72 percent contained an individual's full name and address, 40 percent provided a full credit or debit card number, 32 percent divulged the card's expiration date, 20 percent held bank account numbers and sort codes, and one trash can even had a signed blank check.
- *Lock your mailbox.* Better yet, call 888-567-8688 to opt out of credit card solicitations altogether.
- *Guard your passwords and care for your cards.* Sign any new credit cards immediately. Don't attach your pin numbers to bankcards, and never carry a Social Security card. Carry only the cards you really need.
- *Consider using distinct passwords for various bank and brokerage accounts and any Internet site where personal information is communicated or stored.*
- *Know your bank's policy on fraud.* Is there a policy for reviewing fraudulent activities? If you can prove it wasn't you, will they work toward a consumer-friendly resolution? Conditional or provisional credit should be given in all fraud cases.
- *Monitor your credit report and consider subscribing to an alert service.* By the time identity theft is discovered—an average of 14 months after the crime, according to Equifax—a thief can wreak havoc on your credit standing.

Monitoring your credit report annually is a good start, but it gives scam artists months between your reviews to open new accounts. So choose an online credit monitoring service like http://www.privista.com to notify you instantly when someone tries to open an account in your name or when one of your credit cards gets hit with a surprisingly large purchase. Choose a service that monitors all three credit reporting agencies and that alerts you in real time—not quarterly or monthly.

- *Be aware.* Stay alert to the information that you release, be aware of changes to accounts or credit, and guard all your transactions as if they were personal and confidential—and maybe they'll stay that way.

End Note$

A leading source of information on identity theft is the Federal Trade Commission's Web site (http://www.consumer.gov/idtheft). It includes tips on how to minimize your risk, what to do if you're a victim, and how to file a complaint, among other useful information.

EILEEN S. FREIBURGER, CFP® (El Segundo, California)

TIP 14 THERE ARE DEBTS ON MY CREDIT REPORT THAT AREN'T MINE. WHAT NOW?

Q. I requested my credit report, and there were credit cards listed that I'd never heard of. What do I do now?

A. Find out if it's an error. But if you suspect your identity has been violated, get organized immediately. Start with a legal file that has six to eight partitions, and mark the sections as indicated below.

Section 1: Police report. It may take time and diligence to have the police take your report, but do it. Eventually, every store will ask for an affidavit and a police report.

Section 2: Credit bureau statements. Contact the fraud departments of Equifax, Experian, and TransUnion, the three major credit bureaus. If you haven't received one already, request a copy of your credit report from each and look for any unusual or unexplained activity. Request that a fraud alert be placed in your file, and ask that creditors call you before opening any new accounts or changing your existing accounts.

Section 3: Call log. Start a logbook of all related calls. Keep a separate, color-coded page for each store, fraudulent transaction, or financial institution involved. Always speak directly with the fraud department.

Call your bank if you suspect that your banking relationship has been broached. You can place a stop payment on missing checks, or you can contact the major check verification companies directly to request that they notify retailers who use their databases not to accept your checks.

Call credit cards, department stores, and other creditors to let them know that you are a victim of identity fraud and that you wish to close your account and clear your name. Always keep track of the date, time, contact person, and topic of each call and consider following up each call in writing.

Section 4: Correspondence. Keep copies of everything from e-mails to certified letters as you plod through the process of clearing your name. The FTC provides a sample letter on its Web site (http://www.ftc.gov) to get you started. Again, differentiate your transactions or institutions by using different colors of paper.

Make a cover sheet for each company and indicate the next step and date. Organize your correspondence so you'll know at a glance when your case has been passed from a store's fraud department to the credit bureaus. Then make sure that the credit bureaus actually follow up. You're not done until your credit report reflects Closed/Fraud or some other notation indicating that you were not at fault.

Section 5: Affidavits. Every institution will require you to sign an oath and give detailed information. Most require that your signature be notarized (most banks provide free notary service for customers).

Section 6: Clearance letters. Have ready access to copies of all letters indicating that accounts have been closed or disputed charges and debts have been cleared. You may need these in the future if the wrong information resurfaces or if errors are not corrected.

End Note$

Here are a few useful Web sites and telephone numbers.

- Federal Trade Commission (http://www/consumer.gov/idtheft) or the Identity Theft Helpline (877-ID-THEFT, 877-438-4338). The FTC serves as the federal clearinghouse for complaints by victims of identity theft. While they do not resolve individual consumer problems, filing a complaint helps them investigate fraud and can lead to law enforcement action.

- Identity Theft and Protection (http://www.identitytheft.org)
- TeleCheck (800-710-9898)
- Certegy, Inc., previously Equifax Check Systems (800-437-5120)
- International Check Services (800-631-9656)

EILEEN S. FREIBURGER, CFP® (El Segundo, California)

TIP 15 MANAGING AND LEVERAGING YOUR DEBT

Q. I've heard different opinions on debt ratios and debt management. Is some debt OK?

A. Yes, it's OK to have some debt; however, it's important to distinguish between *good* debt and *bad* debt. *Good* debt, like mortgages and student loans, offers a tax deduction for the interest paid and often is used to buy an appreciating asset like a home or business. Generally speaking, most other debt is *bad* debt.

Think what you do when you run into debt; you give to another power over your liberty.

—BENJAMIN FRANKLIN

Advantages to Having Debt

Liquidity. A line of credit sometimes can be used to reduce the need for a high balance in liquid assets. For example, if you have only three months' living expenses in your emergency fund instead of the six months you might need, a line of credit can make up the difference in case of emergency.

Increasing your FICO scores. Having a credit card that you pay off on a timely basis actually boosts your credit score, but be sure to use a card with a low interest rate.

Leverage. Debt, when used properly, can leverage your purchasing power and magnify the return on an investment. Let's say you buy a home for $200,000, put down $40,000, and borrow the remaining 80 percent or $160,000. Several years later, you sell the house for $240,000. That's a $40,000 gain or 100 percent return on an initial investment of only $40,000. If you had paid for the house in cash, your gain would still be $40,000, but with a cash outlay of $200,000, your return would only be 20 percent.

Debt's Disadvantages

Leverage. When used inappropriately, debt can downwardly leverage or magnify losses. A prime example of this is borrowing on margin against stock investments. Sudden declines in investment values can trigger margin calls and magnify your losses. For example, with a $10,000 investment account, you can buy $20,000 worth of stock on margin (50 percent leverage). If you used that margin to purchase 1,000 shares of stock at $20 per share, and the price increased by 10 percent to $22 per share, your gain would be 20 percent on your investment ($22,000 sales price minus $10,000 margin minus $10,000 original account value equals $2,000 or 20 percent of your original account). However, if the price falls by 10 percent to $18 per share, your loss would be 20 percent and your account would now be worth $8,000. Investing on margin should be undertaken only by skilled investors who can closely monitor their holdings and quickly take action in case of negative outcomes.

You assume that things will not change. When you borrow, you assume that today's salary will continue (or increase) and that you will be able to repay the amounts you borrow. However, you might discover that you want to change careers, or your job may be eliminated, etc. If you have significant debts, you may be unable to adapt easily to the needed lifestyle changes.

Interest. Debt is not free. Even if the interest is tax deductible, it's still an expense. If you are in a lower tax bracket, every dollar of interest is worth only a 10-cent to 15-cent reduction in taxes. It is not wise to "buy more house" simply because you think you will save more on taxes, no matter what tax bracket you are in.

Managing Debt

Debt ratios. A general guideline is 28 percent to 36 percent debt-to-income ratio. The 28 percent, or front ratio, is calculated by dividing your total monthly housing expense (includes principal, interest, taxes, and insurance) by your total monthly pretax income. It should not exceed 28 percent. The 36 percent, or back ratio, is your total monthly housing expense (as calculated above) plus all other monthly debt, divided by your total monthly pretax income. It should not exceed 36 percent.

Before you borrow in excess of these amounts, seriously ask yourself if it's wise. You may prefer, for instance, to buy a less expensive home and use the savings to furnish it.

Cheap interest rates. As this book goes to press, interest rates are at an all-time low, and many low-interest rate options are available, especially on student loans, home equity loans, and mortgages. Locking in a low fixed rate now can be advantageous, because most people anticipate interest rates will rise in the future.

Pay off mortgage or save for retirement? If you have a mortgage fixed at 6 percent and are in a combined 35 percent federal and state tax bracket, your effective rate is 4 percent. If you're confident of achieving more than 4 percent after-tax returns on your investments over the long term, save for retirement before paying off the mortgage early. On the other hand, if you think long-term, after-tax returns will be less than 4 percent, go ahead and pay off the mortgage.

Home equity line or credit card consolidation? A major advantage of a home equity line of credit (HELOC) over ordinary credit card debt is that the interest is generally tax deductible. Also, consolidating your credit card debt with a HELOC looks better on your credit report than if consolidated with a credit card consolidation program.

The major disadvantage of using a HELOC to pay off credit card debt is that you convert unsecured debt into debt secured by your home. If you fail to make payments on the HELOC consistently, you could lose your home. Another danger is that you may rack up charges on your credit cards again—if you don't close them—finding yourself saddled not only with the HELOC but with credit card debt as well.

GLENDA K. MOEHLENPAH, CPA, CFP® (San Diego, California)

TIP 16 DROWNING IN DEBT? HOW TO GET OUT AND STAY OUT

Q. What can I do if I feel as though I'm drowning in debt?

A. First, let's explore some of the warning signs of imminent drowning.

- You only pay the minimum balance due every month.
- Occasionally you miss or are late with payments.
- You receive late fees, over-the-limit fees, and finance charges on your accounts.
- You use the grace period on a regular basis.
- You use a credit advance on one card to make the minimum payments on others.

- You're denied credit.
- You can't sleep due to worrying about your debt.

You do have options. Here's a closer look at some of them.

Bankruptcy

While bankruptcy forgives many debts, some—like child support, federal income taxes, and some student loans—are not erased.

Chapter 7 bankruptcy allows you to keep certain minimal exempt assets as determined by the state in which you live, and it eliminates many debts. Nonexempt assets are liquidated, and creditors share the proceeds.

In Chapter 13 bankruptcy, creditors agree to take a lower amount than the balance due, and your assets are not liquidated as long as you make the required payments. This option is generally available only if you have a steady income.

Either form of bankruptcy remains on your credit report for up to ten years, and it may affect your ability to obtain rental housing as well as future credit.

Credit Negotiation

Many creditors will negotiate directly with you for a lower total payment or reduced interest rates to help you avoid filing for bankruptcy. To the extent that actual debt (and not just future interest) is forgiven, the debt forgiveness is considered to be taxable income.

Debt Consolidation

Certain organizations, like Consumer Credit Counseling Services (http://www.cccsintl.org), will contact creditors on your behalf to negotiate for lower balances and generally lower interest rates. You pay a nominal fee to use their services. Credit consolidation may be considered a negative on your credit report and reduce your overall credit score.

Debt Repayment

Repaying debt impacts your credit score positively. While this method isn't easy, people who choose this path indicate a tremendous sense of accomplishment and satisfaction when they are finally debt free. To accomplish debt repayment, you need to use a budget.

Targeting Debt to Pay First

Over the long term, you will be better off financially if you pay off the debt with the highest interest rate first. However, for a sense of immediate accomplishment, you may wish to knock off debts with the lower balances when you can.

Budgeting for Debt Repayment

In establishing a debt repayment budget, you first need to determine your sources of cash inflows and discretionary and nondiscretionary cash outflows.

Cash inflow. While your primary source of cash inflow is probably employment, when you need money, remember that personal possessions can be sold. You can find buyers online at Web sites like eBay (http://www.ebay.com), at garage sales, pawnshops, or through local trading magazines to raise cash in an emergency.

Nondiscretionary cash outflows. These include your rent or mortgage payment, utilities, minimum and target debt repayment, taxes, child support, food, gas, and auto and home (or renter's) insurance. Set up monthly reserves to save for payments like auto insurance that may not be monthly.

Discretionary cash outflows. These include dining out, entertainment, personal care, clothing, gifts, and charitable contributions.

Stretching your pennies. If your cash inflows are insufficient to cover your outflows, you must increase the cash inflows, reduce the outflows, or both. Some possible options include getting a second job, taking in a boarder, carpooling or using public transportation, downsizing living quarters, taking your lunch, clipping coupons, and more.

Don't give up. Take action today to enjoy peace of mind and a brighter financial future.

GLENDA K. MOEHLENPAH, CPA, CFP® (San Diego, California)

TIP 17 WHEN RETHINKING THE RULES MAKES SENSE

Q. Many books on personal finance offer general guidelines for determining how much to save, where to invest, and how to make better money management decisions. Sometimes the guidelines don't seem right for me. Is there ever a time to stretch the rules—or even break them?

A. Financial planners and personal finance books frequently use general guidelines for recommendations, but one size does not fit all. Sometimes it makes sense to rethink the rules. Below are a few examples.

Emergency Funds: More or Less—and Where

The general rule is to keep the equivalent of three to six months' of expenses in an emergency fund. That's fine on average, but for some, a larger or smaller safety net makes sense. That includes people whose livelihoods are prone to downturns and prolonged unemployment. On the other hand, a two-income family with stable jobs, substantial assets, access to a home equity line of credit, and no large credit card balances may need to stash away less.

How you invest your emergency funds is another matter. Many people think their emergency funds should be in ultrasafe accounts, such as checking, savings, or money market accounts. Unfortunately, that means forgoing any meaningful growth opportunity on, potentially, a lot of money. These accounts pay very low interest, and you may not need to use them for years.

Investing money in a mutual fund may be worth the risk in your situation, because your money will have a chance to grow. Fund selection, however, is very important. Consider a conservative bond or balanced mutual fund with low expenses (the Vanguard family of funds is one source (http://www.vanguard.com). Be smart. Don't take unnecessary risks with your emergency funds. Remember that a rainy day fund is not sound if its roof has a leak.

Retirement Accounts as a Part of Your Emergency Preparedness Plan

Sometimes, building a large emergency fund should be balanced against adding to your retirement account. If your employer has a generous matching contribution to a tax-deferred plan, such as a 401(k) or 403(b), you might be better off placing a priority on funding your 401(k) rather than adding to your taxable emergency fund.

A retirement account also would be available if you lost your job or became disabled. The 10 percent tax penalty on premature withdrawals might be offset by your lower tax bracket as a result of your reduced or nonexistent income. If you had a personal hardship but still retained your job, you also might be able to access part of your money through a loan from your 401(k) plan. It would have to be repaid on a regular basis with interest, but essentially you would be repaying yourself the interest.

Similarly, funding your IRA every year may make more sense than funding a taxable emergency fund. While an IRA doesn't have the potential added benefit of a matching contribution from your employer and you cannot take out a loan against it, you still could be ahead because of tax-deferred or tax-free growth and possible tax deductibility of the original contribution.

Consider a Blended Approach for Your Safety Net

If you're still not comfortable deviating from the three-month to six-month guideline for emergency funds, consider a blended approach to your safety net. For example, combine a money market account with a short-term bond fund, laddered certificates of deposit (CDs with varying maturity periods), etc. A more aggressive but potentially much more rewarding strategy would be to keep one-third of your reserves in cash equivalents like the ones above, one-third available through a home equity line of credit, and a third in funds that you could access through your 401(k) and/or IRAs.

Home-Buying Guidelines: When to Stretch or Reinterpret the Rules

Experts offer lots of guidelines for how much home you can afford. But if you live in an area of expensive housing, national guidelines might not apply. Or what if you have other financial priorities, such as funding your children's education or retiring early? A less expensive home than the traditional guidelines allow may make more sense.

Similarly, the general guidelines may be to rent, not buy, if you plan to move within three years, because closing costs and Realtor fees overwhelm any tax savings or potential appreciation. What happens, though, if you expect a transfer in two years and your employer has a policy of reimbursing closing costs?

Here's another scenario. Experts often recommend financing your home with a long-term, fixed-rate mortgage to lock in costs and hedge against inflation and rising interest rates. But, if you expect a large sum of money with which you could pay off the mortgage or plan to sell the property within a few years, an Adjustable Rate Mortgage (ARM) could be significantly cheaper. Once again, individual circumstances are more important than guidelines.

Life Insurance Guidelines: When to Stretch or Reinterpret the Rules

Some general guidelines for determining the face amount of life insurance you need include buying seven to ten times your annual income and buying more death benefit if you have dependents. But, if your family has two incomes, lives a generally thrifty lifestyle, and saves regularly, you may need less. Your estate plans and personal objectives may also warrant rethinking the amount of life insurance you carry. For instance, if you have no children but wish to leave a charitable legacy, you can easily and effectively do so by purchasing a life insurance policy and naming the charities or organizations as your beneficiaries. Do you have a large estate? You may wish to purchase a life insurance policy to pay estate taxes upon your death so that your heirs receive their full inheritance.

Instead of accepting a general guideline, it makes sense to do a needs analysis of your situation.

ROGER STREIT, MBA (Montclair, New Jersey)

TIP 18 BEST BOOKS ON PERSONAL FINANCE

Q. I'm interested in learning more about personal finance. What are some good books?

A. Books on personal finance abound, but it can be tough trying to choose the right one for you. In addition to this book, here are 18 others to consider.

1. *You* Don't *Have to Be Rich: Comfort, Happiness, and Financial Security on Your Own Terms,* by Jean Chatzky (Portfolio/Penguin; 375 Hudson Street, New York, NY 10014; 212-366-2000). Chatzky, who is with NBC's *Today Show* and *Money* magazine, creates an insightful book that shows how to make financial decisions to make you truly happy, no matter your financial means.
2. *The Richest Man in Babylon,* by George Clason (Signet/Penguin; 375 Hudson Street, New York, NY 10014; 212-366-2000). The book jacket on this collection of parables written in the 1920s says it's, "the greatest of all inspirational works on the subject of thrift, financial planning, and personal wealth." This may or may not be the case, but it's a classic and well worth reading. The advice is just as sound today as it was 80 years ago when the book was written and 5,000 years ago in Babylon.
3. *Your Money or Your Life: Transforming Your Relationship with Money and Achieving Financial Independence,* by Joe Dominguez and Vicki Robin (Penguin; 375 Hudson Street, New York, NY 10014; 212-366-2000). This

is another classic and a bestselling book on how to get control of your money and your life. The authors help you take a look at how you handle your money and whether your financial management reflects of your values. This book can change your life.

4. *The Millionaire Next Door,* by Thomas Stanley and William Danko (Fine Communications). Contrary to what many may believe, most millionaires are not flashy. This book gives you a good profile of a typical millionaire, how they got there, and how you can learn from their habits. Who knows, you might even be the next Millionaire Next Door.
5. *Saving Money: A Smart and Easy Guide to Saving Money,* by Barbara Loos, (Silver Lining Books; 122 Fifth Street, New York, NY 10011; 212-633-4000). Formerly published under the title, *I Haven't Saved a Dime, Now What?!,* this book has been repackaged and sold under the Barnes & Noble Basics label. It is an enjoyable walk through the often puzzling and worrying world of money.
6. *Retiring: An Easy, Smart Guide to an Enjoyable Retirement,* by Hope Egan and Barbara Wagner (Silver Lining Books; 122 Fifth Street, New York, NY 10011; 212-633-4000). Formerly published under the title, *I'm Retiring, Now What?!,* this book has also been repackaged and sold under the Barnes & Noble Basics label. It discusses all you need to know to retire worry-free, from planning your retirement to making your money last and deciding where to live. Designed to make retirement more fun, the book even includes the inside track on travel for seniors.
7. *The New Retirementality,* by Mitch Anthony (Dearborn Trade Publishing; 30 South Wacker Drive, Chicago, IL 60606; 312-836-4400). This book will help put into perspective the notion of traditional retirement—the myths and realities of what we want when we say *retirement.* This book will help you paint a detailed portrait of your own perfect future and show you how to achieve it.
8. *The Budget Kit,* by Judy Lawrence (Dearborn Trade Publishing; 30 South Wacker Drive, Chicago, IL 60606; 312-836-4400). This pioneer budget book has been in print for over two decades and just released again as a new fourth edition. It's an excellent, practical, and easy-to-use workbook to help you organize, plan, track and manage your cash flow. The 240 pages are packed full of a year's worth of user-friendly worksheets for outlining a budget and tracking expenses every month. It even includes worksheets for debt payoff, windfalls, child support, online subscriptions, and gifts.
9. *Seven Stages of Money Maturity: Understanding the Spirit and Value of Money in Your Life,* by George Kinder (Dell Publishing/Random House; 1745 Broadway, New York, NY, 10036; 212-782-9000). This is a book that searches for the spiritual meaning in wealth; it tells the stories of three

composite characters. You learn how to evolve through the seven stages (innocence, pain, knowledge, understanding, vigor, vision, and aloha) necessary to achieve financial and emotional security.

10. *Affluenza: The All-Consuming Epidemic,* by John De Graaf, David Wann, and Thomas Naylor (Berrett-Koehler Publishers, Inc.; 235 Montgomery Street, Suite 650, San Francisco, CA 94104; 415-288-0260). The term *affluenza* suggests a disease from overconsumption. The theme of the book is that we and our society are consuming more than we should—and we are not any happier for it. This message is a major wake-up call for many of us.
11. *101 Tax Saving Ideas,* by Randy Gardner and Julie Welch (Wealth Builders Press; 800 West 47th Street, Suite 430, Kansas City, MO, 64112; 800-410-1829). This useful, expertly written book is a great guide for ideas on how to save money on taxes—it's not a dry, technical tax manual. It could very well save you some money, time, and headaches on your next tax return.
12. *Who Gets Grandma's Yellow Pie Plate?*, by Marlene Stum (University of Minnesota Extension Service; http://www.extension.umn.edu/). This is a sensible, down-to-earth guide on how to handle the distribution of family items from one generation to the next. The goal is to have the process be a celebration of the deceased person's life, rather than allowing emotions to harm or destroy family relationships.
13. *A Random Walk Down Wall Street: The Best Investment Advice for the New Century,* by Burton Malkiel (Norton W.W. & Company, Inc.; 500 Fifth Avenue, New York, NY, 10110). This is an investment classic, originally published in 1973. It has just been updated and now takes into account the dot-com meltdown. Among other topics, Malkiel gives an entertaining history of past market bubbles and explains why it's not worth trying to beat the market. There is also a life-cycle guide to investing.
14. *The Only Investment Guide You Will Ever Need,* by Andrew Tobias. (Harcourt; 15 East 26th Street, New York, NY, 10010; 212-592-1000). This guide has been updated many times and has been available for more than 20 years. This easy-to-read book covers many of the basics of personal finance, from investments and life insurance to Social Security.
15. *4 Steps to Financial Security for Lesbian and Gay Couples,* by Harold Lustig (Random House Publication Group; 201 East 50th Street, New York, NY, 10022; 212-751-2600). Because gay and lesbian and nonmarried heterosexual partners do not have legal marriage status, there are different approaches to the proper titling of assets, tax planning, and estate planning. This book is a good overall guide with sound advice. The concepts apply to all nonlegally married couples.

16. *The Essence of Success: 163 Life Lessons from the Dean of Self-Development,* by Earl Nightingale (Nightingale Conant Corporation; 6245 West Howard Street, Niles, IL, 60714; 800-560-6081). This classic collection of lessons touches on many topics, many of which relate to money. Setting goals, being creative, managing risk, making the most of opportunities, and other topics are covered. Each lesson is only a few pages long, so it is easy to read a few lessons at a time.
17. *Protecting Your Wealth in Good Times and Bad,* by Rick Ferri, CFA® (McGraw-Hill Trade, PO Box 182604, Columbus OH 43272, 877-833-5524). *Protecting Your Wealth* is an essential guidebook to a secure savings and investing strategy. Step by step, this book walks you through the process of developing and implementing a sound lifelong plan to grow and protect your hard-earned assets.
18. *Bogle on Mutual Funds: New Perspectives for the Intelligent Investor,* by John Bogle (Dell, 1745 Broadway, New York, NY 10036, 212-782-9000). This book explains the various investment markets and different types of mutual funds (bond stock, balanced, money market). It tells you how to understand and evaluate risk and gives advice on how to construct an investment program for whatever purpose you have in mind.

End Note$

All of these books can be found online at http://www.amazon.com or http://www.barnesandnoble.com and at most major bookstores.

JAMES J. PASZTOR JR. CFP® (Greensboro, North Carolina)

TIP 19 BEST SOFTWARE AND SYSTEMS FOR MANAGING YOUR PERSONAL FINANCES

Q. I am interested in a software program or some other system to assist me in streamlining my finances. What do you suggest?

A. Once you've organized your personal finances with the help of a home filing system, it's time to consider automating the management of your personal finances. Plenty of tools are available to help you with everything from reconciling checking accounts, paying bills, and budgeting to managing investments, tracking loans, buying insurance, or even paying taxes. Here's a look at some of them.

Software for Staying Organized

Quicken and Microsoft Money. Two of the most popular programs today are Microsoft Money and Quicken. Both are well recognized and tested and can be practical tools for managing your finances. Different versions of each provide specific features depending on your needs. Versions can range from basic/standard to premier/deluxe, and they can be packaged for either personal/home use, business use, or both.

The basic/standard versions are entry-level products designed for people new to personal finance software. They include basic features to track bank accounts, including scheduling and paying bills online, downloading financial statements, reconciling accounts, budgeting, and tracking spending patterns. You also can track, download, and analyze other accounts like credit cards, investments, and loans.

The advanced versions of Quicken and Microsoft Money are more robust, right for those who take a more active role in financial management, investments, and planning. All the benefits of the basic version are included along with features for investing, tax planning, and tax reporting. The extras enable you to create and track holdings, performance, and cost basis history of your investment portfolios and perform retirement and tax planning projections yourself.

The personal and small business versions include everything in the other versions as well as features to help you manage your small business finances. They help you automate the tracking of your business cash flow, inventory, receivables, and payables. They also automatically categorize tax-related items for your small business.

If you want to manage your money personally, then a software program such as these will be a valuable asset. Be prepared, however, to take the time required to input your financial information as you get started and also as you use the program. You can take heart in the fact, however, that it will eventually be time well spent, when you are able to download current information from your bank, credit card, and investment accounts; manage your cash flow; pay bills online; and utilize other features to make your life easier. If you are working with a financial planner, they may be willing to help you set up your Quicken or Money program, assign accounts that make sense for your personal situation, teach you how to use the program, etc.

For more information, visit http://www.quicken.com/quickensw or http://www.microsoft.com/money. In addition, you may wish to read Paul Lemon's book, *Ten Weeks to Financial Awakening: A Guidebook to the Creation of Your Own Financial Plan Using Quicken Software* (Beavers Pond Press).

Mvelopes spending management system. The Mvelopes Personal software program is based on the traditional envelope method of cash flow management. Rather than just helping you to reconcile your checking account and develop a budget based on what you want to do (like Quicken and Microsoft Money do), Mvelopes helps you develop and focus on your spending plan and helps you enforce the discipline you need to accomplish your financial objectives. If you are having a difficult time controlling your cash flow, this program can help get you on track. You will create spending accounts, or envelopes, and allocate your monthly income into each account based on a spending plan you construct in advance. Mvelopes allows you online access to gather all your daily financial transactions and account balances, assigns each transaction to an envelope/spending account by category, and then reduces the amount of money available from that account in real time, automatically, anytime you want. You will know exactly how much money you have remaining in each of your budgeted expense categories on any given day of the month. Remember, if you can measure it, you can manage it. Mvelopes Personal is the only tool of its kind to illustrate exactly where you stand at any moment with regard to your spending plan.

For a low, monthly fee, Mvelopes Personal has an online bill-paying service; asset tracking and management; and outstanding, unlimited user support and coaching services. Estimates are that people fritter away about 12 percent of their income. By better managing your cash flow, you can channel these resources to help achieve your long-term financial objectives.

To learn more, visit http://www.mvelopes.com.

Systems for Staying Organized

Nolo personal recordkeeper. If organization doesn't come easily to you and you need to cut through the financial-paperwork clutter, consider the Personal RecordKeeper software program. It makes it easy to organize various categories like insurance records, investments, medical and health care information, business interests, deeds and tax records, credit card information, and emergency contact information. You also can create a home inventory system and keep track of your estate planning documents.

The software lets you know what you have and where it is stored so you'll be less likely to misfile important personal and financial information.

For more information, visit http://www.nolo.com/lawstore/software/index.cfm.

Homefile® home organizer kit. This system includes 22 file divider cards that can be set up in a portable file box or in a file cabinet. The cards include categories like bank accounts, credit, expenses, insurance, investments, medical, residence, retirement, and taxes, just to name a few. Each card will show you what to file there, alleviating confusion. Also, the divider cards tell you when you can discard paperwork, meaning that you no longer have to keep unnecessary items.

This company also offers other financial document collectors, including a Safe Deposit Box Organizer and 31-Day Bill Organizer. More information is available online at http://www.homefile.net.

Prosperity for Life financial organizer binder. This system will help you accumulate the information you need to create a financial plan. It guides you through the process of completing two very important components of your plan: your net worth statement and your cash flow statement. It provides a centralized place for the important documents that you will need at tax time and in the event of a disability or death. It also serves as an important reminder of financial tasks that need to be done.

For more information, visit http://www.prosperityforlife.org.

Clearly Organized personal financial system. This is a binder with 42 specially printed envelopes and pouches organized into four different sections. As with the Homefile® Kit and the Prosperity for Life organizer, every document can be kept in one place, meaning that you will always know where you have filed a receipt, bill, or statement related to your personal finances. Also, the system may help make paying bills and taxes more simple and efficient.

It can work in conjunction with a software program like Quicken, Microsoft Money, or Mvelopes by helping you to manage all the paperwork, including receipts, bills, statements, and other records. It also will provide the backup you may need come tax time or if audited.

For more information, visit http://www.clearlyorganized.com.

Dome® simplified home budget book. More than a budget book, this oldie but goody may be all you need to manage your finances. While it focuses primarily on assisting homeowners in saving money, you may find value in the varied tips and simple organizational strategy offered. The book contains a completed example page, tax tips on how to cut interest costs on personal loans, how to figure out the operating cost of a car, and many more money-saving ideas. The book is undated—you fill in your own dates—so it is good for a full year from the time you start using it.

It's generally available at traditional office supply stores, or visit http://www.officedepot.com.

The Budget Kit, by Judy Lawrence, is a comprehensive, practical, and easy-to-use workbook to help you organize, plan, track and manage your cash flow. The 240 pages are packed full of a year's worth of user-friendly worksheets for outlining a budget and tracking expenses every month. It even includes worksheets for debt payoff, windfalls, child support, online subscription, and gifts. It is available from Dearborn Trade Publishing (http://www.dearborn.com/dfp/Trade_Home.asp).

CAROLANNE CHAVANNE, CFP® (Laguna Niguel, California)

TIP 20 TOP WEB SITES FOR LEARNING ABOUT PERSONAL FINANCE

Q. What Web sites are helpful for learning about financial planning issues?

A. The good news is that a wealth of financial planning information is easily accessible via the Internet. The quantity of information, however, includes highly commercialized sites focusing on product sales pitches, which yield little useful information, to sites that provide objective, unbiased information. Below are some quality sites with practical, easy-to-understand information on various financial planning topics.

College Funding

- *http://www.savingforcollege.com.* This College Planning Resources link includes a lot of information on college funding, with access to a college savings calculator and a nationwide college tuition database. This is considered by many to be the best Web site on the subject of college funding.
- *http://www.financenter.com/consumer.* Use the College Planning Calculator for general planning help and for budgeting college living expenses.
- *http://www.quicken.com/taxes.* Learn about available education funding plans and the general tax implications for each.

Debt Management

- *http://www.nolo.com and http://www.myvesta.org.* These sites offer general information on topics like debt and bankruptcy, overspending, credit repair, strategies for repaying debts, and debt collections.
- *http://www.cccintl.org.* This site offers various consumer services, such as information on consumer credit counseling and credit fraud, a summary of consumer rights, Fair Credit Reporting information, and links to related resources.

- *http://www.credittalk.com.* Learn about the basics of budgeting, credit reports, helpful credit tips, and tools for help managing your money.
- *http://www.quicken.com/planning/debt.* Get ideas to reduce your debt.

Estate Planning

- *http://www.nolo.com/lawcenter.* The Wills and Estate Planning link provides access to plain-language articles on topics such as estate planning basics, funeral planning, and various legal documents.
- *http://www.agingwithdignity.org.* Learn how to ensure that your wishes will be followed in the event of a serious illness, how to talk with loved ones and your physician about your wishes, and where to obtain resources for family caregivers. Also, you can access links to related sites. Check out their "Five Wishes" brochure.

Finding a Financial Planner

- *http://www.GarrettPlanningNetwork.com.* The nation's premier organization of hourly, fee-only planners offers information on how planners differ. Enter through the Consumer button; includes a Find a Planner function.
- *http://www.napfa.org.* For a questionnaire that you can use to interview potential financial planners, check out the Consumer Tips link; includes a Find a Planner function.
- *http://www.cfp-board.com.* The organization that awards the CFP® marks of distinction offers insights on how planners are credentialed.
- *http://www.fpanet.org.* For a questionnaire that you can use to interview potential financial planners, click through to the Consumer leg of the site; includes a Find a Planner feature.

Home Ownership

- *http://www.bankrate.com.* Has assorted general consumer information, including current mortgage rates for a specific location, calculators to help you determine how much house you can afford, and a glossary.
- *http://www.askjeeves.com.* The First Time Home Buyers Program contains solid information related to buying and financing a first home.
- *http://www.financecenter.com/consumer/calculators.* Use the features under the Home Financing link to compare loan terms and lenders, analyze

whether paying points or making extra payments is best, and determine in general terms how much you can borrow.

Retirement

- *http://www.quicken.com/taxes.* The Life Events link under Tax Planning provides general consumer information on issues like Social Security and taxes, changes in retirement laws, tax impact of early withdrawals from retirement plans, and inheriting an IRA.
- *http://www.nolo.com/lawcenter.* The Retirement and Eldercare link provides access to helpful information on assorted topics such as Social Security, retirement plans, Medicare, Medicaid, and long-term health care.

More Senior Issues

- *http://www.aarp.org.* This site focuses on retired people or those planning for retirement and provides access to a wide range of useful information. Be sure to check out Learning, Life Answers, and Money and Work.
- *http://www.medicare.gov.* Learn about eligibility and benefits, compare health care options, download Medicare publications, and locate participating providers in a specific area.
- *http://www.ssa.gov.* Access a wealth of information related to Social Security, obtain general planning information, and apply for benefits online.

Taxes

- *http://www.irs.gov.* Access a comprehensive database of information, obtain recent tax news, and download forms and publications.
- *http://www.quicken.com/taxes.* Obtain plain-language summaries of recent tax law changes, access tax planning tips, and use the calculators for general tax planning.

DEIDRA FULTON, CPCU (Plano, Texas)

Chapter

2

RISK MANAGEMENT

TIP 21 MINIMIZING YOUR FINANCIAL RISK WITH INSURANCE PRODUCTS AND LEGAL CONTRACTS

Q. We are living on a limited budget, but know we need certain kinds of insurance to protect ourselves and our assets. What are the major types of insurance, and under what situations would we need them?

A. Mitigating financial risk with insurance products is essential to most Americans' financial well being. Financial plans, after all, are best when built on a strong foundation. Look at the great pyramid of Ghufu at Giza in Egypt. Built more than 4,000 years ago, its foundation is of the highest quality limestone, which has provided the stability and strength to last through the ages.

Your financial pyramid's foundation also should provide stability and strength, regardless of your age or economic situation. Here's a brief look at some risk-management tools and how each contributes to a strong financial foundation. You can learn more about each in detail later in this chapter.

Property/Casualty Insurance

Earthquakes, fires, floods, and mudslides along with theft and vandalism affecting your home, and auto accidents can occur at any time. Make sure you have sufficient coverage from an insurance company with a good rating. Note also that standard property/casualty policies do not always cover risks that may be specific to a particular area, such as floods or mudslides. You may need to purchase a rider or separate coverage. For example, flood insurance is provided through the federal National Flood Insurance Program, but policies are issued through traditional property and casualty insurance agents. Periodically review and update your policies, too.

Be sure to firm up what can be an expensive crack in your pyramid's foundation by purchasing an umbrella liability policy.

Health Insurance

The two primary types of health insurance are medical insurance and long-term care insurance.

1. *Medical insurance.* The costs of medical/hospital insurance can seem high, but a serious illness, accident, or injury could bankrupt you. Get a good policy and pay the premiums.
2. *Long-term care insurance.* You work diligently to accumulate assets that will, you hope, provide a lifetime income and a possible legacy for your heirs. An extended stay in a nursing home could destroy that plan. You can transfer all or most of that risk to an insurance company by purchasing long-term care insurance. You may want to consider a plan for not only yourself but also your parents.

Disability Insurance

One likely gaping hole in the foundation is income-continuation insurance. If you have an accident or become ill and can't work, how much monthly disability income will you receive? For how long? Think of yourself as a money machine that provides the income that pays the bills. Insure yourself to the maximum allowed. The potential to earn income is usually one's most significant asset.

Life Insurance

How much life insurance is enough? While some general guidelines apply, you should buy an amount that would allow your family to maintain its lifestyle, assuming that is your family's objective. A variety of cost-effective policies are available, and you can learn details via the Internet. Be sure that the policy you buy is from a strong, reliable company with sterling ratings. Refer to the end of this chapter for Web site resources.

Other Risk-Mitigation Tools: A Will or Revocable Living Trust

Mitigate another risk with a properly executed Will or revocable Trust. It's not insurance related, but it's important to your financial well-being. In many states, if you die without a Will *(intestate),* the state will dictate the terms of your estate distribution and appoint guardians for your children. The guardian may not be the person or people you had in mind, and your financial assets might not be managed or distributed as you wished.

A Revocable Living Trust commonly is used to (1) avoid probate, (2) allow the Trustee(s) (generally you and your spouse) to manage your assets while living, and (3) facilitate decision-making and the legal process in case of incapacity. The Trust agreement has provisions for distributing the Trust assets after your death, similar to a Will. Because it is revocable, you, the grantor, can change terms and remove assets freely. Even if you use a Revocable Living Trust, it's important also to have a Will (sometimes called a Pourover Will) because all your assets many not be titled in the Trust's name.

MARY ANN SHEETS-HANSON, CFP® (Walnut Creek, California)

TIP 22 THE PURPOSE AND VARIETIES OF LIFE INSURANCE

Q. Why purchase life insurance? What kind should I buy?

A. The primary purpose of life insurance is to manage the financial risk of premature or untimely death. In addition to providing death benefits, life insurance also can offer living benefits.

The Advantages

The death benefits of life insurance may include the following:

- Replacing income and providing financial security for heirs
- Paying off outstanding debt, including the mortgage
- Meeting ongoing alimony/child support payments
- Covering final expenses like a funeral and medical bills
- Providing for estate liquidity and/or payment of estate taxes
- Making charitable gifts
- Protecting a business against financial hardship incurred at the death of a key employee

Living benefits of life insurance may include the following:

- Forced savings/emergency funds
- College expenses
- Supplemental retirement income

The Three General Categories of Life Insurance

The types of life insurance are *term* (death benefits only), *universal* (death and living benefits), and *whole* (death and living benefits). Each has advantages, and one size doesn't fit all.

To understand better the differences between the types of life insurance, think in terms of renting an apartment, buying a condo, or purchasing a home. Term insurance is like renting. As long as you pay your rent, you have a place to live. You usually have the choice of renting month-to-month or signing a short-term or long-term lease. At the end of the first year or lease period, the rent usually increases. And, no matter how many years you pay rent, you don't build equity. Like renting, term life insurance is less costly to get into, but the monthly premiums go up as you age. Term policies are available for differing periods of time, but they expire either at the end of the coverage period or when you stop paying premiums. A term policy pays out if you die during the coverage period, but it's worth nothing if you don't.

Universal life is like purchasing a condo or townhouse. Generally, the cost is higher than renting but less than purchasing a single-family home. And, as when you buy a condo, some monthly costs like association fees go up, and they never end even when the mortgage is paid off. But you are building equity, and if you decide to sell, you likely will have accumulated cash and profit. Just as with buying a condo, universal life insurance costs more to get into and includes some additional fees, but you build up equity in your insurance policy. The policy then has permanent value, even if you do not die during the coverage period.

Whole life is like purchasing a single-family home. The cost is usually greater than the condo, you'll likely need a larger down payment, and the monthly payments will be higher. However, over the long term, the accumulated equity in your home can be substantial. In addition, you may decide to pay off the mortgage so you will not have house payments during your retirement years. With whole life insurance, you pay more in premiums for your death-benefit coverage; however, you not only receive death-benefit coverage but also an opportunity to accumulate equity value over the life of the policy.

This analogy illustrates why term insurance is often called *temporary* coverage, and universal life and whole life *permanent* coverage. While many people go through life just fine using term life insurance, others need permanent protection and may have reason to build up equity through life insurance.

Determining the Policy That's Right for You

Term life can be cost-effective for people with a pure life insurance need for a specific period of time. Universal and whole life policies may be right for those who need to combine a life insurance and savings element, or who have a lifetime need for insurance. The latter, for example, could include providing estate liquidity, paying estate taxes, or paying heirs of a key business partner in the event of their death.

When deciding what's right for you, augment professional advice with your own research and, possibly, a second professional opinion. Then look at the options and make the decision that's best for you.

Read the following pages and weigh your options carefully before making hasty decisions that you may regret later.

MARY ANN SHEETS-HANSON, CFP® (Walnut Creek, California)

TIP 23 MORE ON COMPARING TYPES OF LIFE INSURANCE

Q. I would like to know more about the various types of life insurance that are available. Can you help me?

A. Understanding the various types of life insurance can help you make a better informed decision. Below are the major types of life insurance contracts you are likely to encounter.

Term Life Insurance

Term insurance offers the most coverage for the lowest premium and is the most economical if it's needed for a specific period of time, such as while you have a dependent spouse and children.

Three popular types of term insurance are the following:

1. *Annual Renewable Term (ART).* Has a preset and unchangeable death benefit; contract renews annually; premiums increase each year; best if you have a short-term need of about five years or less.
2. *Level term.* Higher premiums than ART in first years; premiums and coverage remain level for stated time period—10, 15, 20, and sometimes 30

years; at end of period, it may be possible to convert your term policy or buy a new term policy, although proof of insurability will be required; some contracts allow ongoing coverage at high premiums.

3. *Decreasing term or mortgage insurance.* Face amount or death benefit decreases annually while the premiums remain the same; insurance protection ends when the face amount decreases to zero; useful if life insurance need declines over time, for example if college expenses wind down or you pay off your mortgage. Often, you can find level term policies that are as economical as decreasing term policies, but you maintain level coverage.

Advantages of term life insurance. This type of policy is substantially less expensive than whole or universal life insurance and offers pure death protection, and some policies can be renewed or converted, although usually at higher premiums. The disadvantages include no benefit if you outlive the specified period plan and no savings element.

Universal Life Insurance

Universal life insurance combines term life protection and a cash-value fund that accumulates tax-deferred. This product and its cousin, variable universal life, are the insurance industry's answer to critics who suggested that consumers would be better off to buy term and invest the difference.

The life insurance company deducts certain expenses and the pure insurance protection cost from the premiums paid. The balance of the premium earns interest in a cash-value fund, similar to a savings account. These contracts include both a guaranteed and a current interest rate. All the costs of the contract, the cash value, and current rate of interest earned are listed in your annual statement. Because the costs and benefits are revealed, universal and variable universal life plans are sometimes referred to as *unbundled* insurance contracts.

Advantages of universal life insurance. These contracts have cash value that earns tax-deferred interest at competitive market rates, and premiums can be flexible. You can even skip making premium payments as long as the accumulated cash value covers the cost of the pure insurance protection. Depending on the contract, you also may be able to increase or decrease the contract death benefit according to your needs. Policy loans are available at fairly competitive interest rates.

Disadvantages of universal life insurance. Rates paid by the insurance company may drop as low as the contract guaranteed rate, and you may have to pay additional premiums to keep the contract in force. Also, your contract may not have the most competitive insurance rates or be the most effective savings vehicle.

Variable Universal Life Insurance

Variable life insurance is like universal life in many ways, combining term life protection and a cash-value fund. The big difference is that, rather than earning a rate of interest, the cash portion can be invested in a variety of vehicles like equity and bond mutual funds, cash, and real estate securities. Unlike universal life, you choose the investments and assume the investment risk. The life insurance company offers you a selection and pays various mutual fund companies or third-party money managers to invest and manage the money, according to the policy contract.

Advantages of variable universal life. You're guaranteed the minimum death benefit if the minimum required premium is paid; you can change your investment allocation, keep professional investment management, enjoy tax-deferred earnings, and there's potential for cash in the account to accumulate quickly due to equity growth.

Disadvantages of variable universal life insurance. Exposure to market risk may put your policy in jeopardy, forcing payment of additional premiums to keep the contract in force. Also, your contract may not have the most competitive insurance rates and/or not be the most cost-effective or flexible investment vehicle.

Whole Life Insurance

Whole life insurance insures you for life. Some contracts are called 20-Pay or Life 65, which usually means the premiums are paid for 20 years, or to age 65. All others are generally paid for your lifetime. Basically the premium you pay the first month, quarter, or year remains the same. While premiums are initially higher than term or variable universal policies, whole life contracts come with many guarantees.

Advantages of whole life. Guaranteed premiums, interest, and death benefit; lifetime protection; cash value compounds, which can be substantial after about ten years; policy loans available at rates guaranteed in the contract; forced, tax-deferred savings with the benefit of FIFO (first in, first out) withdrawals; and, if protection is needed for ten or more years, may be cost effective.

Disadvantages of whole life. Compared with term or universal plans, the premiums are higher; premiums are not flexible; only guaranteed interest—not the current rate—is disclosed in the contract, and you should be ready to pay the required premiums for at least ten or more years.

Partnership Life Insurance Plans

There are two types of partnership plans: first-to-die and second-to-die. Both insure two lives with one contract, usually cost less than two individual policies, and provide flexibility in the amount of premiums paid. The insurance carrier will blend dividend-paying whole life with term insurance. If you choose a blend that contains more whole life, the premiums will be higher versus a plan that has less whole life and more term insurance.

First-to-die plans work well for married couples or partners in either personal or business relationships. The death benefit will be paid to the surviving partner at the death of the first partner. If death is simultaneous, each partner's contingent beneficiary will be paid the full death benefit.

Second-to-die plans pay the death benefit at the second death and often are used to pay estate taxes that come due after the death of the second or surviving spouse. It's usually cost-effective to fund and leverage a charitable gift. Premiums are based on a joint equal age, and if one of the spouses is in poor health or medically uninsurable, the good health of the second spouse equalizes the underwriting risk.

Shop Carefully

Most companies offer a variety of contracts. Shop carefully and ask informed questions. It's important to purchase from a company with sterling ratings. Ratings agencies include Standard & Poor's (http://www.standardpoors.com), Moody's Investor Service (http://www.moodys.com), Fitch IBCA (http://www.fitchicba.com), and A.M. Best (http://www.ambest.com).

Remember, as with housing, cheapest isn't necessarily what you want or need over the long run. Meet with your financial advisor to analyze your needs and options. You're insuring the financial value of your life. When the resources are needed, they must be available.

MARY ANN SHEETS-HANSON, CFP® (Walnut Creek, California)

TIP 24 A CLOSER LOOK AT TERM AND WHOLE LIFE INSURANCE

Q. I've decided to purchase life insurance. Should I purchase a term or whole life insurance policy?

A. The right answer depends on your financial situation and how you plan to use the life insurance. This section will provide some basic information and guidelines that, hopefully, can help you make a wise decision.

Term and Whole Life Defined

Life insurance is most often purchased to offset the impact of premature or untimely death. Term life pays a death benefit if the insured dies within a certain time period or term. If the insured dies outside of the term, a death benefit is not paid. A term policy's premium is based on the life expectancy of the insured and the costs incurred by the insurance company (including a commission to the selling agent, if the policy is not structured as no-load).

Whole life insurance combines the pure insurance aspect of term insurance with a savings account and requires a higher premium than term. The coverage is effective for your entire life. It primarily differs from term life in that it guarantees a death benefit payment as long as the policy is in force and the premiums paid. That's why it requires an attached savings account. As the savings account grows, the policyholder gradually becomes more "self-insured," through the savings account built into the policy.

Cash Value Life Insurance Compared with Other Investment Options

As mentioned above, the main difference between term and whole life is the savings element or *cash value* of the whole life policy. Because the cash value component is a long-term investment, it needs to be compared with other investment alternatives. Here's a closer look.

Transaction costs. Investment management costs for most policies are similar to those of mutual funds. Remember that you are buying life insurance and must pay for the cost of the death benefit as well. Sales commissions are significantly higher for a cash value policy than for a term life policy. Whole life policies also typically have surrender charges that go to the agent and insurance company should the policy be canceled before a certain time has elapsed, generally ten years. Therefore, whole life savings accounts can be a high-cost investment vehicle.

Expected rate of return. In most whole life policies, the savings account is invested in cash, bonds, and other loans. Because stocks and other equities have, over longer periods of time, outperformed bonds and other debt instruments, you may be losing out on investment performance. Variable universal life policies are a way to incorporate equity investments into a life insurance policy, but the policyholder assumes the investment risk.

Taxation. The cash value of a whole life policy grows tax-deferred. If the cash value is held until death, the proceeds are considered tax-free life insurance benefits to your heirs. However, if withdrawn prior to death, gains are taxed as ordinary income, at rates that are typically higher than capital gains taxes. If you don't need the lifetime coverage for estate planning or other reasons, other savings vehicles may provide more flexibility and the potential for higher returns than a whole life insurance policy.

For example, if you qualify for a Roth IRA, you can get similar tax-sheltering properties because Roth IRA gains are tax-deferred. Unlike the whole life savings account, the Roth IRA allows for tax-free withdrawals once the owner reaches age 59½ and/or the account has been open five years. Annual contributions to Roth IRAs are limited, however, and you may be able to shelter more in a whole life policy than you can in a Roth IRA.

Control of investment options. Outside investments often allow greater investment options and flexibility than whole life policies.

General Guidelines for Purchasing Life Insurance

- Buy insurance that covers the time frame corresponding with your exposure to risk. If you need death protection for a term of 30 years or less, term insurance may be your best option.
- Have the primary benefits of a whole life policy by buying term and using the premium difference to pay off debt or invest in a Roth IRA.
- Consider using whole life insurance as a tax-sheltered investment vehicle if you have exhausted other tax-advantaged possibilities like a Roth IRA, traditional IRA, 401(k) or 403(b) (for retirement savings) and/or a 529 Plan or Education Savings Account (for education savings). But compare whole life with an annuity, which is also a tax-sheltered investment vehicle to determine which product might be more appropriate for your circumstances.
- If you are unsure of your needs-based time frame, buy a convertible term policy that enables you to convert a traditional term policy to a whole life policy. Be aware, however, that a conversion option comes at a price.

- Purchase low-load insurance policies to minimize your insurance costs. Use the Internet to research options or work with an independent insurance consultant who represents a number of companies that provide high-quality, low-priced life insurance coverage. A quick check on competitive policies can be beneficial. See references to specific Web sites later in this chapter.

SHERYL D. GARRETT, CFP® (Shawnee Mission, Kansas)

TIP 25 HOW MUCH COVERAGE YOU NEED TO PROTECT YOUR LOVED ONES

Q. I want to buy life insurance. How do I determine the right amount of death protection to buy?

A. While the average consumer enjoys shopping for life insurance about as much as buying a used car, the process does not need to be as cumbersome or mind-boggling as some may make it seem.

The Basics

Despite all the motivated insurance agents out there, most Americans are underinsured. To help you determine how much insurance you actually need, let's go back to the basics.

A general guideline is that you should have at least five to seven times your salary in insurance coverage. But no two situations are the same, so you need to do your homework to find out what's best for you.

The Internet offers many resources to help you calculate the insurance you need. While these sites offer helpful calculation tools, they still may not yield the best answer because they are based on general guidelines.

When evaluating how much life insurance to purchase, consider your current age and health, debt load, the educational needs of your children or grandchildren, your total assets, and the ages of your spouse and children.

How Much Is Enough for the Breadwinner?

Consider this real-life needs analysis developed using a professional software program. John and Jill Sample, both 31, have been married two years and expect a baby in three months. Both are employed, but Jill plans to become a full-time mother when the baby is born. John's income is $80,000, enough to live comfortably, and Jill's is $32,000 (which will stop when the baby is born). They just purchased a $250,000 home with $50,000 down and have a $200,000 mortgage. They have $5,000 in credit card debt. They have $10,000 in mutual fund investments and $4,000 in emergency money (they are rebuilding that to $50,000). John's 401(k) plan is worth $15,000, and Jill's is worth $7,500. John already has life insurance provided by his employer for twice his salary, or $160,000. Jill also has employer-provided insurance for $50,000, which will terminate when she leaves the company.

If John died suddenly, Jill would need enough life insurance coverage to eliminate all their debts, provide living expenses while she raises the child, pay for the child's education, and help provide for her living expenses through retirement. For the purposes of this example, let's assume $25,000 for funeral and final medical expenses, plus $2,500 in probate and administration costs surrounding John's death. Let's also estimate that $50,000 needs to be invested at John's death in a separate account to fund college education completely for the child. We also want to be sure there is $50,000 in the emergency fund.

If John were to die "today" (or in the next three years), he would need slightly more than $1 million in capital to pay for his immediate expenses, fund his baby's education completely, and provide for his family's living expenses. This assumes that Jill does not have an earned income again at some point. After subtracting their available capital, Social Security Death Benefit, and existing life insurance benefits from his work-related policy, John still needs an additional $822,004 in life insurance to meet his $1,007,259 capital need. John would be wise to purchase at least $800,000 in 20-year term life insurance. The 20-year term is a good choice because his insurance needs will reduce drastically once his child is out (or nearly out) of college.

Determining Life Insurance for a Stay-at-Home Spouse

If Jill were to die suddenly, John might have to quit his job or provide full-time care for their child. Let's assume he would keep working and pay for childcare—at least $1,500 a month. He also needs to have at least $50,000 in an emergency fund. Analyzing the details, Jill would need at least $100,000 in 20-year term life insurance to fund the child's college education and fund their emergency fund. The cost of childcare will easily add another $100,000 in death benefits need.

End Note$

No one enjoys talking about the possibility of unexpected death, but it does occur and should be planned for. You likely will be more comfortable after going through the process and purchasing the proper amount of coverage, knowing that your loved ones will be able to maintain their lifestyle if the unexpected happens.

JAMES H. CHRISTIE, CFP® (Bridgewater, New Jersey)

TIP 26 THE DOS AND DON'TS OF DISABILITY INSURANCE

Q. What is disability insurance? Do I need it?

A. Like life insurance, disability income insurance is designed to protect your income. But in this case, the income lapse would be due to your inability to work as a result of an illness or injury. If you work for a living and need your income to live on, you need disability insurance.

Financial Impact of Long-Term Disability

A disability can be more economically devastating than death. Not only does your income stop, but expenses usually increase. In addition, at most any age, the chance of disability is far greater than the chance of death. If you are 35 to 65, the chances of a total disability of three months or more are 33 to 70 percent. Though the majority of disabilities are short term, nearly 30 percent of all cases are permanent. So ask yourself: What would happen financially to you and your family if you became disabled and could no longer work, for a few weeks or forever?

Even if your employer offers disability insurance, the coverage may not be enough to keep you financially solvent. Self-employed people must, of course, obtain their own policies. And government programs provide few benefits. To receive Social Security, a worker must be totally and permanently disabled and be unable to work in any gainful activity anywhere in the country. These criteria make it notoriously difficult to collect benefits, and the amount collected is very low. Workers' Compensation pays only for disabilities arising out of and in the course of employment.

Disability Income Needs Analysis

How much disability insurance do you need? Generally, as much as you can get—unless you have other sources of nonemployment income or investments to fall back on and are willing to reduce your standard of living drastically. Insurers usually provide a maximum benefit of 65 percent to 70 percent of your income.

If you pay for the policy, the benefits will be tax free; if your employer does, benefits are taxable. If your employer offers disability insurance and you are not automatically enrolled for it, sign up as soon as possible.

Coverage available under group plans is sometimes broader than that offered by individual policies, and the cost is usually a lot lower. Some group policies cannot be converted to individual policies. If you anticipate frequent job changes or worry about developing a condition that would make you ineligible for future coverage, or you want to more adequately insure yourself, consider supplementing group coverage with an individual policy.

The cost of coverage, whether a group or individual policy, depends on factors like occupation, age, sex, length of time for which benefits are payable, extent of coverage, size of benefits, and length of waiting period. If you're 30 to 40, the cost probably will be 2 to 3 percent of your gross annual income. For example, if Bill, 36, makes $50,000 a year, he will pay a $1,000 to $1,500 annual premium that would entitle him to a $30,000 to $32,500 annual benefit if he becomes disabled.

While paying these premiums sounds expensive, especially because it's something you may never use, the peace of mind it brings can be well worth the cost of maintaining the policy.

STEVEN THALHEIMER, CFP®, MA (Silver Spring, Maryland) and
STEVEN LYDDON, CFP®, MBA (Kansas City, Missouri)

TIP 27 HOW TO BUY A GOOD DISABILITY INSURANCE POLICY

Q. What should I look for when buying an individual disability insurance policy?

A. Five features are critical in evaluating or selecting a disability income insurance policy: definition of disability, elimination or waiting period, monthly benefit payment, maximum benefit period, and renewal provisions.

Definitions of Disability

Choose the policy with the broadest definition that is available and affordable.

- *Any occupation.* Unable to perform the duties pertaining to any gainful occupation. This strict definition of disability based on occupation is used to determine eligibility for Social Security disability benefits.

- *Modified any occupation.* Unable to engage in any occupation for which one is reasonably fitted by education, training, experience, and prior economic status.
- *Own occupation.* Unable to engage in the principal duties of one's own occupation.
- *Split definition.* This means own occupation, generally for two years, followed by modified any occupation.
- *Income loss definition.* This is based on a comparison of postdisability income with predisability income. Duties or occupations in which the insured is able to engage are not significant factors.

Elimination or Waiting Period

The waiting period before benefits are paid is like a deductible, forcing the insured to bear part of the loss. Its purpose is to eliminate coverage for short-term, nonserious disabilities. Frequently, elimination periods are 30, 60, 90, or 180 days. Choose a waiting period commensurate with the number of sick days you maintain at work, any short-term disability coverage you may have, and the amount of your emergency savings.

Monthly Benefit Payment

A policy should restore your income to what it was before disability, but insurers typically limit coverage to 65 to 70 percent of monthly wages. Benefits of employer-paid policies generally are taxable to you.

Maximum Benefit Period

Benefits usually are payable to age 65 but can vary according to the cause of the disability.

Renewal Provisions

A policy can be noncancelable, guaranteeing the insured the right to renew for a stated number of years or to a stated age (normally 60 or 65), with the premium guaranteed at renewal. Or the policy can be guaranteed renewable, which guarantees renewal rights and permits premium adjustments. Other renewal provisions include conditionally renewable, so that the insurer may terminate the contract by not renewing it under certain conditions stated in the contract; renewable at company's option, which has no guarantee of continuation; no renewal provision; or cancelable with the insured given a number of days notice.

Other Provisions

- *Guaranteed insurability.* Allows an individual whose income increases after the policy is purchased to increase the amount of coverage at specified dates after the inception of policy, regardless of physical health.
- *Cost of living adjustment benefit.* Disability benefits are increased annually, based on the Consumer Price Index or a simple or compounded percentage specified in the policy. Policies using simple interest will cost less but may provide inadequate protection from inflation over longer periods, for example 20 years or more.
- *Additional insurance rider.* This is a variation on the Cost of Living rider and Guaranteed Insurability option that automatically increases policy benefits by 5 percent each year.
- *More choices.* Some other options that can affect premiums and policy selection include obtaining counseling or therapy; presumptive disability clause, where the loss of the use of two bodily members (e.g., use of both legs) or the loss of sight is considered a total disability; residual and partial disability; rehabilitation provision; and exclusions.

Financial Strength of the Insurance Company

Because a disability policy may pay benefits for 30 years or more, the financial strength of the company is an important factor in selecting a policy. A more expensive policy from a financially strong company may be a better deal than a cheaper one from a company that may not be around to pay the benefits.

Probation Period

This is the period of time a policy must be in force to cover specified perils or illnesses. This protects the insurance company from having to cover certain preexisting conditions and other adverse situations.

STEVEN THALHEIMER, CFP®, MA (Silver Spring, Maryland) and

STEVEN LYDDON, CFP®, MBA (Kansas City, Missouri)

TIP 28 FINDING AFFORDABLE HEALTH INSURANCE IF YOU DON'T HAVE GROUP COVERAGE OR ARE SELF-EMPLOYED

Q. How do I find affordable health insurance if I am self-employed or just need to secure my own policy?

A. Individual health insurance policies can be expensive. It is important to compare your options carefully. Before comparing policies, though, decide your coverage needs, the monthly premium you can afford, the potential risk you will accept, and the health of your family.

Then develop a checklist to compare different policies. On a blank sheet of paper, list the basic features, benefits, and costs down the left side of the page. At the top of the page, write the top three or four policies you're considering. Make a grid, and check the appropriate box if a policy offers that feature or jot down the number or dollar figure as appropriate.

Let's take a closer look at the various kinds of health insurance.

Types of Individual Health Insurance Policies

The individual health insurance market offers the same plans as the group market, including traditional fee-for-service arrangements, health maintenance organizations (HMOs), and preferred provider organizations (PPOs). Each plan has its own features.

Fee-for-service. Insurance companies pay fees for the services provided to the insured in these plans, which also are called indemnity plans. These offer the broadest choice of doctors and hospitals. Usually, this type of insurance requires the insured to pay the provider up front for medical services, then submit forms to the insurer to be reimbursed. You pay a monthly premium, an annual deductible (for each individual), and coinsurance after your deductible is met (for example, you pay 20 percent, while the insurer pays 80 percent). Most plans have caps, which limit the amount you will have to pay for medical bills in any one year, not including your premiums.

There are two types of coverage, basic (pays toward hospital room and care costs, surgery, and some doctor visits) and major medical (provides coverage for expensive illnesses or injuries, subject to policy limits).

Health Maintenance Organizations (HMOs). These prepaid health plans are the least expensive and the least flexible. You pay a monthly premium, and the HMO provides comprehensive care for you and your family, including doctors' visits, hospital stays, emergency care, surgery, lab and X rays, and preventive care. Usually, your choice of doctors and hospitals is limited, and you may be assigned a doctor from those who have agreements with the HMO to provide care. There may be a small copayment (e.g., $10 or $20) for each doctor visit and generally higher for emergency room treatment, but there are no claim forms to file. You may be assigned a physician or be allowed to choose one to serve as your primary care doctor. This doctor monitors your health and provides most of your health care, referring you to specialists only if needed.

Preferred Provider Organization (PPO). This combines services of both the above. Like an HMO, a limited number of doctors and hospitals are known as preferred or in-network providers, and you choose a primary care doctor to monitor your health care and cover most preventive care. You can use doctors who are not part of the plan and still receive some coverage (referred to as out-of-network); however, you will pay a larger portion of the bill yourself. Also, like a fee-for-service plan, a coinsurance percentage means that you will share in the cost of your medical coverage.

Comparing Plans

If you are leaning toward a more well-rounded plan, make sure that you are getting what you pay for. Read the fine print. Will your plan pay for X rays? Will it cover your doctor's visit if you have the flu? Will it cover prescription drugs?

Use a checklist of services to compare several policies. That checklist could include hospital care, doctor visits, and well-baby care, as well as costs like premiums, deductibles, copayments, maximum out-of-pocket expenses, and more.

Resources for Group Policies

Don't overlook membership in various associations, alumni or civic groups, churches, and professional or chamber of commerce organizations as a possible way to save money on health insurance. They may offer group policies, often at better rates than you can obtain on your own.

End Note$

Finding a cost-effective individual health policy can be tricky. Talk to other people in the same circumstances. You can contact a licensed independent insurance agent/broker in your area who specializes in individual health policies, or you can begin your research online. Internet sources include the following:

- http://www.nase.org
- http://www.healthinsurance.org
- http://www.ehealthinsurance.com
- http://www.insure.com

SHER MILLER, CPA, Sher Miller Financial Services (Dallas, Texas) and
MARTIN MESECKE, CFP® Self Worth Financial Planning (Dallas, Texas)

TIP 29 CONTINUING HEALTH INSURANCE COVERAGE IN EARLY RETIREMENT AND FOR SELF-EMPLOYMENT

Q. I'm retiring from the corporate world and will be starting my own company. What do I do for health insurance coverage?

A. Even for retirees with portfolios large enough to accommodate a sustainable withdrawal rate, health insurance remains a big concern. The odds are good that you will pay far more for health insurance when you retire (or if you become self-employed) than when you were employed. That is because most employers subsidize the cost of health insurance, many paying 50 to 100 percent of the actual cost of their employees' health insurance.

Check out http://www.dol.gov/dol/topic/health-plans/index.htm. This interactive Web site is a resource to help employees and their families make informed decisions about their health benefits when facing life and work changes.

Options for Medical Coverage

If you've lost medical coverage due to employment termination, you have several options.

- Seek group coverage through a spouse's plan or through an association with which you are affiliated.
- Consider an individual policy, although it may involve a physical examination and may not cover a preexisting condition.
- Look into COBRA, which requires employers—in certain cases—to provide continued group insurance under the Consolidated Omnibus Budget Reconciliation Act of 1985 (COBRA). Coverage typically lasts for 18 months but, in special cases, may extend for 36 months. The employee must pay full premiums plus administrative costs, which could run as high as 2 percent of the premium.

More on COBRA

For more information on COBRA, contact the U.S. Department of Labor.

- Employee Benefits Security Administration (EBSA)
  Division of Technical Assistance and Inquiries
  Room 5619 North
  200 Constitution Avenue Northwest
  Washington, DC 20210
- Division of Technical Assistance and Inquiries, 202-219-8776
- Toll-free Employee and Employer Hotline, 866-444-EBSA (866-444-3722), ext. 3272
- http://www.dol.gov/ebsa

What to Do When Your COBRA Benefits Expire

Fortunately, Congress passed a law called the Health Insurance Portability and Accountability Act of 1996 (also known as HIPAA or the Kennedy-Kasenbaum bill), allowing people who have exhausted their COBRA benefits to obtain individual (nongroup) health insurance policies for themselves and their dependents without restrictions on "preexisting conditions."

Although Congress has guaranteed that you can get insurance, it has not mandated how much you pay for it.

To qualify for HIPAA coverage, you must have credible continuous coverage with no gaps in coverage. If you have a break of 63 days or more, you're ineligible. Make sure you get a "Certificate of Group Health Plan Coverage" from your COBRA benefits insurer. You will need this to qualify for an individual policy.

The cost of health insurance depends on where you reside, your health history, and your age. Planning before you leave your current job will allow you the most flexibility in determining the best options for health insurance coverage.

JOHN POCHODYLO, CFP® (Phoenix, Arizona) and **RICK EPPLE,** CFP® (Minnetrista, Minnnesota)

TIP 30 UNDERSTANDING LONG-TERM CARE INSURANCE—ASSET PRESERVATION AND AGING WITH DIGNITY

Q. What do I need to know about long-term care insurance to make a decision about whether or not to buy it, and if I do, how do I evaluate a policy?

A. Understanding long-term care insurance can be a challenge because each company and policy has its own features and benefits. Some common questions about long-term care insurance follow.

What Is Long-Term Care Insurance, and Why Do I Need It?

Long-term care insurance is designed to cover the costs of caring for individuals with one or more chronic health conditions from which they are generally not expected to recover. It is not traditional medical insurance; rather, it covers skilled, intermediate, and custodial types of care, which focus primarily on assistance with activities of daily living or supervision related to cognitive impairment.

To qualify for benefits in most states, you must require substantial assistance with two of six activities of daily living or need substantial supervision due to cognitive impairment.

Depending on the state, current care costs can range from $30,000 to $100,000 a year and up. If you're 60 years old today, by the time you're 85, the costs will be closer to $100,000 to $550,000, due to inflation.

People who save to pay for this care will pay for it with after-tax dollars. Medicaid may be an option, but it's only available if you meet very strict requirements. Long-term care insurance benefits paid by tax-qualified policies that meet government specifications are free from income tax. Also, premiums paid on a tax-qualified policy may be partially deductible as a medical expense under itemized deductions on your income tax return.

Reasons Not to Purchase Long-Term Care Insurance

Don't purchase long-term care insurance if you

- truly cannot afford the premium.
- could not afford a premium increase of 10 to 20 percent.
- have limited assets.
- have only Social Security or Supplemental Security Income as an income source.
- have trouble paying for utilities, rent, food, medicine, or other important needs.
- can afford and prefer to pay care costs on your own.

Reasons to Purchase Long-Term Care Insurance

You should buy long-term care insurance if you want to maintain your independence, retain more control over your care choices and the quality of care, or preserve your income and assets as much as possible.

Decisions Associated with Buying Long-Term Care Insurance

- *Where do you want your care to take place?* Most policies provide for care in a nursing home, an assisted-living facility, an Alzheimer's facility, an adult day care center, or in your own home.
- *For how long do you want to receive benefits?* Options most often include two, three, four, five, six, seven, or ten years or a lifetime. Make sure the benefit period is not split between facility care and home health care, unless you are insured for life time.
- *How much money do you want as a daily benefit?* Most policies provide from $50 to $300 or more, offered in $10 increments. The daily benefit is always at 100 percent for nursing home care but can be less for assisted-living facilities and/or home health care.

  The majority of policies pay *actual expenses* up to the daily benefit amount. If a company pays the *prevailing cost* for like services to individuals with similar health conditions in your locale, the amount could be less than your actual expenses. For an additional premium, you can purchase an indemnity benefit that pays the full daily benefit amount regardless of your actual expenses.
- *How long do you want to wait after you start receiving care for the insurance benefits to begin?* This elimination period is similar to a deductible on medical insurance. Longer waiting periods will reduce your premium.
- *What, if any, protection from inflation do you want?* Because the costs associated with long-term care increase faster than the average rate of inflation, consider purchasing inflation protection. Most policies offer 5 percent simple or 5 percent compound inflation protection.

Understand the Wording

Some words to watch for include *substantial assistance* and *substantial supervision.* The more lenient definitions are standby assistance for daily living activities and presence of another individual for cognitive impairment. More restrictive definitions are hands-on assistance for a majority of the time and verbal supervision and cuing for a majority of the time, or continual supervision. The more restrictive the definition, the harder qualifying for benefits will be.

Also, look at who determines if you qualify for benefits and develops your plan of care. Many policies require only that a licensed health care practitioner of your choosing certify that you need assistance and will need it for longer than 90 days. A few policies require that a care advisor, employed by the insurance company or by an agency with which the insurance company has a contract, be used.

Finally, as with other types of insurance, the company you select should have a top financial rating. It also should have been in the long-term care insurance business for at least ten years with a good history of paying claims.

More Resources

- The National Association of Insurance Commissioners publishes "A Shopper's Guide to Long-Term Care Insurance" (http://www.naic.org/insprod/catalog_pub_consumer.htm#ltc_guide).
- Check out the list of Web sites at the end of this chapter.

LOUISE A. SCHROEDER, CFP® (Stillwater, Oklahoma) and **JIM BLANKENSHIP,** ChFC (New Berlin, Illinois)

TIP 31 OBTAINING A GOOD AUTO INSURANCE POLICY

Q. Am I paying too much for automobile insurance?

A. Low-cost insurance is no accident, literally. The only way to know for sure if you are paying too much is to shop around and compare policies. Here are some tips to help you obtain the best policy and lowest rates possible.

Shop Around

Insurance rates for the same coverage differ dramatically from company to company based on factors like driving history and personal data. Mature adults generally are more attractive than teens to the insurance companies. If you have not had an accident or received a traffic ticket within the last two years (both of which can hurt your insurance record), get competitive bids. Your maturity and good judgment may be rewarded. If you have an accident and can pay the repairs out of pocket, without filing a claim, simply report the accident to your insurance company. After a couple of incident-free years, at renewal time, ask about a discount.

Also, if you stay accident free, raising your deductible saves on premiums. If the same policy has a $250 deductible, annual premiums are $1,621; $500 deductible, $1,403 premium; and $1,000 deductible, $1,301 premium.

Drop Some Coverage

For example, drop all but liability coverage on an older auto, which has lost most of its value. If the vehicle is worth less than $2,000, it may not be worth paying for comprehensive coverage.

Drive a Less Expensive Car

A number of magazines and automobile associations publish information about which cars are most likely to be stolen. Also, check the cost of insurance for any car you're thinking about buying. When you get a new vehicle, be sure to tell your insurer about its installed safety features. Airbags, antilock brakes, and antitheft devices often reduce premiums.

Get Discounts

Some professional organizations and automobile club memberships entitle you to a premium discount on renewal. Insurers may offer multiple policy discounts, safe-driver discounts, or premium reductions based on commute distances. Even some professions, like engineering, are considered safer risks and therefore qualify for policy discounts.

Don't Underinsure

Underinsuring is the wrong way to lower insurance costs. States have insurance minimums, but remember that the per-accident injury protection in liability insurance may not cover the cost of common injuries. Make sure your coverage is enough to protect your assets in case of a lawsuit. Some states also require underinsured or uninsured motorist coverage. Don't skimp on it.

Buy from a Highly Rated Company

A lower-quality insurance company is more likely to lowball a quote, inflate your premium at renewal time, then not make good on a claim. For more information, check out the resources at the end of this chapter.

BOB STOWE, CFP®, CFS, MBA (Plano, Texas)

TIP 32 PROTECTING YOUR INSURANCE RECORD PAYS

Q. What does *protecting my insurance record* mean?

A. It means paying minor repairs and fender benders out of pocket to keep a claim off your insurance record.

How It Works

Protecting your record can keep your insurance premiums down, because filing a claim for even minor losses may mean that your insurance company assesses policy surcharges or penalties after negligent accidents or certain moving violations. Let's say you inadvertently back into a steel pole. The result is a small dent in the car's bumper and rear quarter panel. The repair estimate totals $700; the collision deductible on your automobile policy is $500. What should you do?

Does any net insurance recovery offset the loss of a potential loss-free discount? Or does any net claim payment outweigh the potential surcharge that may be assessed against your policy for the typical three-year period? In the example above, the $200 potential insurance company reimbursement may not be worth taking the chance that your rates would go up.

In another scenario, a car runs a red light and hits your vehicle. No one is injured, but your vehicle sustains moderate damage. You exchange insurance and contact information with the other driver and recognize the name of his insurance agent, your neighbor. The other driver says that he has full coverage under his auto policy, and you are inclined to believe him. Do you file a claim with your own company, or do you pursue repairs through the other party's carrier? Does your answer change in any way if you or another family member has filed a claim under your own policy for a separate incident earlier in the year? These situations are the types of factors you should consider.

Of course, occasions arise when the issue is moot, such as when you are responsible for an accident with a third party or when the damages are not minor. Policy contract provisions require that you notify the company of the loss as soon as possible, so it can begin gathering relevant information, investigating the facts, assessing damages/extent of injuries, etc.

Plus, you would not want to jeopardize the valuable supplemental defense coverage provided in most liability policies by failing to notify the company promptly.

These examples focus on automobile policies, but the concept applies to other types of property and casualty insurance, such as homeowners insurance. Insurance companies have gotten more sophisticated at monitoring claims and sharing this data. If a homeowner files several claims in succession for small items such as lightning strikes or damage from a fallen tree, they may find that the policy will be much more expensive at renewal time, or that the insurance company may not renew the policy at all. Also, when the property is sold, an adverse record of claims can make it difficult for the new owner to obtain coverage on the property.

DEIDRA FULTON, CPCU (Plano, Texas)

TIP 33 HOW TO PROTECT ONE OF YOUR BIGGEST INVESTMENTS

Q. How do I know if I have appropriate homeowners protection?

A. While your home is probably your largest single asset, it's also a potential source of a liability claim against you. It's important to have adequate homeowners insurance coverage for damage and liability claims.

You should work with a trusted insurance professional and have a basic understanding of homeowners coverage. First, let's discuss perils.

Covered Perils

Most homeowners policies cover 12 basic *named perils:*

1. Fire
2. Lightning
3. Windstorm
4. Hail
5. Theft
6. Aircraft
7. Vehicles
8. Vandalism/malicious mischief
9. Explosion
10. Volcanic eruption
11. Riot or civil commotion
12. Smoke

Broad named perils also include falling objects; weight of ice, snow, and sleet; accidental discharge of overflow of water or stream; sudden and accidental tearing apart, cracking, burning, or bulging of steam, hot water, air-conditioning, or automatic fire protective sprinkler system, or from within a household appliance;

freezing of a plumbing, heating, air-conditioning, or automatic fire sprinkler system, or of a household appliance; and sudden and accidental damage from artificially generated electrical current.

General Exclusions

Homeowners policies have eight general exclusions that prevent coverage for a loss, although it's possible to buy riders to cover some of these exclusions. The exclusions include ordinance or law (condemnation), earth movement (earthquake), water damage (flood), neglect (abandonment), intentional loss (any intentional damage), nuclear hazard, power failure (interruption of power), and war.

What's Covered: Property and Liability

Each policy has a property and a liability section. Let's look at what is covered within each section.

Dwelling and other structures. Base your coverage amount on the replacement cost of the home excluding the value of the land. Other structures coverage is generally a set percentage of the building amount. At a minimum, your mortgage company will require the coverage amount to match or exceed your mortgage loan balance.

Personal property. Coverage generally is a set percentage of the building amount, with *limited* coverage for jewelry, firearms, silver, computers, artwork, and more. You can get additional coverage with a rider/endorsement to your policy or a separate personal property floater policy.

Loss of use. This covers increased costs to you if the property is temporarily uninhabitable.

Personal liability. This protects you and your family from the cost of legal actions or claims for injuries or property damage by people other than those who reside in the home. You should have at least $100,000 in coverage, and $300,000 is commonly recommended. Depending on your other assets, even more may be advisable. It can be purchased through a separate *umbrella* liability policy.

Medical payments. This pays the cost of minor accidental injuries occurring on your property and minor injuries caused by you, your family, or pets without determining fault. Coverage from $1,000 to $5,000 is provided by most policies.

Other Things That You Need to Know

The standard claims settlement method is the actual cash value method (current replacement value less depreciation), but consider replacement cost coverage.

Maintain building coverage at 100 percent of the replacement cost, and keep in mind periodic increases in coverage to compensate for rising costs of material and labor and/or rising property values.

In your safe deposit box, keep a detailed home inventory supported by pictures or video as adequate evidence in case of loss.

Also, compare premium costs for a range of deductible amounts.

BRENDA L. SHERBINE, CPA/PFS (Hamilton, Montana)

TIP 34 PROTECTING YOUR FAMILY FROM CATASTROPHIC LOSS WITH AN UMBRELLA POLICY

Q. A friend told me I should have an umbrella insurance policy. What is that, and how can it help my family?

A. Personal umbrella insurance is additional liability coverage to protect you from catastrophic financial losses that could wipe out assets. It fits over your auto and homeowners insurance policies like an umbrella to provide added coverage payable after your primary insurance coverage is exhausted.

How It Works

While at a dinner party in your home, a guest falls and has a major injury. Your homeowners insurance pays the liability on the claim up to its $100,000 limit. But your guest sues for $1 million. How do you pay the other $900,000?

The answer is an umbrella insurance policy, which typically comes in increments of $1 million to $5 million, and is reasonably priced—perhaps $200 to $300 a year for $1 million in liability coverage. An umbrella policy may extend over your home, auto, boat, aircraft, and other nonbusiness assets and covers you for damages to other parties whether bodily injury, mental anguish, shock, sickness, disease, disability, false arrest, false imprisonment, wrongful eviction, detention, libel, defamation of character, or invasion of privacy.

Umbrella insurance does *not* cover your obligation for worker's compensation and disability benefits, your property damages, or product failure.

How to Purchase Coverage

Umbrella insurance usually is available through your current insurance provider or another provider. If you opt for a stand-alone policy, you should not need to move your homeowners or auto insurance, too. To alleviate any gaps in liability coverage, make sure your auto and homeowners insurance policies have coverage up to the deductible on the umbrella policy.

End Note$

Your insurance professional or financial planner can help you determine the right amount of coverage. A general guideline: Round up your net worth to the next million.

When you realize that you can be sued for everything you have, it pays to insure your entire net worth—especially when the premiums are generally so affordable.

SHERRY HINRICHS (Santa Rosa, California)

TIP 35 BEST WEB SITES FOR INSURANCE INFORMATION

Q. Which Web sites are best for learning about insurance and obtaining policy quotes?

A. The Internet, with its many options, has leveled the playing field. Now you can obtain information that once was available only to insurance professionals and financial planners.

Insurance Information

Here are some of the best insurance information sites to find solid educational content, policy quotes, or links to quote services. Doing your homework ahead of time can save you money on premiums—and headaches down the road.

- *About Disability Insurance (http://www.about-disability-insurance.com).* Provides descriptions of the major features of a disability insurance policy and links to other Web sites.
- *E.F. Moody (http://www.efmoody.com) life and disability insurance analyst.* Features financial information as well as an overview of insurance.

- *Federal Emergency Management Agency flood insurance information (http://www.fema.gov/nfip/whonfip.shtm).* The only option for flood coverage, this site provides information about the coverage and how to get it.
- *Health Insurance Information (http://www.healthinsuranceinfo.net).* A resource to maintain health insurance once COBRA coverage expires; see the Consumer Guides for Getting and Keeping Insurance for each state.
- *Insurance Information Institute (http://www.iii.org).* Provides the public with information about insurance and the insurance industry.
- *Insure Kids Now (http://www.insurekidsnow.gov).* Provides information on free or low-cost health insurance to children of lower-income families who do not have health insurance.
- *Medicare (http://cms.hhs.gov/midicaid/consumer.asp).* Medigap plan comparisons, Medicare health plans comparison, consumer publications; also, includes directories of potential sources of additional assistance with care expenses.
- *National Association of Insurance Commissioners (http://www.naic.org).* Consumer interest site featuring a directory of state insurance regulators and catalog of educational publications.

Insurance Rating Agencies and Helpful Sites

- A.M. Best Company (http://www.ambest.com)
- Anthony Steuer Insurance Services (http://www.tonysteuer.com/res_RatingServices.html)
- Coalition against Insurance Fraud—Scam Alerts and Insurance Fraud Hall of Shame (http://www.insurancefraud.org)
- Fitch Ratings, Ltd. (http://www.fitchratings.com)
- Moody's Investor Services (http://www.moodys.com)
- Standard and Poor's Corporation (http://www.standardandpoors.com)
- Weiss Research (http://www.weissratings.com)

Shopping Sites to Compare and Obtain Quotes

- http://www.insweb.com
- http://www.insure.com
- http://www.ehealthinsurance.com
- http://moneycentral.msn.com/insure/welcome.asp

P. PAULINE PRICE (Bronx, New York)

Chapter

3

PROPERTY OWNERSHIP, MORTGAGES, AND TITLES

TIP 36 SHOULD I BUY OR LEASE A VEHICLE?

Q. I'm confused by vehicle ads that promote leasing and buying. How do I know which is the best approach for getting a new vehicle?

A. Don't just follow the lead of auto industry advertising. A better approach is to test your choices against the following criteria and then make a decision that best fits your circumstances.

Comparing Buying versus Leasing

On the whole, buying a car or truck is a better deal than leasing for most people. You know the cost of purchasing a vehicle. At the end of the financing period, it belongs to you. Also, during the financing period (and later when you own it outright), you control what's done with the vehicle. That's not the case with leasing. Think of leasing as a long-term rental car with limits on mileage, wear and tear, customizing, and early termination of the lease. Exceed any of the limits and conditions, and you could face fees and penalties, and you won't know what or how much until the end of the lease term.

Leasing could make sense, however, if two or more of the following apply:

- You have a business and can claim vehicle lease payments as a business tax deduction.
- It's important that you drive a new car every two to three years.
- You keep your cars in excellent condition.
- You have no plans to modify the vehicle.
- You won't exceed the mileage limits of the lease.
- You don't mind always having a car payment.
- If it turns out that the vehicle doesn't suit your driving needs, you are willing to grin and bear it or pay the penalties for terminating the lease early.

Feature	**Leasing**	**Buying and Financing**
Down payment	None or small	Usually required; the more that's paid up front, the smaller the monthly payment
Monthly payments	Continuous, usually less than for buying	End when the loan is paid off
Vehicle modification	Not allowed	You can do what you want, when you want
Mileage limits	Usually 12,000 to 15,000 miles/year	Unlimited
Wear and tear	If in excess of contract limits, penalties due at end of lease	No limits
Early termination	Fees and penalties apply	There usually are no prepayment penalties
End of term	Lease again, or purchase the currently leased vehicle; payments continue	Payments stop
Ownership	None	Ownership equity builds with each payment; vehicle is owned at the end of the financing period

Whatever you decide, don't be intimidated by salespeople. They need you as a customer. Know what you want and what you are willing to spend before you attempt to make a deal. Visit dealerships, compare vehicles and prices, research the Internet for pricing and options, and leave your emotions at home. Negotiate in a realistic, win-win manner. First, negotiate the vehicle's price, including options and service programs. After you have agreed on price, tell the salesperson whether you want to lease or buy.

MARY GIBSON, CFP® (San Juan Bautista, California)

TIP 37 HOME SWEET HOME—SHOULD YOU RENT OR BUY?

Q. Is it better to buy or rent a place to live?

A. Your choice depends on several factors. While financial factors can be carefully weighed and measured, the intangibles of owning property may appeal most. Home ownership remains an essential part of the American dream.

Tax Breaks for Home Purchases

Home ownership offers a number of tax breaks. On your Schedule A, under the Itemized Deductions section, you can deduct mortgage interest (on your principal residence and a second home), property taxes, points paid on a new loan, and points paid on a refinanced loan (must be amortized over the life of the loan). When selling your home at a profit, gains of up to $250,000 per person ($500,000 for married couples filing jointly) are tax-free, if you have lived in your principal residence at least two of the last five years. Better yet, you can use this same exemption again after living in another home for at least two years of the last five.

Return on Investment

Is the return on investment an incentive to own versus rent? Let's do the math. A typical down payment is 20 percent of the home's value. For a $150,000 purchase, that's $30,000. If that same home's value increases 2 percent next year to $153,000, the return (ignoring taxes) is more than 2 percent because of the leverage from the down payment. Divide that $3,000 (increase in value) by $30,000 (the down payment), and it leaves you with a 10 percent return.

Breakeven Home Purchase Guidelines

As a general guideline, to cover the costs of buying or selling a property (mortgage, appraisal, application, inspection, moving, title insurance, legal costs, real estate commissions) plus the regular costs of home ownership, a property has to appreciate about 15 percent. That generally takes five years, depending on location and markets.

Of course, you need to consider other factors when calculating your total return, such as closing costs, mortgage interest, equity build-up in the home, repairs and maintenance while owning the home, and tax savings. Leverage can work to your advantage with a home purchase as long as the home appreciates.

Qualifying for a Mortgage

General mortgage qualification guidelines state that you can spend up to 28 percent of your monthly, gross, pretax income for housing (front-end ratio) and that the monthly cost of all debt (including housing) cannot exceed 33 percent (back-end ratio).

First-time buyers often get loans with a 10 percent or less down payment. Veterans can get VA loans. HUD, FHA, Freddie Mac, and Fannie Mae are other government programs that assist first-time homebuyers.

If you can, avoid Private Mortgage Insurance (PMI). It adds $50 to $150 to the monthly payment and probably is required if the down payment is less than 20 percent. You can avoid PMI by getting an 80 percent first mortgage, putting 10 percent down, and getting the seller to carry a 10 percent second mortgage.

Other Factors to Consider When Buying a Home

Let's say that you sell your primary residence and move to your vacation home on the beach, pocketing a large, tax-free gain. Home prices skyrocket, and it's too crowded at the beach, so you sell the beach house and get another large chunk of cash tax-free. Then you move to Kokomo, Indiana, which has one of the lowest housing costs in America, and live happily ever after.

Unless you live in an area that has escalating home prices, you may never see a sharp spike in your home's market value. But that's OK. Slow, steady growth is good, too.

Wherever you live, the essential rule in home buying is location. If you're buying a first home, start small with the lowest-priced home in the best neighborhood, then work to fix up and maintain your home so it keeps pace with other properties in the neighborhood. Check out the school districts. Good schools make a difference when you sell.

If you're thinking about a condominium or townhouse, check the quality of construction carefully, especially the soundproofing. Talk to other condo residents, check that most units are owner-occupied, and review the financial status of the complex to make sure the homeowners association is doing its job to maintain the property and control expenses.

Advantages of Renting Your Residence

For some, renting may be advantageous. You pay no maintenance, property taxes, or repair costs if something breaks. Estimates are that for every dollar a homeowner spends to buy a home, they spend $1.50 on interest, repairs, maintenance, property taxes, and other costs.

Renters can save or invest the money that a homeowner typically would spend on a new roof, property taxes, or landscaping. They often have access to amenities like pools and exercise facilities and enjoy a sense of community. Nice homes may also be available for rent in good neighborhoods at reasonable prices. If you relocate to a new city, consider renting first as a way to learn about the community before buying.

ROBERT BUBNOVICH (Irvine, California)

TIP 38 HOW TO GET EVERYTHING TO WHICH YOU ARE ENTITLED FROM YOUR HOME

Q. What are some of the tax incentives for home ownership?

A. Many people buy a home just for financial and tax incentives that can include mortgage interest tax deductions, property tax deductions, capital gain exclusions, and penalty-free IRA withdrawals for first-time homebuyers. Owning a home also may enable you to itemize your deductions, which opens up an array of other deductible expenses.

Mortgage Interest and Property Tax Deduction

For each dollar that you spend toward your mortgage interest and property taxes, you are entitled to subtract a dollar from your adjusted gross income. Use the following formula to calculate your potential savings:

Monthly Mortgage Interest Payment
+ Monthly Property Tax Payment
= Subtotal
× Your Effective Tax Rate
= Monthly Tax Savings

Monthly House Payment
– Monthly Tax Savings (calculated above)
= Real Cost of Monthly House Payment

In the first year of home ownership, you may be entitled to an additional tax break if you paid any points, also called origination fees, to the lender to get your mortgage loan. The points are considered prepaid mortgage interest and can be deducted as additional mortgage interest. You can amortize them over the term of your mortgage or take them in the first year of home ownership.

Capital Gain Exclusion

The government allows you to exclude from taxable income up to $250,000 ($500,000 if you're married and file jointly) of gain on the sale of your home. You qualify for this exclusion as long as you have owned and used the home as your principal residence for at least two of the past five years.

Penalty-Free IRA Withdrawals for First-Time Homebuyers

If you have an IRA, you may be entitled to withdraw funds from the IRA penalty-free for the down payment on a home. But the early withdrawal is subject to income tax on any previously untaxed distributions. A distribution from a Roth IRA is not subject to the early distribution penalty or income tax, but it must first meet a five-year holding requirement. Before withdrawing any funds, be sure that you have met the requirements to qualify for this distribution treatment and that you have weighed the potential effect on your retirement savings.

TODD SHEPHERD, CPA, MBA (Leawood, Kansas) and
ALAN M. SCHAPIRE, CFP®, CPA/PFS (Media, Pennsylvania)

TIP 39 ASSESS ALL YOUR FINANCIAL GOALS TO DETERMINE THE RIGHT MORTGAGE AMOUNT

Q. I talked with a financial planner about how much mortgage I could afford, but when I applied for a mortgage, the broker told me I could afford more. What gives?

A. Mortgage lenders and financial planners often have different ideas on how much mortgage a person can afford. The planner will often suggest a lower amount.

Be Cautious of Standard Guidelines

Mortgage lenders are in business to lend money and have lots of experience assessing credit risks. Guidelines—mortgage debt should be less than 28 percent of gross income, total debt less than 36 percent—are based on lending as much money as possible while maintaining an acceptable default rate. The guidelines provide for a basic standard of living in addition to the mortgage, but do not, on a case-by-case basis, account for individual needs and circumstances. A financial planner looks at many factors, from sending the kids to college to vacation preferences and retirement issues. Mortgage companies also focus on the mortgage time frame, not your lifetime or long-term goals such as building a retirement nest egg. Your financial planner, on the other hand, does factor such goals into a recommended mortgage amount. From a financial planning perspective, it's important to factor lifetime goals into the mortgage company's affordability calculations.

BRAD BOND, CFP® (Murrysville, Pennsylvania)

TIP 40 CHOOSING THE BEST TYPE OF MORTGAGE LOAN

Q. I am about to purchase/refinance a home. What type of loan should I choose?

A. Consumers today have plenty of options. Among them are fixed-rate mortgages for terms of 30, 20, or 15 years; adjustable-rate mortgages (ARMs) and balloon mortgages; FHA/VA loans; and niche programs such as first-time homebuyer, 100 percent programs, and loans for the credit challenged.

Let's take a closer look at a few of those options.

Fixed-Rate Mortgage

As this book goes to press, rates are at historic lows. With fixed-rate mortgages, the rate, payment, and term remain constant from the day you sign the note regardless of market fluctuations and inflation. The payment is less with a 30-year mortgage than a 15-year one, but you also pay more interest. For example, with a 5.5 percent fixed-rate $150,000 mortgage of 15 years, the monthly payment is $1,226 and total interest paid is $70,613, while a 30-year loan carries an $852 monthly payment and $156,606 in interest.

Choose a fixed-rate loan if you plan to stay in your home for more than seven years or if you if you like knowing that the monthly payment will not change.

Adjustable-Rate Mortgage (ARM)

An ARM has a fixed rate and payment for the initial specified time (less than 30 years); then it can change every year after that. With a 3/1 ARM, for example, the payment and rate is fixed for the first three years, then can fluctuate annually based on an index like the one-year Treasury Securities Index, LIBOR (London Interbank Offered Rates), or COFI (Cost of Funds Index). Lenders also add a margin, most commonly 2.75 percent, to determine the new rate. ARMs have caps on how high a rate can change per adjustment—most often 2 percent over the starting rate.

Balloon mortgages are more risky. The payment and rate are fixed for the initial term, after which the loan principal balance is due. At that point, you either pay off the loan or refinance at current market rates. Unlike the ARM, there is no cap.

ARMs or balloons make sense if you relocate frequently or plan to stay in the home a short time. Choose an ARM carefully if this is your first home. The lower initial rates mean that you can qualify for a more expensive home, but remember, the payment can rise, and you need to be prepared. Many lenders qualify you for your ARM loan based upon the initial rate plus the first cap.

FHA and VA Loans

The Federal Housing Administration (FHA), an agency within the Department of Housing and Urban Development (HUD), was established in 1934 to increase home ownership in America among the middle class. It helps to do that with less-stringent loan qualifications, such as 3 percent down payment, higher qualifying ratios (29/41, whereas conventional loans are 28/36), more flexible qualifying guidelines, limitations on buyers' closing costs, and allowing closing costs to satisfy part of your down payment requirement.

The Veterans Administration (VA) also guarantees loans to eligible veterans that are made by private lenders like banks and mortgage companies. To determine if you are eligible for a VA loan, you should request a certificate of eligibility from the VA. VA loan features include no down payment, no monthly mortgage insurance premiums, and limits on closing costs. For more information, visit http://www.homeloans.va.gov.

Niche Programs

Many lenders have special programs for first-time homebuyers. These programs offer special interest rates, give credits toward closing costs, expand your purchasing power by allowing higher qualifying ratios (33/38), and even have 97 or 100 percent financing.

First-time homebuyers should always ask lenders if they offer special programs or cash incentives.

Loans for the Credit-Challenged

If you have had credit problems, don't despair. Certain lenders have mortgage financing for you. You'll pay higher interest rates, but often, if you try to improve your credit score, you can refinance later on.

LEE A. SPADONI, CFP® (Naperville, Illinois)

TIP 41 PRIVATE MORTGAGE INSURANCE (PMI)— HOW TO AVOID UNNECESSARY PREMIUMS

Q. I don't have 20 percent to put down when I buy a home. What is PMI?

A. Private mortgage insurance (PMI) allows people to purchase a home with a smaller-than-usual down payment. In return for the smaller down payment, the borrower pays a premium (included in the monthly mortgage). So, while your down payment is lower, your monthly payments may be higher ($20 to $100 on a $100,000 loan) because of the added cost of the insurance. In essence, you are paying for the lender to carry an insurance policy on your mortgage loan in the event of your default. While mortgage interest is tax deductible, PMI is not.

Options Available

Ways to avoid PMI include getting a mortgage with a higher interest rate that requires no PMI from you. The lender purchases the mortgage insurance, and you pay the additional cost through higher interest rates over the life of your loan.

The way you finance your home also can make a difference; 80/10/10, for example, means that your primary mortgage is for 80 percent of the home's value, the second mortgage is for 10 percent, and you make a 10 percent down payment.

Calculating the cost benefit of paying PMI versus structuring your financing to avoid PMI must be done on a case-by-case basis, so that consumers avoid overpaying when all is said and done.

How and When to Cancel PMI

For most loans that originated after July 29, 1999, when the Homeowners Protection Act of 1998 became effective, lenders must cancel PMI when the loan value falls below 78 percent (the borrower has paid off 22 percent) of the purchase price. If lenders neglect to do this, it is up to the homeowner to follow up.

If your loan originated *before* July 29, 1999, ask a lender to cancel the insurance once you exceed 20 percent equity. You can save money by having the PMI canceled ahead of time, if you can prove you have achieved 20 percent equity based on the home's appreciation.

State laws for canceling PMI vary. If your loan is considered high risk, you have not been current on your payments within the last year, or you have liens on the property, expect more resistance to cancellation. Contact the lender for the requirements to cancel under these conditions.

BONNIE A. HUGHES, CFP® (Rome, Georgia)

TIP 42 DETERMINING WHEN TO REFINANCE

Q. With interest rates so low, there is a lot of talk about refinancing. How can I determine if now is the right time to refinance my mortgage?

A. There are many reasons to consider refinancing your mortgage, including a lower interest rate, a lower monthly payment, a shorter loan term, and extra cash for home improvements or debt consolidation.

When Refinancing Makes Sense

Before you refinance ask yourself three questions:

1. How long do you plan to stay in the home?
2. How much can you reduce your interest rate?
3. How much will it cost to get the new loan?

Though you often hear that it makes sense to refinance your mortgage if you can reduce your rate by at least 2 percent, that guideline is too high in most cases. Often, a person can benefit from lower interest rate differentials, depending on how long they plan to remain in the home, so analyze your *breakeven point.*

Reaching Breakeven on Cost of Refinancing

After any new or refinanced mortgage takes effect, there is a period of time called the breakeven period. If you don't plan to stay in the home long, refinancing may not be beneficial. In general, the larger the rate reduction, the shorter the breakeven period. The higher the loan costs, the longer the breakeven period. Ideally you would like the breakeven period to be less than two years.

To estimate the breakeven period, look at how quickly the principal is repaid on the loan. Compare the refinance costs to the sum of the monthly payment savings and the difference in the mortgage principal balances. At the point where the savings exceed the refinancing cost, you have reached the breakeven point. There are many calculators on the Web that can assist you with comparing loan options. You will need to compare the two loan amortization schedules to see the difference in mortgage balance amounts for different time periods (three months, six months, etc.).

The same analysis can be applied to the question of whether you would be wise to pay points in order to obtain a lower rate. The best calculators take into account several factors, including your refinancing costs, tax bracket, how rapidly principal is paid down, the time-value of money, and the rate your money could earn if you did not use it to refinance. Keep reading for a listing of helpful Web sites.

Changing from a 30-Year to a 15-Year Loan

Reducing the term of your loan is an easy way to reduce your rate and save thousands of dollars in interest. As noted above, analyze the breakeven period. Reducing the term can be accomplished without a significant increase in the monthly payment, when the rate difference is large enough.

If the monthly payment will significantly increase, be careful that you are not overextending yourself. Being "house poor" is no fun. Is your employment secure? Can you handle the larger payment if unemployed? Also, keep in mind that making regular extra principal payments on a 30-year loan offers you flexibility and can save thousands of dollars of interest, too.

Swapping an ARM for a Fixed-Rate Mortgage

This is a tough decision that requires speculation about where rates are heading. Also, consider how long you plan to stay in your home, the cost of a new loan, and how today's interest rates compare to historical rates. Ultimately, only you can decide what's comfortable for you.

Taking Out Cash on Refinancing to Consolidate Debt

Consolidating debt (e.g., credit card balances) at a lower, tax-deductible interest rate usually makes a lot of sense on paper. In real life, though, it can turn a short-term problem into a long-term debt. Also, this serial borrowing strategy often repeats itself, with the homeowner habitually racking up debt, pulling out the equity in the home, and jeopardizing a debt-free retirement.

If you must consolidate, make sure that you have addressed the issues that made it necessary to consolidate your debts in the first place. Remember: You are putting your home up as collateral. If consolidation is your goal, it may be more cost effective to use a home equity loan or credit line due to lower loan acquisition costs. If you choose an equity line of credit, avoid making interest-only payments. It works the same as it does with credit cards: if you only pay the minimum, the balance will never go away.

Finding the Best Loan

Once you decide that refinancing is cost effective, consider using a mortgage broker to find the best loan. A good broker can shop many lenders effectively and is especially helpful if your credit is less than perfect. Be diligent in comparing costs, and when you decide to lock in the rate, be sure to get it in writing. Insist that your mortgage broker disclose all sources of compensation, including the broker's markup (how much higher your rate is than the wholesale rate). You might look for a broker who will work on a flat-fee basis.

Following are some helpful Web sites:

- http://www.mtgprofessor.com
- http://www.mortgage-x.com
- http://www.hsh.com
- http://www.bankrate.com

SHERYL GARRETT, CFP® (Shawnee Mission, Kansas)

TIP 43 REFINANCING A MORTGAGE AND TAKING OUT A LINE OF CREDIT

Q. Interest rates have dropped since I purchased my home, and I need money to make improvements to the house. Should I refinance my mortgage?

A. Whether or not to refinance depends upon several factors, including the change in the interest rates, the remaining term of your mortgage, and the cost of the refinancing. There are also some cash flow and income tax considerations.

The Basics—Interest Rate, Points, and Mortgage Term

A general rule for refinancing is that the new rate be at least 1 percent less than your existing rate to make it advantageous to refinance considering the costs involved. Points or prepaid interest charges for a new mortgage are also a critical factor. One point equals 1 percent of the total amount borrowed. You can buy down your interest rate by paying additional points or buy down the points by paying a higher interest rate. In a refinance transaction, you generally want to avoid paying points for several reasons, including the tax treatment of points in a refinance.

You also need to consider the term or life of the existing loan and the new loan. You may decide to refinance because of lower rates, your current loan has a balloon provision, you currently have an ARM, or to extend the loan term.

Home Remodeling/Expansion Considerations

If you're thinking about making home improvements, a home equity line of credit, home equity loan, or refinancing your mortgage for a higher amount can be helpful.

A home equity line of credit allows you to draw money from the bank on an as-needed basis, up to the maximum amount of the line. Interest rates generally are tied to and fluctuate with the Prime Rate, so the monthly payment changes.

Home equity loans are for a fixed term and interest rate. The entire amount of the loan is drawn when the loan is established. Lines and loans generally require less paperwork and involve fewer loan fees and closing costs than traditional mortgages. Home equity interest is tax deductible as long as the loan does not exceed $100,000.

If you decide to refinance your mortgage, the mortgage interest is generally tax deductible. If you pay points on the refinance, the points on the amount of the loan used for the remodeling or expansion are deductible. However, the points attributable to the existing loan must be amortized and deducted over the life of the new loan.

End Note$

Always allow yourself some financial flexibility. You don't want mortgage and/or home equity payments to create undue hardship if your monthly income suddenly drops. Look for a loan with no prepayment penalties, and consult a qualified tax advisor to accurately evaluate the tax ramifications of changes in your home mortgage.

ALAN M. SCHAPIRE, CFP®, CPA/PFS (Media, Pennsylvania)

TIP 44 SAVE MONEY BY REFINANCING, THEN PUT THE SAVINGS TO WORK FOR YOU

Q. We recently refinanced our home and have improved our cash flow by $200 a month. What should we do with the funds created as a result of our reduced mortgage payment?

A. Depending on your current mortgage rate, refinancing at today's lower rates can indeed result in a reduced monthly payment. There are several good options on what to do with your additional cash flow.

Good Uses for Savings from Refinancing

- *Increase retirement savings.* Increase your retirement account contributions to the level that maximizes your employer's match. That's *free money,* like a guaranteed return of, generally, 25 to 100 percent. Do not pass up this opportunity to build personal wealth.
- *Pay down credit card and consumer loans.* Many credit cards have rates in excess of 18 percent. Pay off credit card debt, and you've got an 18 percent after-tax return on your investment.
- *Open a Roth IRA.* It's one of the best wealth-building tools available if you qualify. (See the Chapter 5 on retirement planning for more information.)
- *Create or add to your emergency fund.* Put the money into a liquid, low-risk account like a savings or money market account.
- *Shore up insurance coverage.* Buy additional, low-load term insurance or disability insurance.

TIMOTHY BROWN, MBA, CFA® (Oakdale, Minnesota)

TIP 45 USING YOUR HOME'S EQUITY WISELY

Q. Some of my neighbors seem to be remodeling their homes, taking grand vacations, and buying fancy cars. I've been told they are using home equity loans to finance these things. I do not want to squander my hard-earned equity. Can you give me some guidelines for using my home equity wisely?

A. Congratulations. If you are in the fortunate position of having a substantial amount of home equity, you have most likely been doing a good job of managing your money and building your financial future. When interest rates are low and property values are appreciating, many people feel the urge to pull money out of their home equity. Following are suggestions for using your home equity wisely to further your financial goals.

Debt or No Debt?

No doubt about it: it is better to have no debt and no monthly mortgage payment than to have a large monthly obligation and limited flexibility to pursue future opportunities. Do not squander your home equity—if you need it, use it, but use it wisely.

It is critical to ensure that repaying a home equity loan will not negatively impact other plans, especially your retirement plans. Before getting a home equity loan, know how much you need to save and invest monthly and the rate of return you must earn on your investments to meet your retirement goals. If your retirement plans show that you need to invest more to reach your objective, investing more in a tax-deferred retirement account is probably the wisest course of action.

Making Smart Choices

Some wise uses of home equity include the following:

- *Debt consolidation.* The interest is tax deductible.
- *Investments that increase in value.* Make sure an addition or renovation will increase your home's value. Studies show that remodeling a bathroom or the kitchen often pays off in home resale value, whereas remodeling the basement or adding a deck provides less return on investment.
- *Education funding.* To fund future needs, first determine the estimated cost of your children's education. Then, depending on when your children will enter college, determine how much must be set aside, and at what rate of return, to meet your college funding goals. Now you know how much you need to borrow against your home equity to fund an investment account today to meet your projected college funding needs. Investing these funds in a tax-advantaged college savings program, such as a 529 Plan, could make sense. The correct strategy depends on your specific situation and factors such as the likelihood of your children being eligible for financial aid.
- *A home equity line of credit.* Also known as a HELOC, this is good to have in place in the event of an emergency or to seize an opportunity. A HELOC is simply a line of credit secured by a second mortgage on your home, and

it is accessed via a checkbook and/or debit card. The size of the HELOC is limited by the amount of equity you have in your home.

TIMOTHY BROWN, MBA, CFA® (Oakdale, Minnesota)

TIP 46 MORTGAGE ACCELERATION—HOW TO DETERMINE IF IT'S RIGHT FOR YOU

Q. I think I would like to pay off my mortgage early. Should I spend my extra money this way?

A. You've touched on a long-standing debate. The answer involves your personal circumstances and feelings about debt. Crunching your particular numbers is the best method for determining if prepayment makes sense for you. Remember that the primary benefits to prepaying a mortgage are realizing substantial savings on interest and the peace of mind one that comes with paying off a debt. It has no effect on the sales value of your home.

Consider the following in determining what's best for you:

- Can you afford extra payments?
- If you might move again, why bother?
- Will you lose an important tax deduction?
- Can you get a better after-tax return on your investment elsewhere?

Let's look more closely at the details.

I Can't Afford to Prepay My Mortgage

Accelerating your loan repayment reduces the total amount of interest you must pay the lender. Like any effective savings plan, just getting started is important. Even $100 a month, or about $3.50 a day, can save thousands of dollars in interest over the life of the loan. Simply pay the extra principal yourself each month. Do not pay extra for mortgage prepayment plans that charge fees for doing the same thing.

I May Move Again

Moving makes little or no difference in accelerating your mortgage repayment because every dollar you apply toward reducing your loan balance will come back when you sell your home.

Loss of an Important Tax Deduction

Losing the tax deduction is not relevant if you earn more by paying off the mortgage early and saving the interest. The math here is pretty easy. When you send in $1 for interest on the loan expecting to get 27 cents relief on your tax return, you're still out 73 cents.

Better Returns Elsewhere

You definitely can get better returns on your cash if you pay down a high-interest credit card instead of accelerating your mortgage payment. You may also do better by investing in the stock market, but there are no guarantees. It would be difficult to obtain a higher after-tax yield on a guaranteed, fixed account than what your mortgage costs.

End Note$

Other considerations include the very real concern about locking up cash that might be needed for other things. When you review your total financial plan, make sure that you have the cash flow needed for all your goals before committing to an early payoff.

BONNIE A. HUGHES, CFP® (Rome, Georgia)

TIP 47 REVERSE MORTGAGES HELP CASH-STRAPPED SENIORS ENJOY RETIREMENT

Q. My wife and I are 68, and our house is paid for. We barely make ends meet on Social Security and have no extra funds for home repairs or emergencies. Would a reverse mortgage make sense for us?

A. Many seniors share similar circumstances—their largest asset, their home, is paid off or nearly paid off, but they are cash strapped and unable to enjoy their retirement years fully. In the past, the only alternatives were to refinance the home, which is difficult unless you can show the ability to make the payments, or to sell and move to something less expensive. Reverse mortgages present a third possibility, but the first step is to consider the alternatives.

Look at All Your Options

Most people, understandably, want to stay in their own homes. But don't just assume that you will. For example, do you know what your house is worth? Do you know the cost to buy or rent a new home? Have you looked into the cost and feasibility of moving into an apartment, an assisted-living facility, or other alternative housing? Are you eligible for Supplemental Security Income (SSI) or other assistance programs? Could you qualify and make the payments on a low-cost home equity loan? Before considering any type of major refinancing or selling your home, review these and other possibilities.

How Reverse Mortgages Work

This mortgage allows homeowners, age 62 and up, to borrow against their home's value and receive a lump sum, monthly cash advances, or advances from a credit line. No income is required because no payment is made until the borrowers die, sell their home, or permanently move out. In the meantime, the monthly interest is added to the amount(s) borrowed.

Generally, the older you are, the more you can borrow, and the greater the appraisal of your house, the higher the loan. However, the National Housing Act, section 203-b, has mandated county-by-county limits; in 2003, the highest reverse-mortgage loan available in urban areas was around $280,000.

On a regular mortgage, each monthly payment increases your equity and lowers the loan balance. With a reverse mortgage, the amount owed increases each month and the equity decreases. (Of course, if the homes in your area are appreciating, that will add to your equity.) With a reverse mortgage, you remain the homeowner. You are still responsible for insurance, taxes, and upkeep. And, while you cannot be foreclosed, failure to keep the property up or pay taxes could trigger default on your reverse mortgage.

Different Types of Reverse Mortgages

The Home Equity Conversion Mortgage (HECM) is the only reverse mortgage insured by the federal government (through the Federal Housing Administration). Unless you qualify for a specialized state or local government loan as discussed below, the HECM program is usually the best consumer option for reverse mortgages.

The FHA stipulates to HECM lenders how much you can borrow, based on your age and home value. The HECM program holds down loan costs, which can be substantial. And the FHA ensures that lenders meet all their obligations. As a general rule, HECM programs provide the largest loan advances and the most payout options.

Some companies offer proprietary reverse mortgages that might allow you to borrow more than the FHA limit. However, you are likely to pay more in closing costs and interest. Compare such a loan carefully with its HECM counterpart. For help, visit http://www.hecmcounselors.org/request.

Many states and localities offer targeted versions of reverse mortgages that should be considered. Deferred Payment Loans (DPLs) provide a single lump-sum payment to improve or repair your home. Property Tax Deferrals (PTDs) provide annual loan advances just to pay property taxes.

Further Considerations

- *Closing costs.* Money from the reverse mortgage can pay closing costs, which are added to the loan and paid back at the end of the loan. There is an origination fee, up to 2 percent of the home's value or the county's 203-b limit. For smaller loans, lenders are allowed to charge up to $2,000. These costs are sometimes negotiable, so it pays to shop around. Other costs include title search and insurance, appraisal fees, credit checks, and the like. Because the up-front costs are heavy, reverse mortgages make the most sense if you plan to stay in your home for a long time.
- *Can I end up owing more than my house is worth?* All HECM reverse mortgage products (and most others) have a cap or nonrecourse limit. For example, if your house is worth $175,000 and your reverse mortgage loan balance is $200,000, the lender can only collect $175,000. This feature is paid for through a Mortgage Insurance Premium (MIP) which costs 2 percent of the home's value and .5 percent added to your interest rate. The Mortgage Insurance Premium also ensures that you will receive the promised loan advances and will not have to repay the loan for as long as you stay in the home.

End Note$

Reverse mortgages are complex, and even to qualify for an FHA-insured HECM, you must discuss the loan, free of charge, with an FHA-approved counselor. For more information, call 800-569-4287.

A few helpful Web sites include the following:

- AARP (http://www.aarp.org/revmort)
- National Center for Home Equity Conversion Mortgage (NCHEC) (http://www.reverse.org)

- U.S. Department of Housing and Urban Development (http://www.hud.gov/buying/rvrsmort.cfm)

NEIL P. COLLINS CFP® (Melrose, Massachusetts)

TIP 48 HOLDING TITLE ON YOUR PROPERTY

Q. What is the best way to hold title on my real property?

A. How you hold title has legal, estate, and tax consequences. Each state has its own laws and regulations, so where you live and/or where your property is located determine your options. Ask your attorney, financial planner, or CPA to assist you in this essential decision.

Some Examples

Here are a few examples based on California law.

As an individual, you may hold real property either as sole owner or in co-ownership, with several variations on each.

Sole ownership is ownership by an individual or other entity capable of holding title, a single person, an unmarried person, domestic partners, or a married person as their sole and separate property.

Co-ownership of real property occurs when two or more persons hold title. That includes: community property, joint tenancy, tenancy in common, Living Trust, or community property with right of survivorship. Let's look more closely at the kinds of co-ownership.

Holding title as community property. California is one of nine community property states. Others are Nevada, Louisiana, Wisconsin, Texas, Arizona, Washington, Idaho, and New Mexico. Community property is real property acquired by a husband and wife or by either one of them. Real property is presumed to be community property unless otherwise stated. Both spouses have the right to dispose of one-half of the community property. If a spouse does not exercise their right to give one-half of the property to someone other than the other spouse, then the half goes to the surviving spouse without administration. If the right is exercised, the half is subject to administration in the estate.

Holding title as joint tenancy. Joint tenancy is when two or more people, who may or may not be married, own property equally together. The joint tenants do not own distinct shares in the property; if one of them dies, the other(s) will continue to own the property, with the title immediately going to the surviving joint tenant.

Tenants in common. As tenants in common, two or more people own a property together. Each co-owner may hold an interest that is not equal, and has a distinct share that he or she can pass on to anyone at his or her death, or sell without permission of the other co-owners.

Living Trust. Both sole ownership and co-ownership can use Trusts Revocable Living Trust to hold title in real property. The grantors of the Trust retain complete control of all the assets in the Trust, including the management rights and responsibilities allowing real property to be bought and sold easily. If the grantor/trustee of the Trust becomes disabled, a successor trustee would take over management of the Trust and property held in it without obtaining a court-appointed conservator or guardian. On the owner's death, the Living Trust allows the Trustee(s) to transfer assets directly to the named beneficiaries without probate, saving valuable time, trouble, and money.

Community property with right of survivorship. The newest form of holding title in California is community property with right of survivorship. A husband and wife must specifically declare this in the transfer document. Then, on the death of one spouse, the property passes to the surviving spouse, outside of probate.

Also, note that in California, it is illegal for your real estate broker, loan agent, or title and escrow officer to advise you on how to hold title, making it even more important to seek independent, professional guidance.

SHERRY HINRICHS (Santa Rosa, California)

Chapter

4

EDUCATION FUNDING

TIP 49 WAYS TO SAVE FOR COLLEGE

Q. What options are available for us to save for our children's college education?

A. The most important thing is to begin saving, even if it's $25 a month. As your income increases, boost the amount you save.

Savings options are plentiful and confusing. Some plans pay interest and preserve your initial contribution or allow you to control how the savings are invested. Others do not. Adding to the confusion, how you save can affect your child's financial aid options (keep reading for more information on the financial aid formulas).

Many Ways to Save

The following are a few ways to save:

- Section 529 Savings Plans
- Prepaid tuition plans
- Series EE and I savings bonds
- Custodial accounts (Uniform Transfers to Minors Act—UTMA; Uniform Gifts to Minors Act—UGMA)

- Taxable accounts in a parent's name
- Coverdell Savings Accounts (formerly known as Education IRAs)
- Retirement plans (401(k), traditional IRA, and Roth IRA)
- Life insurance

KATHY DOLLARD, CFP®, MBA (Boxborough, Massachusetts)

TIP 50 HOW MUCH TO SAVE FOR COLLEGE

Q. How much do I need to save to send my child to college?

A. How much you need primarily depends on the choice of college and its cost, the anticipated increase in the cost until your child reaches college age, and the likelihood of your child receiving financial aid.

Cost of a College Education

The average nationwide cost of college attendance (tuition and fees, not including room and board) for the 2003–04 school year was $19,710 for a four-year private college and $4,694 for a four-year public university for an in-state resident (*Trends in College Pricing, 2003,* © 2003 by College Board). Add about $7,000 if the student attends an out-of-state public university, for a total of $11,740.

Multiply the national average annual cost by four years, and it costs $18,776 (for a public university) to $78,840 (for a private college) to send one child to four years of college today, not including annual price increases or room and board. The good news is that many students receive some sort of financial aid. The bad news is that much of the financial aid is in the form of loans, very few of which pay the full cost. If cost is an issue, set your child's expectations regarding college no later than junior high school.

College Costs Rise Every Year

In the 2003–04 school year, average public university tuition and fees increased 14.1 percent; private college costs rose 6 percent. Historically, college costs have climbed at about twice the annual inflation rate.

Larger Incomes for College Grads

The average income in 2000 for someone 18 and over with a bachelor's degree was $51,700, according to the U.S. Census Bureau. For a person with only a high school diploma, the average income was just $27,100. In 1975, the average college graduate made 57 percent more than the average high school grad. By 2000, the average college graduate's income was 91 percent more than that of the high school graduate (after adjusting for inflation).

How Much Do I Need to Save?

If your child is born today, and if college costs increase 5 percent per year for the next 18 years, the projected cost of a year at a public university by the time your child is a freshman is about $30,000. Based on a 6 percent return on your investments, you would need to save about $320 per month for the next 18 years to fund four years at a public university. For a private college, the cost in 18 years will be about $67,000, more than doubling your needed monthly savings to almost $700. Of course, these estimates are based on today's average costs—individual college costs could vary significantly, requiring you to save more or possibly less.

	Public College	Private College
If Your Child is a . . .	You need to save . . .	You need to save . . .
Newborn	$320/month	$690/month
Six-year-old	$440/month	$950/month
Twelve-year-old	$800/month	$1,700/month

The sooner you begin saving, the better. Very few families actually save the full amount needed to pay for college. Colleges generally expect that you will save about one-third of the required amount, borrow one-third, and fund another third from your cash flow while the child is in college.

Don't Allow College Costs to Ruin Your Retirement Plans

As important as it is to save for college, remember that you should make saving for your own retirement your first priority. You should save at least 10 percent of your gross income for retirement—assuming you start early. Then put another 1 percent toward college costs. For example, if your family's annual income is $50,000, try to save $5,000 per year for retirement and $500 a year for college. That breaks down to almost $100 a week for retirement and $10 a week for college. Set up automatic savings plans so you never have a chance to spend this money.

KATHY DOLLARD, CFP®, MBA (Boxborough, Massachusetts)

TIP 51 PROS AND CONS OF A 529 PLAN FOR COLLEGE SAVINGS

Q. Should I use a 529 Plan to save for college?

A. Qualified tuition plans, also known as 529 Plans, are a popular education savings method that feature special tax benefits and allow significantly greater contributions than other options like the Coverdell Education Savings Account. Every state now has at least one 529 Plan. With so many choices, it's important to know the basics about how these plans work and what to consider before you invest.

How 529 Plans Work

Anyone can contribute money to a 529 Plan on behalf of a beneficiary (student), and unlike Coverdell ESAs, contributors are not subject to income limitations, nor are there restrictions on the beneficiary's age. The only requirement is that amounts accumulated in the plan must be used to pay for the qualified education expenses of an undergraduate or graduate program at an accredited institution. Expenses that qualify include tuition, fees, books, supplies, required equipment, and room and board.

The Two Types of 529 Plans: Prepaid and Savings

1. *Prepaid plans.* With prepaid plans, you fund future tuition costs by purchasing college credit hours at today's rates. When the credit hours are used, the plan pays the going rate for tuition at that time. Because the sponsoring state generally guarantees prepaid plans, you're assured the tuition money will be there when you need it. Unfortunately, these guaranteed plans normally cover only the cost of tuition. Recently, some states have discontinued offering prepaid plans. If your state still offers one, check it out. The disadvantage of these plans, however, is that they can affect financial aid eligibility.
2. *Savings plans.* In these plans, your contributions are invested in mutual funds offered by the plan's program manager (like Vanguard, TIAA-CREF, or Fidelity). Some plans allow you to choose the mutual funds. Others have ready-made investment portfolios based on age and risk tolerance, and these are professionally managed by the state or program manager. Remember that investments in 529 Savings Plans fluctuate with the stock market, so they need to be monitored regularly just like retirement savings and other investments. You can change your investment

selections in a plan or move the plan assets to another state's plan once a year.

Requirements and Benefits

Both types of 529 Plans are subject to the requirements of the sponsoring state. Many states allow nonresidents to participate in their 529 Plan.

Among the benefits of a 529 Plan are the following:

- *No federal income tax.* According to section 529 of the Internal Revenue Code (how 529 Plans got their name), earnings from plan investments are free from federal income tax, as long as the funds are used to pay for qualified education expenses.
- *State tax deductions.* Some states allow a deduction for contributions to the state's 529 Plan, others may tax out-of-state Plan contributions, and still others follow the federal rules.
- *Estate planning advantages.* A powerful estate planning tool, 529 Plans allow individuals to make gifts of $11,000 annually to anyone without reporting the contribution or paying a federal gift transfer tax. Under a special provision of the plan rules, an individual can contribute up to $55,000 in one year to the plan without triggering the gift tax. The election treats the gift as if it had been $11,000 per year over a five-year period. The only requirement is that no further gifts be made to that person for the next five years. A married couple can gift up to $110,000 per beneficiary in one year and reduce their taxable estate. A portion of the gift may be included in your taxable estate if you die within the five-year period.

These benefits, coupled with large contribution maximums (more than $200,000 in some states), make 529 Plans attractive savings vehicles. However, if you use the money for anything other than qualified education expenses, you face a 10 percent penalty tax and tax on the earnings subject to that distribution. Special exceptions apply if the student receives a scholarship, dies, or becomes disabled.

Choosing a 529 Plan

Some considerations when deciding on a plan include the following:

- *Eligibility.* Is the plan fully open to nonresidents?
- *Fees and expenses.* Is there a sales commission, an enrollment fee, or annual maintenance fee? Is there an asset-based management fee? What are the annual expenses of the underlying mutual funds?

- *Investment considerations.* Does the plan use age-based or years-to-enrollment portfolios? Is there a fixed or guaranteed investment option? Can you build your own investment portfolio? How often can you change your investments? Who manages the plan investments?
- *Contributions.* What are the minimum initial and subsequent contributions allowed by the plan? What is the maximum contribution allowed? How much is deductible on my state income tax return?
- *Time or age limitations.* Is there any limit on the age of the account beneficiary? How long can the account stay open? Are there restrictions on withdrawing funds from the plan?

A final consideration is the plan's impact on need-based financial aid. Prepaid plans are considered a student resource and result in a dollar-for-dollar reduction in financial aid. However, 529 Savings Plans are considered the owner's asset, not the beneficiary's. If the owner is the parent, up to 6 percent of the account's value will be included in the financial aid formulas. These plans are very new, but it appears that private colleges may treat these plans as a student asset, which will be assessed at 25 percent for financial aid formulas.

There are other considerations as well, so 529 Plans may be most appropriate for families who do not expect to qualify for financial aid or who do not want to count on financial aid.

An excellent Web site with information about all state-sponsored 529 Plans is http://www.savingforcollege.com.

SUZANNE D. FAILS, CPA, CFP® (Stafford, Texas)

TIP 52 SAVING FOR EDUCATION—COVERDELL EDUCATION SAVINGS ACCOUNTS

Q. I would like to take advantage of tax incentives to save for my child's education. What are Coverdell Education Accounts, and how do they work? How do they compare to 529 Plans?

A. The Coverdell Education Savings Account (formerly the Education IRA) provides tax incentives to save for a child's educational expenses. If you are within the income limits, you can contribute up to $2,000 per year for any child under the age of 18. Although the contributions are not deductible, the earnings grow tax-free and are distributed tax-free as long as they are used to pay for qualified educational expenses. If the funds are not used for qualified educational expenses, the earnings are subject to ordinary income taxes as well as a 10 percent penalty.

Where to Open an Account

You can open a Coverdell Account with most banks, mutual fund companies, or other financial institutions that offer traditional IRAs.

Requirements

- Contributions must be made in cash (or a cash equivalent such as a personal check).
- Contributions must be made by the due date of the contributor's tax return (no extensions), usually April 15.
- The same beneficiary can have multiple accounts, but total annual contributions cannot exceed $2,000 (for example, if the parents contribute $1,500 to an account, the grandparents would be limited to contributing $500). Excess contributions are subject to a 6 percent excise tax until they are withdrawn.
- Life insurance contracts are not permitted.
- Contributions can be made only if the beneficiary is less than 18 years old.
- The money must be withdrawn or rolled over to a different family member within 30 days of either the beneficiary turning 30 years old (unless the beneficiary is a special needs beneficiary) or the death of the beneficiary.
- The definition of family member, for the purpose of rollovers, includes the beneficiary's spouse, sibling, or other family member, up to and including first cousins of the beneficiary.

Income Limits

Contributions may be limited or phased out for higher-income individuals based on a person's Modified Adjusted Gross Income (MAGI, the same as Adjusted Gross Income for most people).

For example, in 2004, a single person with a MAGI of less than $95,000 can make the full $2,000 contribution; with a MAGI $95,000 to $110,000, the contribution is prorated; and above $110,000 it's prohibited. For a married couple filing jointly, the phase-out range is $190,000 to $220,000. The income limits change periodically, so check with your tax advisor or IRS Publication 970, "Tax Benefits for Education," for the latest limits.

If you're above the income limits, it's acceptable for another individual who is not—like a grandparent, friend, or even the child—to make the contribution.

Qualified Educational Expenses

The definition of eligible schools has been expanded to include elementary and secondary schools (K through 12), including public, private, or religious schools. Qualifying as higher education are any college, university, vocational school, or postsecondary institution eligible to participate in a student-aid program administered by the Department of Education.

Qualified expenses include the following:

- Tuition and fees, books, supplies, equipment, tutoring, and services for special-needs beneficiaries
- Room and board, uniforms, transportation, and supplementary items and services (including extended day programs). There are limitations on room expenses if a student lives off-campus or is not enrolled at least half time.
- Computer equipment, Internet access, and educational software

Other Important Issues

- You can claim the HOPE or Lifetime learning credit in the same year you take a tax-free withdrawal from a Coverdell Education Savings Account (but not for the same expenses).
- Contributions to a Coverdell Account and a 529 Plan may be made in the same year.
- Coverdell Accounts are treated as a student asset, and withdrawals are counted as the student's income (withdrawals are tax-free) in determining financial aid eligibility.
- Once funds are contributed to a Coverdell Account, they must be paid out to the beneficiary (the gift cannot be revoked). The beneficiary can be changed, however.

End Note$

The most significant advantages of Coverdell Accounts over 529 Plans are that they can be used for grades K through 12 and have more investment flexibility. If your child may be eligible for need-based financial aid in college, try to use up all of the money in the Coverdell Account by December of the child's junior year in high school.

For more information, check out the free IRS Publication 970, "Tax Benefits for Education," at http://www.irs.gov.

BOB NUSBAUM, MBA, (New York, New York)

TIP 53 SAVING FOR COLLEGE WITH UNIFORM GIFTS AND UNIFORM TRANSFERS TO MINORS ACCOUNTS

Q. Tell me about saving for college using Uniform Gifts and Uniform Transfers to Minors Act accounts.

A. Uniform Gifts to Minors Act (UGMA) and Uniform Transfers to Minors Act (UTMA) accounts are custodial accounts that can be set up to transfer assets to minors without incurring gift taxes or requiring the filing of gift-tax returns. The donor of the funds and the custodian of the account may or may not be the same person. UGMA/UTMA accounts must be used for the child's benefit and to cover expenses beyond normal parental obligations (definitions vary state to state).

A UTMA is newer and more flexible than an UGMA, can stay open for a longer time, and allows more types of assets in the account.

Eligible Investment Amounts

For 2004, the annual gift exclusion amount is $11,000, and it is adjusted with inflation in $1,000 increments. Each citizen also has a lifetime exclusion amount related to estate taxes that is above and beyond these annual exclusions. Exceeding the annual exclusion amount in any given year uses up part of the lifetime exclusion amount.

The annual gift exclusion amount applies to an individual donor and an individual recipient. It applies to gift recipients of any age, but the UTMA/UGMA structure is designed to facilitate gifts to a minor through a custodial account, because minors generally cannot hold property in their own name.

As an example, in a household with two parents and two minor children, in 2004 each parent can give up to $11,000 per year of their own assets to each child without exceeding the exclusion amount, or a total of $44,000 per year. If the assets are titled in one parent's name, it is possible for that parent to give up to $22,000 per year to an individual (no limits on transfers between spouses) without exceeding the exclusion amounts, provided that the spouse agrees to gift-splitting as defined by IRS rules. Doing this will require filing a gift-tax return to document the split, although no tax will be owed.

One favorable exception to the $11,000 annual exclusion amount occurs with contributions to a Section 529 Savings Account. In that case, up to five years' worth of gifts can be combined into one year without exceeding the exclusion amounts. However, if any other gifts are made within the five-year time frame, these will use up part of the lifetime exclusion amount and will require filing a gift-tax return. Tax may or may not be owed, depending on whether the entire lifetime exclusion amount has been used up.

Some of the Basics

- Unlike other methods of saving for college, there are no income or other eligibility limitations for UGMA/UTMA accounts.
- Although the funds are in a custodial account, they are considered student assets and any distributions are considered student income. Thus, eligibility for need-based aid can be affected.
- UGMA/UTMA funds can be used for any college expenses, including room and board, or noncollege expenses of the beneficiary, like buying a car or funding a vacation.
- The account custodian controls investment and disbursement until the child reaches the age of majority (18 or 21, depending on the state).
- UGMA/UTMA account funds remain in the donor's estate if the donor is custodian and dies before the child reaches the age of majority. From a transfer and estate planning perspective, it may make sense for someone other than the donor to be the custodian of the account.

Potential Candidates for This Approach to Savings

For some, these accounts are better for reducing the size of an estate than saving for college. UGMA/UTMA accounts can hurt financial aid eligibility and are taxed at a parent's tax rate until the child reaches age 14.

If you have the money, a simpler approach may be to pay the student's tuition directly to the college. Such payments are excluded from the gift documentation and tax provisions and are not limited in amount. But that exclusion only applies to tuition.

C. BRADLEY BOND, CFP® (Murrysville, Pennsylvania)

TIP 54 PREPAID TUITION PLANS

Q. What are prepaid tuition plans, and how do they work?

A. Nearly half the states and a number of private institutions sponsor Prepaid Tuition Plans that allow a person to make lump-sum or periodic payments at current tuition rates to prepay future college costs.

Sometimes, these plans are referred to as guaranteed plans, implying that the plans will keep up with tuition inflation and that future payments will be covered. In reality, most state plans don't provide an ironclad guarantee. The guarantee often is backed only with the plan's assets, which may fall short of covering future obligations.

Eligible Investment Amounts

These vary by state but generally are large enough to cover the expense of four years of college. State-by-state comparisons and investment amounts are available at http://www.finaid.org/savings/state529plans.html.

Some of the Basics

- Some states require owner or beneficiary residency.
- Annual distributions may affect financial aid eligibility.
- Eligible expenses vary by state.
- State maintains investment control. Nonqualified withdrawals are subject to income tax plus a 10 percent penalty.
- The original contribution is usually refundable to the contributor subject to taxes and penalty, although interest may be lost.

Potential Candidates for This Approach to Savings

Prepaid tuition plans may appeal to families with young children or those not likely to qualify for need-based financial aid.

C. BRADLEY BOND, CFP® (Murrysville, Pennsylvania)

TIP 55 SERIES EE AND I BONDS

Q. I understand that U.S. Savings Bonds can be a good way to save for college. What are Series EE and Series I bonds, and how can I use them?

A. Series EE Savings Bonds purchased after December 31, 1989, and the new Series I Inflation Protection Bonds, are another way to pay for college and save on taxes. If the required conditions are met, the interest from these bonds is tax-exempt when used to pay for qualified educational expenses.

Some of the Basics

Individuals can purchase up to $15,000 of Series EE bonds ($30,000 face value) and $30,000 (issued at face value) Series I bonds per year.

- Bonds must have been issued after December 31, 1989, to receive preferential tax treatment; purchaser must be over age 24 at the time of purchase; and bonds must be purchased in the parents' names. If bonds previously purchased are titled incorrectly, there is a procedure to get them retitled, provided that the parents initially purchased the bonds and the parents' income is below the eligibility limits at the time of redemption.

- Redemption must be in the year of qualified expenses. In your records, include the bonds' serial number, face value, issue date, redemption date, total proceeds (principal and interest), receipt from the educational institution receiving the payment, and receipts for qualified expenses.
- Interest on the bonds can be partially or completely tax-free, depending on the parents' income (indexed for inflation) in the year of redemption.
- For tax purposes, bonds are considered a parental asset, and the interest is deemed paid income. The IRS adds redemption interest to your income before determining eligibility for the tax break, also affecting your adjusted gross income (AGI) for financial aid purposes.
- Qualified expenses include tuition and fees but not room, board, and books.
- Bond redemptions are reported on IRS forms 8815/8818.
- Purchasing bonds in smaller denominations provides more flexibility, because any redemption amount that exceeds the amount of qualified expenses loses its tax-free treatment.
- Bond's value is included in the bond owner's estate.

End Note$

Savings bonds may appeal to families that expect to meet the income limitations at redemption, have a low risk tolerance and short time horizon, and are willing to accept the relatively low returns.

More information is available at http://www.savingsbonds.gov or from the Bureau of Public Debt, PO Box 1328, Parkersburg, WV 26106-1328; 877-811-7283; http://www.publicdebt.treas.gov.

C. BRADLEY BOND, CFP® (Murrysville, Pennsylvania)

TIP 56 VARIABLE UNIVERSAL LIFE AS A SAVINGS VEHICLE

Q. Is a Variable Universal Life insurance policy a good way to save for college?

A. The challenge of saving and paying for a child's college education has given rise to a cottage industry of businesses offering advice, services, and products to help families overcome the obstacles in saving for college. In turn, that's led to some creative strategies to enhance potentially the prospects of qualifying for financial aid. Some are effective; others are not. Variable Universal Life insurance is one of those more creative strategies that can be appropriate in very unusual circumstances.

To evaluate whether Variable Universal Life insurance (VUL) is the right college savings vehicle, you should consider the following points.

Your Need for Life Insurance

First and foremost, VUL is life insurance. Do you have a genuine need for it? If not, VUL may not be the best savings vehicle.

Your Tolerance for Risk

VUL is a permanent insurance policy, unlike term insurance. VUL has a death benefit and a savings element or cash value. With a VUL product, the policy's cash values typically are invested in a mix of mutual fund-like subaccounts that allow policyholders to save for their children's anticipated college expenses. Keep in mind, though, the policy's cash value is directly affected by the performance of the subaccounts. A VUL may be a poor choice for investors lacking the stomach for potential market declines or the time horizon to recover from periodic investment setbacks.

Financial Aid Implications

Student financial aid eligibility is based on both the parents' and the student's assessable income and assets. Parents' income is assessed at rates up to 47 percent, the student's income at 50 percent. Parents' assets typically are assessed at 5.6 percent and the student's at 35 percent. The sum total of all this is the Expected Family Contribution (EFC). If it's less than the Cost of Attendance, the student has a financial need. A decrease in either income or assets of parents or the student lowers the EFC, increases the student's financial need, and (presumably) increases the amount of aid awarded.

Some of the more creative strategies in college financial planning have evolved as a way to exploit this formula. VUL is a good example. Life insurance cash values generally are not assessed in the financial aid calculation, but liquid savings are. The solution: Save in the VUL. Moreover, withdrawals from the VUL (to pay for tuition, for example) are not treated as income, thereby lowering total assessable income in the years during which the student is attending college and applying for aid.

Note: Many private colleges use their own aid calculations and their discretion in assessing policy cash values, so transferring lots of cash into a life insurance policy is no guarantee that those values won't be assessed.

Policy Costs

Life insurance policies are complex products with varying levels of costs and expenses. All life insurance policies carry a charge for the underlying death benefit. Most carry additional administrative fees. Many, VUL included, impose charges on or against the value of the cash account. Also, many states levy a tax or surcharge on policy premiums. All these charges easily can eat up the expected benefit from a financial aid perspective. Therefore, any decision to use VUL as a savings vehicle, predicated on an expected increase in financial aid, *must* include an analysis of the cost of the policy and its expected return versus the cost of doing nothing.

Additional Considerations

Taxes. Saving for college via life insurance avoids income taxes on gains in the cash value. Withdrawals from cash value to pay tuition usually are structured as withdrawals up to the policyholder's basis in the contract, then as a loan against any gains in the policy cash value. As long as the contract is not surrendered, the loans are not taxable to the recipient. If the policy remains in force at the time of the insured's death, the loan balance is subtracted from the death benefit payable to the beneficiary.

Fees. If you change your mind, getting out of a VUL policy can be expensive. Life insurance policies sold by full-service brokers or agents often carry steep surrender fees for the first five to ten years. Consider buying a no-load or low-cost VUL policy instead.

VUL's cousin, the variable annuity. Variable annuities are insurance contracts whose value fluctuates with that of its underlying securities portfolio. Like a VUL policy, the variable annuity's value is not included among either the parents' or the student's assets, potentially increasing prospects for financial aid. One popular strategy is for parents to take out a home equity loan (private colleges assess the parents' home equity when determining aid eligibility), then use the proceeds to fund a variable annuity. All the considerations that apply to the VUL as a savings vehicle also apply to variable annuities. But, unlike with a VUL, withdrawals from a variable annuity are not treated as loans, and the earnings are subject to taxes at ordinary income tax rates. What's more, withdrawals from a variable annuity before the owner's age 59½ are generally subject to a 10 percent federal income tax penalty.

End Note$

Under no circumstances is it appropriate for parents to lie about or misrepresent the true amount of their assets and/or income when submitting a college financial aid application. Material misrepresentations regarding the nature and amount of the applicant's or the parents' assets or income can result in severe legal and civil penalties.

TIMOTHY M. HAYES, MBA, CCPS, CMFC, RFC (Pittsford, New York)

TIP 57 SAVING FOR EDUCATION IN A PARENT'S NAME

Q. I want to save for my child's college education, but I also want to retain control of the money in case I need it in the future. What are my options?

A. The good news is that you have many different options to choose from. Let's look at the primary options, with control of the money in mind.

529 Plans

The 529 Plan is a savings plan sponsored by an individual state. Although you name the account's beneficiary, the account remains yours to use if needed (you may pay a penalty to do so). You may change the beneficiary at any time. All earnings are tax-free, if the proceeds are used for qualified education expenses.

If you have state income tax, consider any 529 Plans offered by your state, because you may be able to deduct the contribution on your state income tax return and the plan earnings are tax-free. If your state does not have an income tax, you can shop around for what's best for you. Other considerations that vary by state include: investment options, contribution limits, commissions and fund expenses, creditor protection, and plan fees.

Although you still technically own and control the account, your contributions are considered a completed gift to the beneficiary. A special provision of the 529 Plan allows contributions to be averaged for gift-tax purposes over a five-year period, so you can contribute up to $55,000 ($110,000 if married) to a beneficiary's account in one year without triggering any gift-tax implications. Also, the account is considered to be out of your estate for estate-tax purposes, should you die before the account is exhausted.

Most colleges count 529 Plan assets in the account holders' assets when computing financial aid. However, any dollar amount spent from the plan for your child's education will be considered the student's income.

Traditional and Roth IRAs

A traditional IRA offers a tax deduction for contributions, and the funds may be used penalty-free for higher education. However, you're taxed on any withdrawals at your marginal income tax rate.

Higher-income individuals with a retirement plan at work are not eligible for deductible contributions to a traditional IRA. Additionally, if adjusted gross income exceeds $150,000 for married couples, you are not eligible to contribute to the Roth IRA, either. Even if you're ineligible for the deductible or Roth IRA contributions, you can make nondeductible traditional IRA contributions.

401(k) Plan

Using a 401(k) as an education savings tool allows you to contribute up to $13,000 of your earnings each year tax-deferred. Withdrawals are subject to taxes and a 10 percent penalty, unless you take the money as a loan from the 401(k) plan. If a plan allows, you can borrow up to 50 percent of its value to $50,000, then pay back the loan, plus interest, to the plan over no more than a five-year period.

Savings Bonds

You can redeem savings bonds tax-free for education purposes, but strict rules apply. The bonds must be either Series EE bonds issued after January 1990 or Series I bonds; the bonds must be owned in your name alone or jointly with your spouse, but not in the child's name; and you must have a Modified Adjusted Gross Income of less than $119,750 (in 2004), if married at the time of redemption, to qualify for at least a partial exemption.

Permanent Life Insurance

With a permanent life insurance policy, you pay an annual premium to cover insurance expenses, plus an additional amount contributed to the cash value of the policy. The cash value grows tax-deferred, and you can borrow from this cash value to fund education expenses without owing any taxes. However, the amount you borrow from the policy reduces the death benefit, should you die before the loan is repaid.

Taxable Accounts

A standard taxable account has the most flexibility when it comes to education savings. Account earnings are taxed, but if the earnings are the result of the sale of assets held for more than one year, they'll likely be subject to a lower capital gains rate of a maximum 20 percent (15 percent through 2008).

GLENN BISHOP, CDFA, CMA, MBA (Carrollton, Texas)

TIP 58 HOW TO PAY FOR COLLEGE IF YOU HAVEN'T SAVED ENOUGH

Q. I doubt that I can save the full amount my child will need to cover college costs. If I fall short, what are my other options?

A. You're not alone if you haven't saved enough to cover the full cost of college. Private colleges assume that if parents save for 18 years, those savings will cover about one-third the total cost of a private college education. The remaining two-thirds of the cost generally come from income earned while the child is in school, loans, and financial aid.

Here's a look at how to use current income while your child is in college and at borrowing money to pay for college.

Paying from Current Cash Flow

Because college is such a significant commitment, the student as well as parents should play a role if current cash flow is needed to pay for part of college expenses. The student, for example, could be required to work during vacations. They also may be able to get a work-study award as part of a part of a financial aid package or obtain a part-time job at school.

Cutting back on vacations, making family cars last longer, and putting off remodeling or redecorating projects all help squeeze extra money from regular cash flow. If your student is not living at home, grocery bills, entertainment expenses, and utilities will be lower, too.

Borrowing to Pay for College

The upside is that many lenders are eager to lend money for college. The downside is that they may encourage you to borrow more than you can afford, jeopardizing your retirement or your home.

Student loans: Stafford Loans. Most students are eligible to borrow money through the federal government's Stafford Loan program. If your family qualifies for need-based financial aid, it may come in the form of a subsidized Stafford Loan. You must first complete a FAFSA (Free Application for Student Aid) in January of your child's senior year in high school, although it may be possible to do so through May. Even if you don't think your family qualifies for need-based aid, apply for it anyway.

Everything about the two types of loans (subsidized versus unsubsidized) is the same, including the interest rate, except that with the subsidized loan, the federal government pays the interest while the student is in college. With an unsubsidized loan, if you fail to pay the interest during college, it's added to the total loan at the end (capitalized). You can save hundreds of dollars in interest expense by paying at least the interest due during the college years.

Stafford Loans are easy to obtain; interest rates are low though variable; and the interest may be deductible, depending on your income. The major disadvantage is that students are not allowed to borrow a lot of money through this program. The current annual maximums for dependent students are freshman, $2,625; sophomore, $3,500; junior, $5,500, and senior, $5,500. (Limits are higher for independent students, students whose parents do not qualify for PLUS loans, and graduate students.) That adds up to $17,125 in education-related debt at the end of four years.

With a 6 percent interest rate and loan payoff period of 10 years, the new graduate's loan payment could be $200 per month. According to most lenders, student loan payments should be about 7 percent of the borrower's income, so the new graduate must make about $34,000 a year to manage the loan payment. No wonder so many college grads end up back home with their parents.

Stafford Loans probably make sense if your child (or you) can handle repayment without much trouble. Be sure to shop around for the best deal you can get. Start with the programs your child's college recommends and then comparison shop. Some lenders provide repayment incentives in the form of lower fees and interest rates. You can learn more about Stafford Loans by reading *Loans and Grants from Uncle Sam: Am I Eligible and for How Much?*, by Anna Leider (Octameron Associates, PO Box 2748, Alexandria, VA 22301; http://www.octameron.com). It's updated every year.

Other student loans. A variety of other loan programs, public and private, are available to students. Some lenders will allow students to borrow much larger amounts, often as long as there is a cosigner. Remember: As a cosigner, you are responsible for paying off the loan if your child does not.

Parent loans: PLUS loans. The amount of money that parents can borrow is not nearly as limited. Parents with good credit ratings can get annual PLUS loans (another federal loan program) equal to the cost of attendance less any financial aid. For example, if your child attends a school that costs $30,000 and receives financial aid of $5,000, you could borrow up to $25,000 per year—but should you? This program may look very attractive, but can you afford to borrow $100,000? If you borrowed the $100,000 over four years, with repayment over 10 years at 6 percent, that's a loan payment of $1,110 per month. Could you make those payments and still take care of your other financial obligations?

Parent loans: home equity loans and lines of credit. Home equity loans and home equity lines of credit are other options to fund college. Both are popular because interest rates are low, and the interest on up to $100,000 of the loan may be tax deductible. Higher-income families like the option, because student loan interest deductibility depends on income.

With a home equity loan, you generally borrow a given amount up front, $50,000 for example, and make monthly payments over a predetermined term, usually 5 to 15 years. A disadvantage is that, even if you don't need the full $50,000 up front, you will be paying interest on it—usually at a higher rate than you would earn by keeping the unused extra funds in a savings account until needed.

Don't even think about investing the extra funds in the stock market or high-yield bonds in an attempt to boost your return. That strategy is too risky for money that will be needed in five years or less. Advantages of this type of loan are that you will, theoretically, repay the loan over a fairly short period and the interest rate is generally fixed. Another possible disadvantage is that, if you qualify for need-based financial aid and keep the unused portion of the loan in a savings account or money market account, it may be counted as an additional asset and reduce your financial need.

With a home equity line of credit, you only borrow only what you need by writing a check at the time. So, freshman year, you may borrow only $12,000 and pay interest only on that $12,000. The next year, if you borrow an additional $13,000, you will be paying interest on a total of $25,000—assuming you haven't paid any principal on the initial loan.

The potential problem with this type of loan is that usually you are only required to make interest payments (which can be deceptively low), so it's possible to pay thousands of dollars in interest over many years while never paying down the loan. When the line of credit expires, you have to find a way to pay it off. Although current rates are quite attractive, they are typically variable and likely to go up over the next few years.

Also, remember that, when you take out one of these loans, you are borrowing against the equity in your home. If you're not careful, you could face retirement with large monthly mortgage payments, or even lose your home if the sole breadwinner dies or your home's value falls below the amount of your loan.

How Much Should You Borrow for College?

Every family that's thinking about borrowing should consider this question very carefully. The answer depends on the family's overall financial situation and savings.

A monthly debt-to-income ratio of 36 percent or less is considered healthy, according to *The Ultimate Credit Handbook: How to Cut Your Debt and Have a Lifetime of Great Credit,* by Gerri Detweiler (Plume/Penguin Group, New York; 3rd edition, 2003). However, if you enter—or are close to—retirement with a ratio this high, you probably have too much debt. Let's look at some numbers from a hypothetical family with $100,000 in annual household income.

- Monthly income: $8,333
- Mortgage payment: $2,000 per month, principal and interest
- Homeowners insurance: $50
- Property taxes: $250
- Car payments: $500
- Total monthly debt payment: $2,800
- Debt-to-income ratio: $2,800/$8,333 = 34 percent

While the debt-to-income ratio is within the healthy range, the family easily could slip into a more precarious position by borrowing too much money for college, especially if its income drops. If the family is willing to boost its debt-to-income to ratio to 38 percent by borrowing more money (most lenders wouldn't have a problem with this), that would increase their total monthly debt payments by $367, from $2,800 to $3,167. With a ten-year repayment term, a monthly payment of $367, and an interest rate of 6 percent, this translates into the ability to borrow an additional $33,000, or $8,250 for each of four school years.

Other Options for Parents

- *Borrow from your 401(k) plan.* Most plans allow participants to borrow up to $50,000 or 50 percent of the balance—whichever is less. If you change jobs or get laid off and are unable to pay back the loan, any outstanding amount is considered a taxable distribution, subject to income tax and a 10 percent early withdrawal penalty.
- *Take out a loan against a life insurance policy with cash value.* Check with your insurance agent to determine the interest rates on such a loan and its impact on your policy.
- *Consider having the child attend a community college for two years, then transfer to a state or private university.* This makes sense, especially if a child isn't academically strong in high school or is undecided on a career.

End Note$

Check out http://www.collegeboard.com to access calculators to help with your financial estimates.

KATHY DOLLARD, CFP®, MBA (Boxborough, Massachusetts)

TIP 59 HOW STUDENT FINANCIAL AID WORKS

Q. How will my child qualify for and receive financial aid?

A. The answer depends on the type of financial aid being considered—need-based, merit-based, private financial aid, or tuition discounts.

Need-Based Financial Aid

This is the most common form of aid, and it comes from federal or state governments or from private colleges and universities. Packages can include low-interest loans, grants (money that does not have to be repaid), and/or work-study programs.

Merit-Based Financial Aid

A student can receive merit aid for outstanding performance in a particular area such as athletics, the arts, or academics. Many prestigious schools offer very little merit-based aid compared with their second-tier and third-tier counterparts. Athletic scholarships are limited to NCAA Division I and II schools. Smaller liberal arts schools tend to be NCAA Division III—and are not allowed to award athletic scholarships. You can learn more about athletic scholarships in *The Winning Edge: The Student Athlete's Guide to College Sports,* by Frances and James Killpatrick (Octameron Associates, PO Box 2748, Alexandria, VA 22301; http://www.octameron.com).

Private Financial Aid

Recipients of private aid often satisfy particular requirements set forth by the sponsoring organization, and it often takes research to find these scholarships. Community organizations like the local PTA, garden club, Lions Club, and more give out this type of aid.

Tuition Discounts

These are unique to each school, and you won't know about them until you ask.

Colleges and universities determine whether your child is eligible for need-based aid based on your responses to the Free Application for Student Aid (FAFSA), and/or the PROFILE, and possibly their own unique forms. Public and private schools use the FAFSA to allocate federal aid. Private colleges often require the PROFILE (and sometimes their own form) to determine how money is allocated. To apply for financial aid, you must complete these forms in January and February of your child's senior year of high school—and then every year while the child is in college.

The two types of forms result in two general financial aid formulas—the Federal Methodology and the Institutional Methodology, with many versions of the latter, because private colleges can decide what questions you must answer on the PROFILE (in section Q) and how they will treat that information. In general, both methodologies collect information about the parents' income and assets, the child's income and assets, how many people are in the family and their ages, and whether both parents work.

Some differences in the two methodologies can result in different Expected Family Contributions (EFCs). For example, the Federal Methodology doesn't include the equity in your home, but the Institutional does. The Federal Methodology includes the value of your personal property (cars and more) or any loans, but the Institutional may or may not. Neither formula has traditionally included parents' retirement funds, but some anecdotal evidence suggests that private colleges may be starting to do so.

The result of these calculations is your EFC, which is the amount that your family is expected to pay for one year of college. For example, a family of four with one child in college and one not yet in college, an annual income of $75,000, and no savings might have an EFC of $8,000 per year. Although public universities and private colleges calculate their EFCs somewhat differently, the results generally are in the same ballpark, with the EFC at private colleges higher than at public universities. How much need-based financial aid this hypothetical child might qualify for depends on the cost of the college.

	Private College	**Public University**
Cost of Attendance	$27,700	$12,800
– EFC	$ 8,000	$ 8,000
= Financial Need	$19,700	$ 4,800

The child could be eligible for up to $19,700 in need-based financial aid at a private school, compared with up to $4,800 at a public institution. Keep in mind that, at both schools, at least a portion of any aid is likely to come in the form of a student loan and work-study program, in addition to possible grant money.

End Note$

Just because a student qualifies for a certain amount of need-based aid doesn't mean a school must provide that amount.

A helpful resource for learning how specific schools grant both need-based and merit-based aid is *College Money Handbook,* by Peterson's (Peterson's/Thomson, 2000 Lenox Drive, PO Box 67005, Lawrenceville, NJ 08648; 609-896-1800; http://www.petersons.com) published annually.

KATHY DOLLARD, CFP®, MBA (Boxborough, Massachusetts)

TIP 60 FEDERAL TAX INCENTIVES FOR EDUCATION

Q. Are any tax incentives available to help make college education more affordable for our family?

A. Yes, several important incentives include federal tax deductions and tax credits. The amounts and rules differ with each incentive.

The following information can help you determine your eligibility.

HOPE Scholarship Credit

The HOPE scholarship credit is a by-product of the Taxpayer Relief Act of 1997 that led to the Roth IRA and the Educational IRA (now called a Coverdell Education Savings Account). Married taxpayers (filing jointly) with Adjusted Gross Income (AGI) of less than $83,000 and single taxpayers with AGI of less than $41,000 may claim the HOPE scholarship tax credit. There is a phase out of the credit for those with AGI of $83,000 to $103,000 for married taxpayers, $41,000 to $51,000 for single taxpayers. The credit is not available to taxpayers with AGI above those respective amounts. The amount of the HOPE scholarship credit allowed is equal to 100 percent of qualified expenses (tuition and fees, but not room and board) up to $1,000 plus 50 percent of qualified expenses up to another $1,000, for a total maximum credit of $1,500 per student. The HOPE credit only applies to students who are enrolled at least half-time and who have not completed their first two years of study. The credit cannot be claimed in more than two years for any one student.

Lifetime Learning Credit

Taxpayers can claim a lifetime learning credit, subject to the same AGI limitations that apply to the HOPE credit, for up to 20 percent of qualified expenses (tuition and fees) up to $10,000, for a total maximum credit of $2,000 per taxpayer. If you have three children in college, your HOPE credit may be as high as $4,500, but your lifetime learning credit will never exceed $2,000 per year. Unlike with the HOPE credit, the student doesn't have to be enrolled at least half-time, and there's no limit on the number of years the credit may be taken. However, you may not claim a HOPE credit and a lifetime learning credit for the same student in the same tax year.

Both the HOPE credit and the lifetime learning credit belong to the person who claims the student as a dependent, even if someone else pays the expenses. If no one claims the student as a dependent, the student may claim the credit themselves, even if someone else pays the expenses.

Section 222 Deduction

A deduction for up to $3,000 of college tuition and related expenses is available for tax year 2003 ($4,000 in 2004 and 2005) for married taxpayers with AGI of less than $130,000 and for single taxpayers with AGI of less than $65,000. This is an above-the-line deduction, which means that you do not have to itemize your deductions to take advantage of this incentive. In 2004 and 2005, a deduction for up to $2,000 in college tuition and related expenses is available to married taxpayers with AGI as high as $160,000 and to single taxpayers with AGI as high as $80,000. The Section 222 deduction is not available to taxpayers who claim a HOPE or lifetime learning credit for that student's expenses in the same tax year.

Loan Interest Deduction

Interest paid on student loans for undergraduate or graduate tuition, fees, books, and room and board may be deducted (above the line) by married taxpayers with AGI of less than $100,000 and by single taxpayers with AGI of less than $50,000. The deduction phases out for those married taxpayers with AGI of $100,000 to $130,000 and for single taxpayers with AGI of $50,000 to $65,000. The deduction is not available to taxpayers with AGI above those respective amounts. The deduction is to a maximum of $2,500 per year, with no limit on the number of years in which it's taken. The student must be enrolled at least half-time, and the deduction is available to taxpayers who also claim a HOPE or lifetime learning credit. A student who is not claimed as a dependent may take the deduction on their own tax return.

Other Considerations

Generally, credits are more advantageous for taxpayers than deductions. Credits reduce the taxpayers' liability on a dollar-for-dollar basis, whereas a deduction only reduces the taxpayers' marginal income subject to taxation. Still, it pays to calculate the net tax benefit available under either a credit or a deduction before deciding which incentive to use. If your AGI prevents a deduction or a credit, evaluate whether to give up your dependent's exemption so the student can claim an otherwise unavailable benefit. A qualified college financial planning advisor or tax accountant can help you assess whether this approach makes sense for you.

Coverdell ESAs and Section 529 Plans

Distributions from a Coverdell ESA or a 529 Plan are tax-free if used for qualified higher education expenses. To determine whether any part of a Coverdell or a Section 529 Plan distribution is subject to taxation, qualified expenses must be reduced by the amount of any expenses used to generate a HOPE or lifetime learning credit. For example, assume that you incur $10,000 in qualified expenses and take a distribution from a 529 Plan to cover those expenses. If you claim the $2,000 lifetime learning credit ($10,000 × 20 percent), you must reduce your qualified expenses by $10,000, leaving no qualified expenses to apply to the 529 distribution. As a result, a portion of your distribution may be subject to both income tax and a 10 percent federal tax penalty.

Here's a look at some of the similarities and differences between the Coverdell and 529 Plans.

Feature	Coverdell	529 Plan
Taxation of earnings if used for education	Not taxed	Not taxed*
Deductibility of contributions federal/state	No/No	No/Maybe (varies by state)
Annual contribution limit**	$2,000	None (subject to lifetime limits)
Subject to income limits	Yes (see above)	No
Beneficiary age restrictions	Yes (see above)	No
Can be used for grades K–12	Yes	No
Investment restrictions (generally)	Few	Many (varies by state)
Student asset or parent asset in financial aid formula***	Student	Parent
Revocable contributions	No	Yes

* If current rules are not extended, distributions after December 31, 2010, will be taxed at the beneficiary's tax rate.
** Gift tax rules apply; 529 has a special five-year gifting provision.
*** Federal formula counts 529 assets as the parent's; some private colleges may count 529 assets as the student's; need-based financial aid may be affected.

TIMOTHY M. HAYES, MBA, CCPS, CMFC, RFC (Pittsford, New York)

TIP 61 BALANCING RETIREMENT SAVINGS NEEDS AND COLLEGE FUNDING DESIRES

Q. I know it's important to get an early start on saving for retirement, but with college education costs looming for our children, how do we tackle these competing goals?

A. For many people, funding both a comfortable retirement and college for their children is important. In most cases, however, the better strategy is to prioritize retirement savings over education funding.

This is not to suggest that paying for college is a less important goal. In fact, for some people, paying for a college education might be the highest priority. But, as an investment strategy, it makes sense to focus on your potential retirement needs first. Take full advantage of tax-deferred retirement accounts. Then additional investments can be earmarked for college, and you have the best chance to achieve both of your goals.

There are many ways to pay for the cost of a college education when the time comes—but if you haven't saved and invested properly for retirement, you will be out of luck.

Below is a closer look at the stakes and the solutions.

Sources of Funds

Students can apply for scholarships and grants, take out student loans with reasonable rates and terms, and work part time to help defray costs.

Some parents find that they are near the peak of their earning years when their children enter college, so a chunk of education costs can be paid from out-of-pocket cash flow. Parents also may borrow money from their home's equity at a fairly low rate, and they may even be able to borrow from a 401(k) if necessary.

Advantages of Retirement Savings

To meet retirement goals, it is important to start saving early and utilize tax-deferred, employer-provided programs if available, such as 401(k) and 403(b) plans. In addition to saving on a pretax basis—equivalent to getting a tax deduction—these plans provide the benefit of tax-deferred compounding. Employer plans also provide a convenient and disciplined means to invest on a regular basis and to benefit from "dollar cost averaging" through up and down markets. Because of the *use it or lose it* nature of these accounts, as well as IRAs and Roth IRAs, maximizing annual contributions makes sense.

In some cases, retirement accounts can be used for both retirement and college. For example, withdrawals from Roth IRAs can be made without penalty for qualifying educational expenses, and loans can be taken from 401(k) accounts. For couples having children later in life, the need for college money may even coincide with the start of retirement, and funds can be withdrawn from retirement accounts without penalty.

There also are tax-efficient savings programs specifically for college, like Coverdell and Section 529 Plans. These are excellent programs, but they often offer less time than retirement accounts for the money to stay invested and grow.

Another compelling reason to emphasize qualified retirement accounts is that they are usually excluded from financial aid formulas. In contrast, money held in regular taxable accounts does count in financial aid formulas. Even the Coverdell ESA and Section 529 Accounts could work against receiving need-based financial aid.

Saving directly in a child's name through custodial accounts is another common method for saving for college. Disadvantages, though, include things like the student obtaining control over the account upon becoming a legal adult and college aid formulas that are weighted more heavily against student-owned assets.

WARREN F. MCINTYRE, CFP® (Troy, Michigan)

Chapter

5

RETIREMENT PLANNING

TIP 62 ELEVEN THINGS YOU MUST DO NOW TO ENSURE 24-CARAT GOLDEN YEARS

Q. I'm confused about the economy, my own financial situation, and my prospects for the future. What should I be doing to prepare?

A. A quiet crisis is building in America. While the country has focused on homeland security and the turbulence in the Middle East, millions of Americans are headed for financial derailment. As the Baby Boomers age and begin to retire from the workforce, many will be startled by financial reality. There's still time to avoid a catastrophe; for many Baby Boomers, the only real remedy may be to make significant sacrifices now.

Sobering Realities

It's not news that people are living longer than ever before—we have all been warned that we may spend as much time in our retirement as in our work lives. But with the federal government facing huge deficits, and Social Security and Medicare woefully underfunded, lawmakers face tough decisions if the current system is to remain solvent.

The most pressing concern is that too many Americans are relying on Social Security to provide the overwhelming majority of our retirement income. Many will end up with poverty-level incomes in their retirement years. The average benefit likely will be about $900 a month, and fewer and fewer Americans have company pensions and/or adequate personal savings to augment that.

Compounding the problem, many Baby Boomers don't realize the size of nest egg they will need to maintain their standard of living, let alone how much they need to save and invest systematically to reach that goal. Consider that the average American needs to save at least $230,000 to draw $1,000 a month to supplement Social Security benefits. Unfortunately, less than one-third of American workers have saved $100,000 or more for retirement.

Golden Years or Tarnished Years?

While prior generations enjoyed company-provided pensions that supplemented Social Security and Medicare programs, that's no longer a reality for most people today. Baby Boomers and Gen Xers need to prepare now to fund the majority of their own retirement.

The Sandwich Generation

Boomers have been dubbed the "sandwich generation" for good reason. People between the ages of 40 and 60 find themselves wedged between multiple financial obligations: their children's college tuition, their aging parents' living expenses, and their own retirement saving needs. Some Boomers, who waited to have children later in life, find themselves simultaneously looking at college campuses for their teenagers and nursing homes for parents. To compound the problem, many Boomers continue to live beyond their means, further jeopardizing their financial futures.

Baby Boomer Catch Up

But it's not too late to catch up. New catch-up provisions that allow those over 50 to put away more for retirement through their IRAs or their company's 401(k) plans can help. In addition, a number of other measures can put you on track to a more secure financial future.

You can take some steps now to change your future.

Review estimates of projected Social Security benefits. Look for your Personal Earnings and Benefit Estimate Statement in your mailbox approximately three months before your birthday. It will show your projected benefits at age 62, at your full retirement age, and at age 70. Review it in detail to determine how much you will need to supplement your projected Social Security income.

Maximize retirement plan contributions. One of the best ways to save for retirement is to take advantage your retirement plan at work. A 401(k) allows you to invest money directly from your paycheck, before taxes. In addition, many companies will match a percentage of the employee's contributions. Think of the company match as a tax-free bonus from your employer. But you must participate in the plan to get the bonus. Money in a qualified retirement account grows tax-deferred until you begin to withdraw it during retirement. Self-employed individuals may open a SIMPLE IRA or SEP retirement plan.

Fund your IRAs no matter what. Even if you're covered by another retirement plan, contribute to an IRA. If you meet eligibility requirements, a Roth IRA is generally the best option. Traditional IRA contributions may or may not be deductible, depending on your income and whether you or your spouse is covered by another qualified plan. Even if your contribution is not deductible, it is a great way to invest for your future because it grows and compounds tax-deferred. The *use it or lose it* nature of these accounts is another reason to maximize contributions annually. Retirement accounts, including 401(k)s and all varieties of IRAs, have annual limits. If contributions are not made during the tax year, the opportunity is lost forever.

Invest to meet long-term goals. If you're a late starter, balance risk with potential return. You do not want to jeopardize your financial future by investing too aggressively, but investing too conservatively is risky too.

If you're still seven to ten years from retirement, consider investing a substantial portion of your retirement funds in a diversified portfolio that includes a healthy portion of equity investments. While it may be hard to think about investing in growth-oriented investments in difficult times, remember that over the long term, these investments historically have outpaced more secure investments. As you get closer to retirement, adjust the allocation of your assets toward more conservative investments.

Many issues need to be considered. Even if you feel confident making your own portfolio allocation decisions, consider obtaining a qualified financial planner's advice on portfolio design and asset allocation.

Fund retirement needs first. Make saving for retirement a priority over putting away money for your children's college education. If you don't have enough money to cover tuition bills, your children can apply for financial aid or student loans. That's not an option when it comes to funding retirement. Make sure that you're saving all you can or need for retirement before you earmark substantial funds for the kids' college programs.

Spend less and save more. Track how you spend your money. Evaluate your spending habits, and cut back on nonessentials. For example, cutting out that morning cafe latte saves a couple of dollars each day. It may not sound like much, but $2 invested daily for 20 years at 8 percent interest adds up to more than $36,000. A number of small changes like that can save you big bucks. Determine where you can make cuts, and redirect your savings to your retirement accounts. Better yet, follow the advice offered in one of my favorite books, *The Richest Man in Babylon*, by George S. Clason (New American Library/Penguin Putnam, 375 Hudson Street, New York, NY 10014; http://www.penguinputnam.com). Pay yourself first: arrange to have a fixed amount transferred each month to your mutual fund or IRA.

Consider the new retirement mentality. Read the book, *The New Retirementality*, by Mitch Anthony and published by Dearborn Trade. In this book, Anthony explores significant myths and realities of retirement. According to a survey conducted by the AARP, 80 percent of Baby Boomers say they plan to work at least part time in retirement. Consider taking a course to update your skills or, if you're looking to do something different, focus on developing a hobby or interest that could provide you with self-employment income in retirement. Retiring in stages may be a wise choice financially and emotionally. AARP (http://www.aarp.org) has a wealth of information on financial and lifestyle issues.

Work longer to secure the highest Social Security benefits. When you work beyond your normal full retirement age and delay taking Social Security benefits, your benefit actually increases for each year (until you reach 70) that you do not collect benefits. In many cases, the extra year(s) of employment mean that the wage base on which your benefit is calculated will go up as well, resulting in an even higher monthly benefit.

Take one step at a time. Don't be overwhelmed by what you need to save. Focus on cutting expenses and diverting your savings to retirement savings. Make securing a comfortable retirement a conscious choice. Work toward it daily, weekly, and monthly.

Get professional help. Seeking help now is especially important because declines in the stock market have decimated the savings of many, while low interest rates have hurt retirees living on fixed incomes. Many Americans may feel that they have nowhere to go for independent, objective advice, but a new breed of financial planner has emerged, just over the past few years, that specifically serves Middle America. These planners do not accept commissions or require long-term contracts. They charge by the hour and are happy to provide as little or as much help as their clients need. To learn about the nation's largest group of fee-only hourly financial planners and read related articles by *Wall Street Journal* columnist Jonathan Clements, visit http://www.GarrettPlanningNetwork.com.

Learn All You Can

Some additional sources of good information include the following:

- Financial Planning Association (http://www.fpanet.org)
- National Association of Personal Financial Planners (http://www.napfa.org)
- The Garrett Planning Network (http://www.garrettplanningnetwork.com)
- National Retirement Planning Coalition (http://www.retireonyourterms.org)
- Bloomberg News (http://www.bloomberg.com)

SHERYL GARRETT, CFP® (Shawnee Mission, Kansas)

TIP 63 MANY VARIABLES MAKE RETIREMENT PLANNING A COMPLEX BUT IMPORTANT TASK

Q. How much money will I need to retire?

A. This is the most often asked question in financial planning. It's also one of the most misunderstood and complicated to answer.

Even though most people will spend a third or more of their lives in retirement, many put off planning for it. But whatever your age, you can put together a retirement strategy that develops goals, uses specific numbers and scenarios, and measures your progress. If you have a spouse or significant other, involve them, too. Even though it can complicate the analysis, this should be a joint effort.

To simplify matters, the discussions below assume that you're saving as much as possible in nonqualified and IRS–approved qualified accounts.

A Process for Retirement Planning

Determining how much money you will need for retirement starts with adopting the following process to identify your goals.

1. Determine variables like expected life span, predicted inflation, income sources, age of retirement, living expenses, health care expenses, etc. (See below for more on the variables.)
2. Calculate the numbers.
3. Depending on the results, adjust the variables to obtain more realistic results.
4. Track your progress toward your goals.

Over time, continue to make needed adjustments to your variables and recalculate the numbers.

Steps Needed to Develop Your Strategy

Choose a retirement date. Even if you would like early retirement, be realistic in your choice.

Calculate in today's dollars your annual retirement income need. You can do this by taking a percentage of your present gross household income (planners generally use 80 to 100 percent to run their projections). Keep in mind that, in retirement, you won't need work-related expenses like commuting, meals, parking, payroll taxes, or retirement plan contributions. You also may no longer have a mortgage payment or college expenses, but other expenses like health insurance and health care, elder care, or travel and recreation could increase. List all anticipated expenses by category on a worksheet. One additional variable may be an adjustment for a partner who may have a shorter estimated life span because of health issues, age differential, or heredity.

Determine your anticipated retirement income. Estimate all sources of income and how long each will last. Pensions or other employer-sponsored plans may need cost-of-living adjustments or reductions for joint survivorship.

Determine your anticipated life span. Some key factors include the following:

- What's my expected lifespan?
- What is my family longevity history?
- With major medical and health advances in mind, should I add a few years to my expected longevity (as indicated in the insurance tables)?
- Do I have specific health concerns?

Determine the estimated inflation rate to use in your projections. Inflation rates have been low over the last several years, but since 1926, the average inflation rate historically has hovered at about 3 percent.

Estimate the rate of increase from your income sources. For example, what's the cost-of-living adjustment in your pensions or Social Security benefits?

Determine the value of your retirement investments and their estimated rate of increase. Project your existing retirement resources, taking into consideration any anticipated additional contributions.

Decide your approach to using your retirement capital. Is your goal to deplete all of your funds so that you spend your last dollar on the day you die, or do you want to preserve a given amount for your heirs?

Crunch the numbers to see where you stand. Commercial software programs and Web sites have calculators that can help. But, because retirement projections are complex, it's wise to seek the advice of a qualified financial planner to help you review your assumptions and interpret the results.

End Note$

Your analysis is only a snapshot of the future based on a unique, present point in time. As time passes, your assumptions may prove valid or your circumstances may deviate so that the corresponding variables will need to change. It's a good idea to review your assumptions annually, revise your data accordingly, and then rerun the numbers to verify that your goals still will be met.

WILLIAM L. RODAU, MS, MBA, CFP® (Sussex, Wisconsin)

TIP 64 HOW TO MAXIMIZE YOUR 401(K) FOR A BRIGHTER FINANCIAL FUTURE

Q. How can I take best advantage of my employer's 401(k) plan?

A. If you don't understand or take advantage of a 401(k) plan through your employer, you're not alone. More than 70 percent of Americans with the option to open a 401(k) account at work do not understand or fully utilize this fantastic wealth-building program.

What Is a 401(k)? Why Is It Important?

A 401(k) plan is a defined contribution employee benefits plan that allows tax-deferred retirement savings. The plans are made possible by paragraph 401(k) in the IRS tax code. *Defined contribution* implies that employees contribute their own money by way of payroll deductions.

For most people, a 401(k) is the main retirement option. Your money grows on a tax-deferred basis until you retire, and then you pay taxes on withdrawals at your postretirement income tax rate.

The benefits of a 401(k) as a savings vehicle include: immediate tax savings on contributions, tax-deferred growth of investment earnings, and the possibility of *free money* in the form of matching contributions from your employer. Let's take a closer look.

Benefit 1: Immediate Tax Savings

Contributions to a 401(k) are withheld before taxes, and the plan grows with earnings tax-deferred. Let's say you invest $100 per month annually in your company's 401(k) plan. Assuming you're in the 27 percent tax bracket, that's a little more than $320 in taxes owed on the money if it's not contributed to the plan. In other words, your $1,200 investment in the 401(k) really costs you only about $880 when you account for the tax savings.

Look at it another way. To net $1,200 after taxes to invest outside the 401(k), you must earn $1,524, assuming a 27 percent tax bracket. To learn more about how pretax contributions can affect your take-home pay, visit http://www.401k.com/401k/tools/takehomepay/takehomepay.htm.

Benefit 2: Tax-Deferred Growth

Because interest and dividends in a 401(k) are tax-deferred, they compound tax-free until the investment is withdrawn. Over time, the gap between the value of a taxable and a tax-deferred account, earning the same rate of return, increases sharply.

Benefit 3: The Employer's Match

Often, the greatest advantage of a 401(k) at work is that many employers contribute to their employees' 401(k) by matching a portion of the money contributed by the employee. For example, for each $100 you contribute to the plan,

FIGURE 5.1 *Saving in a Tax-Deferred Retirement Account versus a Taxable Account*

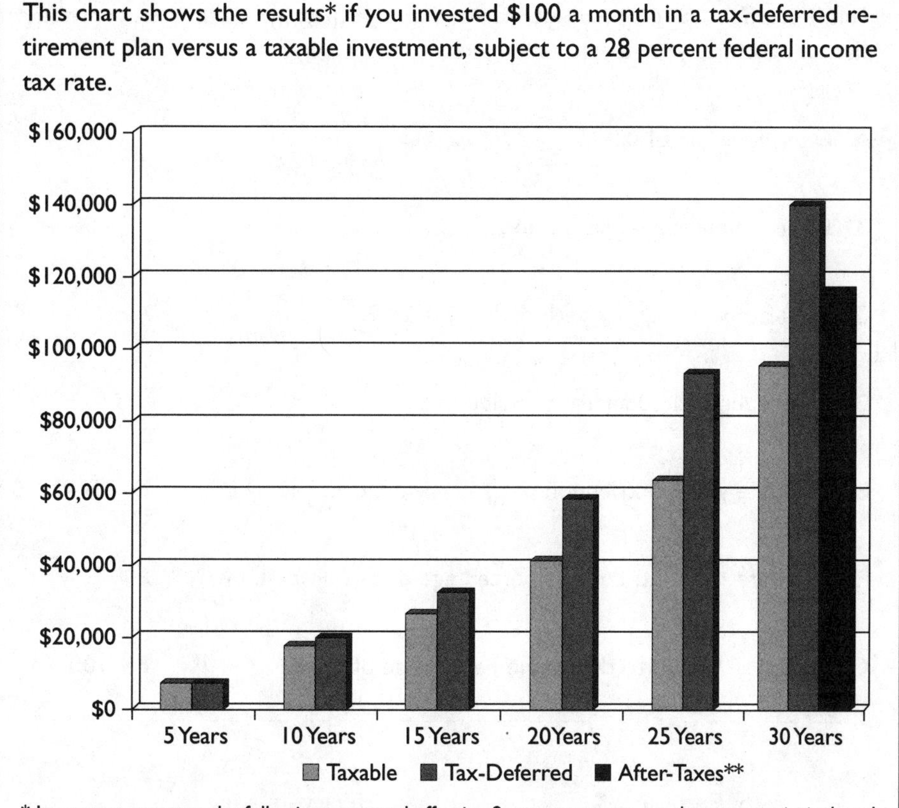

* Investment assumes the following: an annual effective 8 percent return, no changes to principal, and no change to the income tax rate.

** Tax-deferred investment after taxes. Although accumulations in a tax-deferred retirement plan are for retirement, we have illustrated the taxes you would pay on a lump-sum withdrawal after 30 years, given the assumptions. Payout options over time can spread out tax liability.

your employer may add $50 to your account, giving you a total of $150. That's an immediate 50 percent return on your out-of-pocket $100 investment. No tax advantage gives you a better deal.

One tip for anyone who's earning more than $80,000 a year: Be aware of your contribution percentage. If it's too high and you contribute the maximum amount before year-end, you could miss out on a portion of your employer's match. The law allows a maximum annual contribution of $13,000 ($16,000 if age 50 or over) for 2004.

FIGURE 5.2 *Maximizing Your Match*

This worksheet can help you determine how much of your salary to contribute to your 401(k) plan to maximize your employer's match.

A. Enter your annual salary.		$
B. Enter the number of pay periods.		
C. Calculate your pay per period: divide A by B.	A ÷ B =	$
D. Enter your desired annual contribution.		$
E. Calculate your contribution per pay period: divide D by B.	D ÷ B =	$
F. Calculate the contribution's percentage of pay: divide E by C.	E ÷ C =	0._____
G. Multiply F by 100 to determine percentage of pay.	F x 100 =	%

End Note$

If a 401(k) plan is available, do whatever you can to invest in it, even if only a nominal amount each paycheck. In fact, in most cases it's foolish to invest in other retirement vehicles until you have maxed out your 401(k) investment. The table below shows the maximum pretax contributions you can make to your 401(k) plan.

Federal Limits* on 401(k) Contributions

Year	Limit	Catch-Up Limit (for persons age 50+)
2004	$13,000	$16,000
2005	$14,000	$18,000
2006	$15,000	$20,000

* The limits also apply to 403(b)s for nonprofit workers; 457s for state and local government workers; and salary-reduction SEPs, also known as SAR-SEPs.

THERESA LEISTER, CFP®, MBA, CMFC, RFC (New York, New York)

TIP 65 ROLLING OVER A 401(K) OR 403(B) TO AN IRA

Q. Should I roll over my 401(k) or 403(b) into an IRA?

A. If you wonder what to do with the 401(k) or 403(b) you will end up with because you're leaving your employer, consider all your options so you can make a decision that fits your circumstances. Although 401(k) and 403(b) plans differ in some ways, the information below applies to both.

What are your options?

- Leave the money in the current 401(k) if an employer allows that option.
- Roll the money over into an IRA.
- Transfer it into your new employer's 401(k).
- Take the money and pay any taxes and, perhaps, penalty due.

The option you select depends on a number of factors and how they apply to your situation.

Investment Choices

It takes a variety of investments that perform well and have reasonable expenses to grow your money over time. Any plan should include mutual funds split among equities (stocks) that represent value and growth; small, medium, and large capitalization; and domestic and international companies. Bond funds also should be part of the mix, split among corporate and government; short-term, medium-term, and long-term; and corporate bonds of investment grade and high yields.

Check on performance and expenses in your plan's documents. Then compare that data with the rest of the market via Morningstar (http://www.morningstar.com). If you're not satisfied, consider transferring your money into an IRA account with a low-cost brokerage firm like Ameritrade, Schwab, T.D. Waterhouse, or Vanguard. All offer a variety of investment choices.

Need the Money Now?

Your 401(k) and IRA accounts are meant for retirement, but what if you're in a temporary financial bind or are starting a business and need some cash? Loans from IRAs are not allowed, but loans from 401(k) plans are, provided the plan has a provision for it. If it's allowed, generally you can borrow up to $50,000 or half of your account balance, whichever is lower; repayment is by equal monthly payments over five years. If you terminate employment, the loan is due immediately. Check your plan documents or with your plan administrator for the specifics, including fees. If you default on the loan, income taxes are due, as is a 10 percent penalty for an early distribution. The loan interest you pay goes into your account because you are borrowing from yourself. But remember that you will be repaying the loan with after-tax dollars, and those same dollars will be taxed again when you start receiving retirement distributions.

Really Need the Money Now?

401(k) plans may have a hardship feature that allows withdrawal if you have a qualified hardship and you have exhausted other reasonable options. Withdrawals are taxable, and your ability to contribute to the 401(k) is suspended for six months. Check out your plan documents for the details. IRAs do not have hardship withdrawal features, but you can take an IRA distribution and pay income taxes on that distribution. For both the 401(k) hardship withdrawal and the IRA distribution, if you are under 59½ you will pay a 10 percent penalty, unless the money is for disability or certain medical expenses. In addition, a distribution from an IRA avoids the 10 percent penalty if it's used to buy a first home ($10,000 distribution limit), to pay qualified higher-education expenses, or to pay health insurance premiums if you are collecting unemployment insurance.

Periodic Distributions

What if you're not yet 59½ and want to start taking distributions? If you terminate employment after reaching 55, your 401(k) may offer the opportunity to take distributions before 59½. These distributions are taxable, but the 10 percent penalty does not apply. Check your plan documents.

With an IRA, you generally have to wait until age 59½ to take distributions without an early withdrawal tax penalty. However, distributions can start earlier if they are part of a series of substantially equal periodic payments. These payments must continue for at least five years or until you reach 59½, whichever happens later. Distributions are also penalty-free if they occur after death or disability.

Distribution to Beneficiaries

What happens to your 401(k) or IRA when you die?

After death, if your spouse is your 401(k) beneficiary, they have several options, including continuing the 401(k) plan or rolling it over into their IRA. A nonspouse 401(k) beneficiary generally has to take a distribution for the entire balance (usually taxable) within a fixed time, usually five years. Again, details vary by plan, so check your 401(k) plan documents.

With an IRA, your spousal beneficiary has similar options to continue the tax-deferred status. A nonspouse IRA beneficiary can stretch distributions over their lifetime. This benefit can be significant if your beneficiary is a child, as it reduces the immediate tax consequences and gives the money more time to grow.

Protect Your Assets

Federal law protects 401(k) plans from creditors. IRAs are governed by state law and may not be protected the same way.

Rollovers and Transfers

If you roll over the 401(k) to an IRA, don't have the check made out in your name—20 percent will be taken out for federal income taxes. A direct transfer can help avoid this. Open your IRA first, then have the money transferred directly from your current 401(k) to your new IRA. If your current 401(k) cannot do this, then accept a check made out to the IRA, which avoids the 20 percent withholding, and then make sure it gets deposited into your IRA so it can begin working for you as soon as possible.

End Note$

The details don't stop there. Tax laws are complex, as are 401(k) plans. Make sure you understand the implications of what you do. Consult your 401(k) plan administrators, your human resources department, and your financial planner before you take action.

CHARLES TURNER (Highlands Ranch, Colorado)

TIP 66 TRADITIONAL IRAS CAN HELP YOU SECURE COMFORTABLE GOLDEN YEARS

Q. I'd like to save for my retirement. What are the rules for a traditional IRA?

A. A lot of confusion exists about the traditional Individual Retirement Account (IRA) that Congress set up more than 30 years ago. Federal legislators keep changing the rules, changing the names, and adding different IRAs to the mix.

The Basics

If you have earned income and/or alimony, you can shelter current income, save for retirement, and defer income taxes on the money and its expected gains by contributing to an IRA account.

Under current rules for a traditional IRA, you and your spouse (if you have one) may be eligible to set aside $3,000 or more for each of you. Which type of IRA account would be most appropriate for you (and allowed by Uncle Sam) depends on your income level, age, and other retirement plans.

An IRA Is Not an Investment

Don't confuse IRAs with any type of investment. We are talking about a legal structure, not what's inside it—investments. Those innards are vehicles like mutual funds, individual securities, and annuities.

Tax Deductibility and Annual Contribution Limits

Depending on your Adjusted Gross Income (see below), you may be eligible to claim a tax deduction for you and your spouse if you contribute to a traditional IRA. If you or your spouse is not an active participant in an employer retirement plan, you can reduce your income on your tax return by using your $3,000 or more contribution per person (unless you are contributing to a Roth IRA). That amounts to about an $800 tax savings for a $3,000 contribution if you are in the 28 percent federal tax bracket. Congress raised contribution limits from $3,000 in 2002 to $6,000 by 2008 if you are at least age 50. The limit for younger folks caps at $5,000 per year in 2008.

IRAs are subject to deductible *phase-out rules.* If your earned income is too high—phase-out begins at $40,000 for single people or $60,000 for married couples—and you are an active participant in an employer retirement plan, you lose some or all of the deduction opportunity on your tax return.

Eligibility and Withdrawal Rules

More good news: anyone with earned income can contribute to an IRA, although they may not be able to deduct it on their tax return (keep reading to learn about tax deductibility). Contributions still grow with income tax deferred until distribution begins, currently mandatory at age 70½ but possible as early as age 59½ or even earlier without penalty.

You can open or contribute to an IRA by April 15 each year and claim it on your tax return for the prior year.

Now the bad news: like most retirement plans, early withdrawals (or distributions) from IRAs before age 59½ trigger, in most cases, a 10 percent tax on top of your normal income tax rate. That's the case with most retirement plans, too.

IRAs remain an attractive, long-term savings vehicle. To ensure comfortable golden years, people with earned income should make contributing to their retirement accounts to the maximum extent possible a top priority. It's a *use it or lose it* opportunity.

JIM LUDWICK, CFP® (Odenton, Maryland)

TIP 67 ROTH VERSUS A TRADITIONAL IRA—PICKING THE ONE THAT'S RIGHT FOR YOU

Q. How can I determine which IRA is best for me?

A. Let's start by briefly revisiting the definitions of each type of IRA.

Traditional IRA

This IRA provides a tax deduction for a contribution that grows tax-deferred until withdrawn, and then it's taxed at your personal income tax rate. An additional 10 percent penalty is due on withdrawals before age 59½, with the following exceptions: death, disability, substantially equal payments over life expectancy, medical expenses greater than 7.5 percent of your Adjusted Gross Income (AGI), higher education expenses, a first-time home purchase ($10,000 lifetime maximum), and health insurance premiums (if you received unemployment compensation for at least 12 weeks).

Roth IRA

A Roth IRA offers no tax deduction now for a contribution, but it grows tax-free and, at the time of a qualified withdrawal, no income tax is due. For non-qualified distributions, you pay a 10 percent penalty plus ordinary income tax, but only on the earnings in your account, not on the full amount.

Eligibility Factors

If you have earned income (e.g., wages, salaries, professional fees, sales commissions, tips, and bonuses) instead of unearned income (e.g., dividends, interest, and rent) and are under age 70½, you can contribute to a traditional IRA. Your allowable contribution is tax deductible if neither you nor your spouse participates in a qualified retirement plan. If one of you participates in an employer-sponsored retirement plan, your IRA contribution may be deductible, depending on your modified AGI.

You may contribute to a Roth IRA regardless of your age if you have earned income, provided your modified AGI does not exceed certain limits.

Annual Contribution Limits

The maximum allowable annual contribution to an IRA in 2004 is $3,500 (if you include the catch-up provision that's allowed for persons age 50 and older) in either a traditional IRA or a Roth IRA. Spouses must keep separate IRA accounts, and if eligible, each can contribute up to the maximum each year.

Distribution Rules

With traditional IRAs, you must begin withdrawing your money by April 1 of the year after you turn 70½ and you cannot make additional contributions. With a Roth IRA, there's no mandatory age for distributions, and you can contribute as long as you're eligible.

Converting a Traditional IRA to a Roth IRA

Many people find that converting a traditional IRA into a Roth IRA is a viable and compelling option. A full or partial conversion is allowed if your AGI is less than $100,000 and your tax filing status is single or married filing jointly. AGI limits do not include the amount converted, which is subject to ordinary income tax in the year of conversion.

Which Option Is Better?

- Potentially, you might want to choose a traditional IRA if you qualify or need the tax deduction right now and anticipate paying taxes at a significantly lower rate in retirement. A nondeductible traditional IRA is a good option only if you are not eligible to make a Roth or a deductible, traditional IRA contribution.

- Choose a Roth IRA if you don't need the tax break now and meet the AGI limits. It's more flexible, because it allows you to withdraw your original contributions at any time after the account has been open for five years, penalty-free and tax-free, you don't have to take mandatory distributions at age 70½, and earnings for qualified distributions are tax-free. You will earn more over time, after tax, with the Roth IRA than with either the deductible or nondeductible traditional IRAs due to the power of tax-free distributions.

"Start Early" Accumulation Strategy

Would you like to hold $1 million in your IRA by the time you are age 65? If you start early, reaching that goal might be easier than you think, thanks to the magic of compounding.

Contribution ages	Annual contribution amount	**Total investment (5 years @ $3K)**	Rate of return on investment	**Total value at age 65**
20 through 24	$3,000	**$15,000**	10%	**$1,003,013**

End Note$

Which is better—traditional or Roth? After you have accumulated all that money and are ready to tap into it, wouldn't it be nice to get the last laugh on Uncle Sam and keep 100 percent of your Roth withdrawals tax-free? The tax deduction you lost upfront years ago will be long forgotten.

ROBERT BUBNOVICH (Irvine, California)

TIP 68 GETTING OLDER DOESN'T ALWAYS MEAN YOU SHOULD BE MORE CONSERVATIVE

Q. I'm approaching retirement. Should I get out of stocks the older I get?

A. Growing older does not necessarily mean you should pull out of stocks altogether. To understand why, consider the concept of time horizon. Miscalculating or misunderstanding this concept is one of the biggest mistakes an individual can make when it comes to investments.

Investment Time Horizons

The time horizon is the amount of time needed until you begin to use some or all of your investments. For example, if you plan to save for a down payment on a new house in two years, your investment time horizon is two years. If you're saving for a child's first year of college and that child is currently 10 years old, your investment time horizon is 8 years (when the child is age 18 and ready for school).

Applying investment time horizon theory to the retirement planning process means that you understand a key difference between retirement and other investment goals. Most investment goals happen once—car purchases or home purchases, for example. But retirement begins on a certain date and continues over a long period of time. You will need the investment proceeds from your retirement planning over that long period.

Inflation Marches On

Based on historical averages, inflation doubles your cost of living every 18 years and has averaged 4 percent per year over the last several decades. Meanwhile, over the long term, the average rate of return for bonds has been about 6 percent and for stocks about 10 percent. The difference between an investment's rate of return and inflation is known as the real rate of return. You want a high real rate of return for long-term investments.

Combining the facts that most retirements occur over a long time horizon, inflation continues each year, and stocks have a history of outperforming inflation by the largest margin, you arrive at one conclusion: stocks need to be at least some part of most portfolios.

The Five-Year to Seven-Year Time Frame

Historically, it takes stocks five to seven years to complete a full cycle—going from a high, to a low, and back to a new high again. The danger of putting money in stocks for less than a full cycle is that you may catch the down part of the cycle and lose out.

Consider a person, 58, who plans to retire in two years and, therefore, will need to withdraw a small portion of their investments at that time. Meanwhile, the biggest chunk of their money will need to remain invested so that it outpaces inflation. That means stocks. The trick, of course, is to control the percentage you've allocated to stocks and adjust that percentage over time as the time horizons of your life change. This is called *asset allocation,* which is an art all by itself. (See Chapter 7 on investing for more on asset allocation.)

BRYAN CLINTSMAN, CFP® (South Lake, Texas)

TIP 69 WHEN YOU INHERIT AN IRA, UNDERSTAND YOUR OPTIONS BEFORE YOU TAKE ACTION

Q. My mom and I are equal beneficiaries in a $1 million IRA account that belonged to my dad, who died last month. What should we do about the inheritance?

A. In April 2002, the IRS issued final regulations on distributions from retirement plans. Acting completely out of character, it simplified the rules.

The Basics

Let's review a bit about IRAs.

- Funds grow tax-deferred.
- Distributions or withdrawals are fully taxable in the year that the money is taken out (unless from a Roth IRA).
- Distributions from an IRA due to its owner's death are not subject to the 10 percent penalty.

Think of tax-deferred growth as a turbo charger on your investment account. By growing and compounding year after year, tax-deferred, the balance in the IRA grows faster. The longer your money stays in the account, the more turbo charge you get.

Starting Point: Minimum Required Distributions

Before taking any action, find out if your father was taking Required Minimum Distributions (RMD) before his death. Owners of traditional IRAs must begin taking RMD by April 1 of the year after they turn age 70½. If your dad had started taking the RMD, calculate it for the year of his death and withdraw that amount.

One of the first things you and your mom should do is to write a statement saying that you both want the IRA to be treated as *separate accounts,* basically splitting the money into your mom's and yours, even though the money remains in one account. It is very possible that the money will be physically moved to separate accounts at a later date, but this action allows you both to make decisions on your share, independent of one another.

Options for Handling Shares of IRAs

The three options for handling your IRA shares include creating an inherited IRA, taking a qualified disclaimer, or using the five-year rule. Your mom, as spouse of the deceased, has one additional option, a spousal rollover.

You have until September 30 of the year after the death to select your option. If no action is taken by that date, the default option takes effect: the inherited IRA.

Create an inherited (stretch) IRA in your own name. Either of you can take your IRA share and create what is known as an inherited IRA. Remember: This is the default option if you do not elect a different option by the deadline noted above. Also called a stretch IRA, in this option, the beneficiary stretches out the number of years that the money can stay in an IRA account. The required distribution is calculated based on the beneficiary's life expectancy.

In April 2002, the IRS issued new life expectancy tables along with new rules that are surprisingly favorable to the IRA owner and the beneficiary. Let's look at an example of a 30-year-old who inherits a $500,000 share of an IRA on December 31 of the prior year. The single life table for inherited IRAs shows that a 30-year-old's life expectancy is 54.3 years. To calculate the required distribution, the value of the IRA on the December 31 of the prior year is divided by life expectancy. The required distribution for this year would be $9,208.10 ($500,000/54.3). Each year, refer back to the Required Minimum Distribution table for the new factor and divide that number into the prior year's ending balance in the account.

As the beneficiary, you can withdraw any amount during the year, but annually you must withdraw an amount equal to the required distribution.

When you set up the account, be sure it's retitled correctly as follows:

- Your dad's name, deceased
- IRA account
- For the benefit of (your name)
- Your address

Employing the qualified disclaimer option. A disclaimer is the refusal to accept a gift or inheritance. This could be helpful if, for example, your mom is financially secure and doesn't need the money. She could disclaim her share, and it would pass to you. She would pay less income tax because she would not receive any distributions. The balance in the IRA at her death would not be included in her estate, and it would escape any taxes due under current laws. The long-term outcome is that more of the money would remain with the family and less would end up in Uncle Sam's pockets.

If either you or your mom chooses this option, you must file the qualified disclaimer within nine months of the date of death.

Using the five-year rule. This rule says that the inherited account must be completely liquidated by December 31 of the fifth year after the year of the account owner's death. The total account must be withdrawn and all taxes paid. If you choose this option and do not completely liquidate the account in the time frame, you face a 50 percent penalty. This option is not available if the deceased account owner had begun the RMD prior to his death (in this case, the IRA account administrator is not required to offer this option, so check the account documentation).

Spousal rollover IRA. As the spouse of the deceased, your mom can move her share of the IRA into a new account with her as the full owner and subject to all the rights and regulations.

If your dad had begun to take RMD prior to his death and your mom is under the age of 70½, she can stop withdrawals from the account until she reaches 70½, at which time the withdrawals must begin again. But she can use the longer joint life-expectancy table (versus the single one you must use in the inherited IRA option), which means lower withdrawal amounts and lower taxes.

Note: If your mom is older than your dad, it's best to leave the account in your dad's name until he would have turned 70½, then have your mom treat the account as her own. This approach delays the starting of RMD based on your dad's age.

End Note$

Following are a few Web sites that may be helpful:

- http://www.irahelp.com
- http://www.smartmoney.com
- http://www.fairmark.com

For planning purposes, setting up beneficiary designations properly during the account owner's lifetime can eliminate many problems for the family after the decedent's passing. For more information on IRA distributions, penalties, and beneficiary designations, read *101 Tax Saving Ideas,* by Randy Gardner, LLM, CPA, CFP®, and Julie Welch, CPA, CFP® (Wealth Builders Press, 2002).

MARJORIE B. RANDLES EA, CFP® (Argyle, New York)

TIP 70 DECIDING TO TAKE AN EARLY DISTRIBUTION FROM A RETIREMENT ACCOUNT

Q. Due to unforeseen circumstances, I need to tap into my retirement accounts before the qualifying age of 59½. What will happen if I take money from my pension plan at work or from my IRA before age 59½?

A. As a way to encourage the continuation of retirement savings, the government imposes a 10 percent penalty on any retirement money removed by a participant (except in the case of a loan or special qualifying circumstances) before age 59½. The penalty is paid on the taxable portion of this money in addition to the ordinary income taxes due at that time. There may, however, be ways to get around this penalty.

The Bigger Issue

More important, however, is whether you should take money out, even for a qualifying reason. Remember, your money is growing tax-deferred, and you may be getting free money from your employer in the form of matching contributions. Tapping into your retirement savings prematurely can jeopardize your long-term financial future.

What other alternatives are available if you need cash now? Before making a decision on your own to withdraw money from a retirement plan, consult with a financial planning specialist to be sure you look at all the options.

If You Need to Tap Your Savings after Retiring

Choosing a payout option for qualified plan benefits can have a tremendous impact on your future security and lifestyle. A financial planning professional can explain the implications of what's available, including lump sums or some form of an annuity. Carefully consider how each option would affect your cash flow now—and in the future—and the tax consequences of each. (See the next tip for more details.)

CAROL BURROUGHS (Normal, Illinois)

TIP 71 YOUR PENSION—SHOULD YOU TAKE A LUMP-SUM DISTRIBUTION OR MONTHLY ANNUITY PAYMENTS?

Q. I'm retiring and my employer has given me the choice to take my pension as a lump sum or an annuity. What should I do?

A. From a purely financial viewpoint, this decision comes down to deciding whether you can earn more by investing the lump sum from the pension yourself. Unfortunately, determining the breakeven rate of return you need to earn on the lump sum is not easy. It involves determining the present value of your monthly pension payments and requires you to make assumptions about your life expectancy, tax situation, and the discount rate used to bring the future payments back to the present value. Also, your long-term rate of return can have lots of ups and downs, so that variability needs to be factored in.

Taking the Lump Sum

In the stock market's go-go years of the late 1990s, few worried about these complexities. People took the lump sum, thinking that the 20 percent annual returns that the stock market was producing at the time would last forever and that income from an annuity would pale in comparison.

So, while estimating of the rate of return required on the lump sum is still probably a good idea, it is only one part of the overall decision.

Another Option

Looking at the decision another way, first decide how much income you will need in retirement to sustain basic needs without luxuries. Most likely, it will exceed your monthly Social Security payment but will be less than your desired retirement income. Many people wish to annuitize the rest of the basic income they'll need, so they will be able to maintain a minimum standard of living no matter how long they live and no matter what happens to their other assets. One difficulty of this approach is that inflation erodes the purchasing power of monthly income over time, because most employer annuities do not include an inflation adjustment. To counteract this, you may need to make the initial annuity payment higher than would otherwise be necessary. Another alternative is to use an equity-indexed annuity or a variable annuity. However, doing this introduces additional risk to the annuity payment; because you are trying to minimize risk by adopting an annuity strategy, these riskier options are most likely a poor choice.

Beyond the different fundamental approaches, there's more that complicates the lump sum versus annuity decision.

What Happens after Death?

One major difference between an annuity income and a lump-sum distribution is that, if any assets remain from the lump-sum distribution when you die, they can be passed to your heirs. With an annuity, this may not be the case. For example, if you choose a life annuity and die after receiving one payment, your heirs receive nothing. That's because annuities have built-in actuarial assumptions. The money saved by not paying those who die early is used to pay those who live extra long. If you expect to live longer than most people because of a family history of long life expectancy, you may be better off with an annuity payment, particularly if you have few other assets.

In reality, a certain term is often associated with an annuity that guarantees a minimum number of payments, such as five or ten years' worth. Provisions can also allow full or reduced payments to a spouse after you die, thus reducing the sting of an untimely death.

How an Annuity Is Taxed

In many cases, the pension that led to the annuity was fully funded by the employer, and the entire annuity is taxable as ordinary income to the recipient. But in some cases, the employee also contributed. That part of the annuity then represents an employee basis, and so part of the annuity payment is received free of tax.

The Rest of Your Portfolio

Other assets affect the annuity decision, too. If the pension and Social Security are your only sources of retirement income, there's a compelling case for the guaranteed life income of the annuity. On the other hand, because inflation erodes the purchasing power of a fixed income, it may be beneficial to take part of the payment as a lump sum to invest for potential growth and inflation protection.

If, in addition to the pension, you have substantial assets, you may be able to afford the risk in taking the lump sum. But ironically, the other assets also make it less necessary to take on the additional risk, in which case you still may opt for the annuity. Taking the more stable annuity also means you may be able to allocate more of your portfolio to equities, which offer higher growth potential.

Other Alternatives

Outside/private annuity companies that offer low-load or no-load annuities also may offer a higher monthly payment or a better payout option than your employer offers. If you opt for a private company, however, make sure it's reputable and very strong financially. Unlike employer pensions, the Pension Benefit Guarantee Corporation (PBGC) does not protect private annuities. (Read the next tip for more on annuities.)

C. BRADLEY BOND, CFP® (Murrysville, Pennsylvania)

TIP 72 SHOULD ANNUITIES BE INCLUDED IN AN INVESTMENT PORTFOLIO?

Q. What is an annuity and how does it work?

A. Think of annuities as the opposite of life insurance. Instead of a lump-sum payment at death, as with life insurance, annuities provide you with a lifelong income stream. Issuers of annuities, usually insurance companies, invest your contributions. Then, by using actuarially determined life spans, the issuers can forecast the appropriate rate of return for you and the company.

Two Phases to an Annuity Contract

The two phases of an annuity are accumulation, when the funds grow inside the account, and distribution, when they are paid back out.

The growth inside the annuity is not taxed at current rates. Instead, it's deferred until the distribution period. The payment consists of two parts: the return of your original investment (not taxed) and growth in the account (taxable upon distribution). Once your original investment is returned, income from an annuity is completely taxable as ordinary income.

Unfortunately, annuities have evolved into complex products that most consumers have difficulty evaluating. Here's a simplified look.

Types of Annuities

Annuities are categorized as either fixed or variable, and they can be immediate, where the income stream starts within a year, or deferred, where payments begin later.

Fixed annuities. Fixed annuities are similar to bonds and certificates of deposit. They guarantee a fixed rate of return for a stated period of time. Some fixed annuities include an option where rates adjust during the accumulation period. However, the rate becomes fixed during distribution. A straight life annuity provides lifelong income with payments ending at the annuity holder's death.

Payments may be guaranteed for certain periods of time (5, 10, or 15 years), with undistributed contributions returned to a beneficiary at the annuity holder's death. Any option to extend the income stream after your death can reduce your monthly income flow.

Surrender charges on fixed annuities can be high, but these charges decline annually. Despite the extended investment period, fixed-annuity income is taxed as ordinary income rather than long-term capital gains. Dividends from common stocks currently are taxed at lower rates than income from a fixed annuity.

All annuities, variable or fixed, are subject to a 10 percent penalty if redeemed before age 59½. Plus, all annuities are relatively nonliquid compared to bonds or CDs.

If you want a stable income flow, then an annuity from a low-cost, high-yield provider can be a suitable option.

Variable annuities. Variable annuities consist of an annuity contract where your payment is based on the performance of various subaccounts (mutual funds) that you choose. The insurer makes no guarantee as to future returns. In addition to surrender charges, variable annuities incur mortality and expense (M&E) charges along with other fees that further erode your return. With variable annuities, your investment options are limited and often less than competitive due to high operating expenses and/or poor performance. As with fixed annuities, income from a variable annuity does not qualify for long-term capital gains taxation.

One type of variable annuity is the equity-indexed annuity (based on a certain index such as the S&P 500), but the participation level as stated in the contract limits the growth in your account. These variable annuities often have a guaranteed rate, but the M&E and other ancillary fees can mitigate it.

A 1035 exchange allows you to swap an existing annuity or variable life policy. You may want to consider a variable annuity for a 1035 exchange if you have a variable life policy with high expenses and/or poor investment choices. Consider exchanging for an annuity with no surrender charges and low fees, such as TIAA-CREF or Vanguard. Speak with an investment professional to determine if this option is viable for you.

Variable annuities allow your contributions to grow tax-deferred, but that advantage is greatly overrated, because long-term capital gains from other investments are taxed at significantly lower rates. Also, variable annuities do not receive a step-up in basis at death. Tax-efficient, no-load mutual funds or Exchange Traded Funds are a far superior alternative.

Variable annuities do provide some death benefits for your estate, but, like the advantage of tax deferral, those benefits are overrated. A more suitable option for most people is term life insurance coupled with no-load mutual funds.

End Note$

If you decide that an annuity is right for you, choose only a no-load annuity with low operating fees, appropriate investment vehicles, and no surrender charges. Web sites of companies offering these benefits include the following:

- http://www.tiaa-cref.org
- http://www.vanguard.com

BUZ LIVINGSTON (Santa Rosa Beach, Florida)

TIP 73 HOW TO CREATE A STREAM OF INCOME AFTER RETIREMENT

Q. Now that I've determined how much I can withdraw safely from my portfolio, how do I set up my investments to get some money out?

A. This is a common question for people nearing retirement. Most likely, you regularly put money into your 401(k) or IRA and never really considered how best to withdraw it—until now.

Taxable Accounts

Generally, you should spend down taxable accounts first, except if you have large capital gains exposure in a stock(s). From an estate planning perspective, it may be better not to sell the stock(s).

It is easiest to transfer the money you need to live on via a monthly direct deposit from a money market fund.

- *Set up a money market fund within each brokerage account.* Instead of reinvesting interest, dividends, and capital gains, channel those funds into a money market account. Then the money can be transferred to your household checking account.
- *Monitor the money market fund to be sure it always has enough cash for at least three months of living expenses.* Because you will be taxed on the interest/dividends, this strategy provides the cash necessary to pay the taxes.

If there's interest, dividends, and/or capital gains remaining after you withdraw your living expenses, use it to rebalance your portfolio at least annually. If your assets continue to grow, and you foresee not outliving your money, take advantage of the estate planning laws to gift money free of estate tax. (It's more beneficial to gift appreciated stock or stock funds instead of cash to avoid future capital gains taxes.)

If the interest, dividends, and/or capital gains are not enough to meet living expenses, you will periodically need to sell some investments. While some general guidelines for the sale of assets apply, you really need to look at your overall picture to figure out what works best for you. Strategies might include the following:

- *Selling assets to maintain your overall asset allocation.* Example: If bonds represent a higher percentage of your assets than your ideal, reduce your exposure to bonds. If your equity investments have appreciated significantly compared to your fixed-income investments, rebalance your portfolio back to your target allocation. Most advisors suggest rebalancing at least annually.
- *Selling assets that create the least taxable gain.* Examples: Lock in stock losses, offset gains with losses, or sell bonds, which generally have minimal capital gains.

Tax-Deferred Retirement Accounts (401(k), 403(b), IRA, etc.)

Use these accounts for retirement cash flow only *after* taxable accounts are spent down, unless withdrawals are needed to meet Required Minimum Distributions (RMD).

If you're over 70½, set aside your annual RMD in a money market fund within your retirement account. Direct all distributions of interest, dividends, and/or capital gains to be paid out as cash distributions to help replenish your money market fund. Then money from this money market fund can be transferred into your checking account on a monthly or yearly basis.

If the interest, dividends, and/or capital gains are not enough to meet living expenses, you will need to sell assets while maintaining your overall asset allocation. If you're under age 59½, don't forget to factor in the 10 percent early withdrawal penalty as well as income tax payments when determining the amount of money you can spend on living expenses.

Tax-Free Accounts (Roth IRA)

As indicated earlier, use tax-advantaged accounts only after taxable accounts are spent down. Postpone tapping into your Roth IRA assets as long as possible. Generally, Roth accounts should be the last assets you access. Be sure to maintain your overall asset allocation on your total portfolio.

End Note$

Determining how much to withdraw to fund your living expenses and RMD is the first step. Then you can work to simplify the withdrawal process. Remember, utilize the interest, dividends, and capital gains that your investments generate to provide cash to pay taxes, fund living expenses, and meet RMD requirements as much as possible. General guidelines: Tap taxable accounts, then tax-deferred, then Roth.

JOHN POCHODYLO, CFP® (Scottsdale, Arizona) and **RICK EPPLE,** CFP® (Minnetrista, Minnesota)

TIP 74 HOW TO SAFELY DRAW DOWN YOUR PORTFOLIO TO ENSURE THAT YOUR NEST EGG LASTS AS LONG AS YOU DO

Q. Now that I am ready to retire, how much can I safely withdraw per year from my portfolio, and what accounts should I take the money from first?

A. Congratulations, you have made the decision to retire, or you have decided the time is right to determine if and when you can retire. The appropriate amount to withdraw each year depends on your circumstances and goals.

Guidelines

The safe withdrawal rate is approximately 4 to 5 percent, according to several studies. While the studies limited the investment mix to two asset classes (an S&P 500 index fund and short-term fixed income securities), they showed that longer payout periods (30 to 40 years) necessitate that portfolios have heavy concentrations in equities.

For example, if you had a $1 million portfolio, you could withdraw safely approximately 4.5 percent, or $45,000, the first year in retirement. The $45,000 withdrawal would supplement any Social Security and pension benefits you may have. Assuming a 3 percent inflation rate and the same asset balance, next year's withdrawal would be $46,350 (1.03 × $45,000), and so on. Limiting your retirement withdrawals to this safe withdrawal rate offers a good chance of realizing portfolio growth to support your needs throughout retirement.

Assuming the portfolio value increases, you have several options.

- *Do nothing.* If you sleep well at night and are satisfied with your lifestyle, stay the course. Play it safe. Recognize that what goes up can and will go down. Stick with the "safe" withdrawal rate.

- *Increase the withdrawal percentage.* Consider changing it from an inflation-adjusted 4.5 percent to 5 percent in your 70s, 6 percent in your 80s, etc. But be wary of overspending in the first years of retirement. You don't want to outlive your money.

If you do not have the assets required to support your lifestyle and meet the safe withdrawal rate, here are some options to consider.

- Keep working full time a few more years.
- Reduce your living expenses.
- Work part time after you retire.

Generally, retirement assets will last longer if you draw on taxable assets first. Refrain from drawing down the tax-deferred assets like 401(k)s, 403(b)s, and IRAs for as long as possible. This allows the tax-deferred assets to continue to receive tax deferral for a longer period of time. The higher the tax bracket, the more important it is to draw first on taxable assets.

For the taxable category, first draw down assets with a loss or the least amount of capital gain, so you can lock in capital losses for tax benefits and/or reduce the amount of capital gains taxes. Selling investments by matching capital losses and gains also can minimize the total tax impact.

If you never paid taxes on the contributions that you put into your retirement accounts, all distributions will be fully taxable as ordinary income. The order of distributing specific assets within these accounts is immaterial from a tax standpoint. Tax-deferred assets acquired partially with after-tax dollars (nondeductible IRA) should be distributed before the fully taxable retirement assets to defer more income tax liability into later years. All of your retirement assets should usually be distributed before tapping into a Roth IRA.

Exceptions

If you expect to leave assets to your children or other heirs, and if you have unusually large capital gains on certain stocks or mutual funds held outside of retirement accounts, it may make sense to hold the securities and pass these on to your heirs. When you die, the investment's cost basis is stepped up to its current market value before being transferred to your heirs, erasing the capital gains and the built-up tax liability.

JOHN POCHODYLO, CFP® (Scottsdale, Arizona) and **RICK EPPLE,** CFP® (Minnetrista, Minnesota)

TIP 75 COLLECTING SOCIAL SECURITY IN RETIREMENT

Q. Should I start collecting Social Security at age 62 or wait until my full retirement age?

A. Almost everyone asks this question as they approach retirement. The first issue to consider is whether you need the payments for cash-flow purposes. If you do, start the payments as soon as possible. If you don't need them, a number of factors need to be considered, including inflation, risk, opportunity cost, earnings limitations, and tax impact.

How Early Retirement Affects Your Social Security Benefits

Social Security automatically sends annual statements to covered workers age 25 or older, usually about three months prior to the workers' birthdays. The statement provides a benefit estimate for age 62 and for Full Retirement Age (FRA)—65 for those born before 1938, gradually increasing to 67 for those born in 1960 or later. If you start benefits at age 62, they always will be less than the FRA benefits, so that your total expected benefits during your lifetime will be approximately the same either way. You either receive more payments of a smaller benefit or fewer payments of a larger benefit.

Early benefits are 20 percent to 30 percent less than the FRA depending on the number of months to FRA. With your benefit statement in hand, you can work through the items below to make a decision.

Inflation

Any dollar received today is worth more than tomorrow's due to inflation, which continually erodes purchasing power. Social Security, however, takes care of inflation with a Cost-of-Living Allowance (COLA) that applies to everyone at age 62, whether they take benefits or not. Whenever you decide to take your benefits after age 62, the annual COLA adjusts the amount—it was 2.6 percent in 2002.

Risk

The longer you put off drawing benefits, the greater your risk of dying before the total from larger, later payments catches up with that of the smaller, earlier payments you could have elected. To calculate your crossover point, take your projected monthly benefit at both age 62 and at FRA, add the monthly cumulative total during your life expectancy (about age 84 to 86), then find the month when the cumulative FRA benefit either equals or exceeds the early retirement benefit. At this crossover point, you will have collected roughly the same amount under either retirement age. Then, carefully consider your family's longevity and your personal well-being to evaluate the likelihood that you will survive beyond the crossover point.

Opportunity Cost

Most financial decisions involve opportunity cost, in this case the dollar amount you could have realized from taking the benefit earlier and investing it. To determine that, assume an appropriate rate of return for an investment that would have to be sold to replace the Social Security income. Then do the numbers from age 62 until when you expect to need the money.

Earnings Limitations

Effective in 2003, the Social Security earnings limit is $960 per month or $11,520 per year for individuals between age 62 and full retirement age who are receiving benefits. One dollar of every two in Social Security benefits will be withheld for each dollar you earn over the limit. In the year that you reach full retirement age, the earnings limit increases to $2,560 per month or $30,720 per year. After that, there is no limit on your earnings. Exceptions to earned-income limits include pensions, retirement pay, dividends, interest, capital gains, and rental income as well as 401(k) and IRA withdrawals. It may not make sense to begin Social Security if your benefits will be reduced due to other earnings. The earnings limits are adjusted annually and can be found at http://www.ssa.gov.

Tax Impact

Up to 85 percent of Social Security benefits are taxable at your individual income tax rate, which depends on your Modified Adjusted Gross Income (MAGI). If your federal tax rate is 28 percent, you will owe Uncle Sam 28 cents of each $1 of the first 85 percent of your annual Social Security benefits. Also, including Social Security benefits in your AGI may limit the deductions for medical expenses or other itemized deductions that are based on percentages of AGI.

BRENDA L. SHERBINE, CPA/PFS (Hamilton, Montana)

TIP 76 DISABILITY, DIVORCE, AND WIDOW BENEFITS THROUGH SOCIAL SECURITY

Q. I'm familiar with the retirement benefits that Social Security can provide, but what other types of benefits are there?

A. While retirement benefits are the best known of all the Social Security benefits, it's good to have a working knowledge of the other benefits, too, in case you need them.

Disability Benefits

The Social Security Administration pays two types of disability benefits, Social Security Disability Insurance (SSDI, Title II), and Supplemental Security Income (SSI, Title XVI).

SSDI. Title II applies to three types of disabled individuals.

1. A disabled insured worker under 65.
2. A person disabled since childhood (before age 22) who is a dependent of a deceased insured parent or a parent entitled to Title II disability or retirement benefits (includes children of unmarried couples).
3. A disabled widow or widower, age 50 to 60, if the deceased spouse was insured under Social Security.

The benefit is paid to you and certain members of your family if you are insured—that is if you worked and paid into the Social Security system long enough. The benefit is determined based on your earnings. If you become disabled more than six months before reaching full retirement age, your monthly benefit will be equal to your full retirement benefit at the time of the disability. If you become disabled after reaching age 62 and are already receiving a reduced Social Security benefit, your disability benefit also will be reduced.

The same tax rules apply to SSDI as to regular Social Security benefits. Generally, 50 percent of benefits are taxable, but if you have other earnings, the number climbs to 85 percent.

A child, from birth to age 18 (for full-time students age 19), may receive monthly payments based on disability (or blindness) if they meet the following criteria:

- They have an impairment or combination of impairments that meets the definition of disability for children.

- Income and resources of the parents and the child are within the allowable limits. Generally, a family's total SSDI payments will be 150 percent to 180 percent of the individual qualifying for SSDI.

SSI. This is a need-based benefit. Title XVI provides payments to two types of disabled individuals: disabled adults 18 or over, and disabled children under age 18.

The basic SSI amount is the same nationwide. Effective January 2003, it's $552 a month for an eligible individual and $829 a month for an eligible couple. However, many states add money to the basic benefit. SSI recipients usually also receive food stamps and Medicaid. SSI benefit payments are not federally taxable.

Individuals 18 and older may receive monthly benefits based on disability (or blindness) if the following are true:

- The impairment or combination of impairments meets the definition of disability for adults.
- The disability began before age 22.
- The adult child's parent worked long enough to be insured under Social Security and is receiving retirement or disability benefits or is deceased.

Other Disability Payments' Effect on Social Security Disability Benefits

Ordinarily, disability payments from other sources do not affect Social Security disability benefits, unless the disability payment is workers' compensation or another public disability payment.

Workers' compensation payments are made to workers with job-related injuries or illnesses by either federal or state workers' compensation agencies, employers, or insurance companies on behalf of employers.

Public disability payments that may affect the Social Security disability benefit are those paid under a federal, state, or local law or a plan that pays for nonjob-related conditions. The latter could be civil service disability benefits, military disability benefits, state temporary disability benefits, and state or local retirement benefits based on disability.

The Social Security disability benefit is reduced to the extent that the combined Social Security benefit plus workers' compensation payment and/or public disability payment does not exceed 80 percent of your average current earnings. Note that the unreduced benefit amount is counted for income tax purposes.

Divorce Benefits

A divorced person may receive Social Security benefits based on a former spouse's earnings, if the divorce occurred after at least 10 years of marriage, the beneficiary is at least 62, and the former spouse qualifies for benefits. The benefits end generally if the beneficiary remarries, unless the later marriage ends (whether by death, divorce, or annulment).

If the former spouse (and source of Social Security benefits) dies, widow(er) benefits still are available if the marriage lasted ten years or more. Benefits paid to a surviving divorced spouse who is 60 or older will not affect the benefit rates for other survivors receiving benefits.

One of the most important things to remember when applying for Social Security benefits is your personal scenario. You may be eligible for bigger benefits if your former spouse's earned income is larger than yours.

Widow(er) and Other Survivor's Benefits

Most funeral directors will notify Social Security of an individual's death, or you can do it yourself. Those eligible for survivor's benefits include the following:

- Widow(er) may receive full benefits at full retirement age (currently age 65) or reduced benefits as early as age 60.
- A disabled widow(er) qualifies as early as age 50.
- A widow(er) at any age, if they take care of the deceased's child who is under age 16 or disabled and is receiving Social Security benefits.
- Unmarried children under 18, or up to age 19 if they are attending high school full time. Sometimes stepchildren, grandchildren, or adopted children receive benefits.
- Children at any age who were disabled before age 22 and remain disabled.
- Dependent parents age 62 or older.

Those currently collecting survivor's benefits can switch to their own retirement benefits (assuming they are eligible and that the retirement rate is higher than the widow(er)'s rate) as early as age 62.

End Note$

For more information, visit the Social Security Web site, http://www.ssa.gov, stop by your local Social Security office, or call the Social Security Administration at 800-772-1213.

BRENDA L. SHERBINE, CPA/PFS (Hamilton, Montana)

TIP 77 MEDICARE—KNOW YOUR OPTIONS

Q. What is Medicare, and how does it work?

A. Medicare is not Medicaid. Medicare is a federal insurance program for people age 65 and older, certain disabled people, and people with end-stage renal disease. Medicaid, on the other hand, is a jointly funded, federal-state health insurance program for certain low-income and needy people. The original Medicare program consists of two parts, Part A and Part B.

Medicare Part A

Medicare Part A helps cover inpatient care in hospitals, skilled nursing facilities, home health, and hospice care if certain conditions are met. It's a pay-per-visit arrangement and generally does not cover outpatient prescriptions, dental services, hearing aids, most eyeglasses, or long-term nursing care.

Medicare Part B

Medicare Part B is medical insurance to help cover the cost of doctors' services (not routine physical exams), outpatient medical and surgical services and supplies, diagnostic tests, ambulatory surgery center facility fees for approved procedures, ambulance, outpatient therapy, and other professional services as well as durable medical equipment (like wheelchairs, hospital beds, oxygen, and walkers). It also covers some other medical services omitted in Part A coverage. Beware, however: Part B helps pay for these covered services and supplies only when they are medically necessary (as defined by Medicare).

Medicare Costs

Medicare is not free and requires cost sharing in the form of premiums, deductibles, and coinsurance. Generally, people who have worked for 40 quarters or 10 years, are eligible for premium-free Medicare Part A. Deductibles apply, however. Those who have worked less than 40 quarters must pay a premium and deductibles.

Effective January 2, 2004, the monthly premium for Medicare Part B is $66.60, which is deducted automatically from Social Security checks. That amount likely will change every January. In addition to the premium, there's a Medicare Part B annual deductible ($100 in 2004). You must enroll in Part B—preferably when you first apply for Medicare at your local Social Security office or by calling Social Security (800-772-1213).

Medigap Insurance

Because Medicare, like Social Security, is not meant to cover all costs, you can purchase additional insurance known as Medigap or Medicare supplemental insurance through various insurance companies. Just as with any private insurance need, compare policies. Medigap policies only work with the original Medicare plan, the most familiar Medicare option.

Medicare + Choice

Medicare + Choice is an alternative to original Medicare. You must have Medicare Part A and Part B to join a Medicare + Choice Plan. These plans are health maintenance organizations (HMOs), where you choose doctors from among those in that organization, or modified HMOs known as preferred provider organizations (PPOs). A PPO provides an HMO facility but allows member to go to providers outside the network for Medicare-covered services. The PPO option usually costs you more than the self-contained HMO option. Everything covered in the original Medicare Parts A and B is offered by the Medicare + Choice options. In addition, you may be able to get extra benefits like coverage for prescription drugs and more preventive and wellness services.

Private Fee-for-Service

Medicare also offers a private, fee-for service option that allows an individual to go to any doctor or hospital willing to give care and accept terms of your plan's payment. (Check out-of-pocket costs before joining a supplemental private, fee-for-service plan.)

End Note$

Medicare and Medicare benefits, rules, and limitations constantly change. To get the most current information, visit the Medicare Web site (http://www.medicare.gov) or call 800-MEDICARE (800-633-4227).

HELEN T. DELONE, CFP®, Ed.D. (Medford, Massachusetts)

TIP 78 MEDICAID DECISIONS FOR LONG-TERM CARE

Q. What is Medicaid, and potentially how can it help me, or someone in my family, with long-term care costs?

A. Medicaid is a partnership, begun in 1965, between each state and the federal government to provide medical care to the elderly, blind, and disabled poor. Unlike Medicare, eligibility for Medicaid is based on financial need. Medicaid's primary benefit is the safety net it provides for long-term nursing care for those who cannot afford it. Currently, Medicaid covers more than half of the long-term care costs in the United States.

It's an extremely complex system that's handled differently in each state. We can only address the general basics, so check with your state for its unique guidelines. Applications for Medicaid coverage are made with the appropriate state agency. Substantial documentation and paperwork are required.

Eligibility Requirements

Following are the basic requirements for Medicaid eligibility:

- *U.S. citizenship or qualified alien status.*
- *Residency in the state where application is made.*
- *Medical need.* You must need long-term care, usually determined by the inability to perform at least two of the activities of daily living without assistance. The six major activities are dressing; transferring, such as getting from a bed to a chair; using the bathroom; eating; bathing; and maintaining continence.
- *Limited financial resources.* The first of two financial requirements, generally this means that the individual applying for Medicaid cannot have available resources or assets exceeding $2,000. If married, the spouse cannot have more than $89,280 (in 2002) in available resources. Generally, the following count as exceptions to "available resources":
  - *Home.* It's excluded as long as you intend to return there or your spouse resides there.
  - *Vehicle.* The maximum exempt value for an automobile is generally $4,500.
  - *Household goods.* These generally are exempt unless they are of unusual value.
  - *Property or tools.* Those used in your trade or business and necessary for support.

  - *Life insurance.* Only policies up to $1,500 are not included. If the total face value is higher, the cash surrender value counts.
  - *Burial plot.* Prepaid burial expenses and an account designated for funeral arrangements are generally allowed up to $1,500.
- *Income cap.* Almost half the states have an income cap. It varies, but most states fix it at 300 percent of the current monthly maximum Supplemental Social Security benefit ($545 in 2002 or $1,635 a month). Other states are "medically needy states," where income eligibility for Medicaid is the inability to pay the actual cost of private care from the income available.

Watch Out: Impoverishment Strategies Can Backfire

Essentially, to qualify for Medicaid, an individual must exhaust all other assets except their house, car, and household belongings. In the past, Medicaid applicants from middle-income and wealthy backgrounds worked with attorneys and financial planners to figure out ways to "impoverish" themselves (usually by giving away assets to family members), then have Medicaid foot the bill for their long-term care. But Congress has passed two laws that attach criminal penalties to such actions. Despite enforceability and constitutionality issues associated with each, clearly the intent of Congress is that those who can afford their own long-term care should pay for it, not Medicaid.

For Medicaid planning purposes, Medicaid applicants cannot just give away assets so that they can then qualify for coverage. The rules include a look-back period for gifts by an applicant or spouse. Gifts given over the past three years prior to the application (five years if the transfer was made from a Trust) still count as assets in determining Medicaid eligibility.

Other Pitfalls and Mistakes

Another mistake that applicants sometimes make is purchasing an annuity to reduce their assets. That only works when done properly and under certain circumstances. Care has to be taken that the annuity is the proper type and that the income from the annuity will not cause the Medicaid applicant's income level to be too high in the state where the application is being made.

Also of concern is the level of care that Medicaid patients receive. Facilities often have a limited number of Medicaid beds, and some argue that Medicaid patients receive lower-quality care than private payers. That's one reason to consider long-term care insurance—more on that later.

JAMES J. PASZTOR JR. CFP® (Greensboro, NC)

TIP 79 MEDICARE MYTHS AND MISUNDERSTANDINGS

Q. How do I get on Medicare?

A. Medicare is a federal program for all U.S. citizens over age 65 except for those covered by the Railroad Retirement program, who have comparable coverage.

Some people who are under 65, such as the disabled and those requiring kidney dialysis, also are covered. People who do not have a work history or have never married may not be covered (nontraditional couples, for example, with a stay-at-home partner).

Medicare Part A covers hospital expenses. Coverage is automatic. Part B coverage, which is elective, requires you to apply and sign up through your Social Security office. You can do that three months before or after you turn 65. The cost of Medicare Part A ($54 adjusted annually) is deducted monthly from your Social Security benefit.

Why Apply for Medicare Part B?

An individual should sign up for Part B because it covers 80 percent of doctors' bills and other services like labs and X rays; medical equipment (wheelchair) and supplies (oxygen); outpatient surgery; physical and occupational therapy; ambulance services; some limited psychiatry, podiatry, and chiropractic care; and second opinions.

Also covered are 100 percent of annual mammograms, flu and pneumonia shots, Pap tests, diabetic supplies and education and nutrition therapy, colonoscopy, bone density tests, PSA tests, glaucoma screening, and kidney failure treatments.

Part B does *not* cover acupuncture, dental care or dentures, cosmetic surgery, hearing aids or exams, orthopedic shoes (most of the time), outpatient prescription drugs, routine foot care, routine eye care and glasses, annual physicals, health care outside the United States, or custodial care at home or in a nursing home.

Individuals also need to purchase Medicare coinsurance or Medigap coverage to pay for additional benefits needed and the 20 percent that Part B does not cover.

Purchasing Medicare Coinsurance

Keep in mind that 20 percent of outpatient surgery, diagnostic tests, and treatments can be costly.

Medigap coverage is available through private insurance agents and can be purchased on the first day of the month in which an individual turns 65 and is enrolled in Medicare Part B. There is a six-month window known as your *open enrollment period.* During that six-month period following your 65th birthday, no insurance company can deny you coverage or place conditions on your coverage because of health problems.

Medigap comes with ten choices of standardized coverage referred to as Plan A, B, etc., through Plan J. What plan you choose depends on your anticipated lifestyle and personal economics. Do you plan to travel? Some plans will cover you outside the United States. Other plans may limit prescription benefits. Cost is the primary consideration. Keep in mind that what you can afford now is only one part of the decision. The costs will increase with your age and inflation and may change if you relocate to another state.

For example, the total premiums paid for Plan J (the most comprehensive and expensive plan) from ages 65 to 80 may require approximately $47,000, and $66,000 to age 85. Costs in a more expensive part of the country can run almost twice that amount. (This assumes an annual medical inflation rate of 7 percent.)

The Magic Question for Medicare

The magic question to ask your health care provider is, "Do you take assignment?" If the answer is yes, that can minimize your costs. Medicare pays 80 percent of the usual and customary fee, as determined by Medicare. Medicare billing is capped at 115 percent of the doctor's figures. Coinsurance will pay the remaining 20 percent of the approved charges.

For example: The bill is $115. Medicare approves $100 and pays the approved 80 percent. Your coinsurance pays the additional 20 percent of this approved amount. You owe the balance up to the $115 total, which is $15. If the bill were $150, you would owe nothing above the $115, because that represents the 115 percent Medicare billing cap. However, if your doctor takes assignment, you would owe nothing beyond the Medicare and coinsurance payments paid by your insurance coverage.

Some Myths and Misconceptions about Medicare

Doctors welcome new Medicare patients. Some do, but others limit their number of Medicare patients. As reimbursement for services drops, so does the number of doctors willing to serve the senior population. Typically, doctors will continue to see a patient who turns 65 while under their care. However, if you move or seek a new physician, you may be unable to find a practice that will accept you unless you have private insurance.

Medicare will cover my nursing home needs. What it actually will cover is the first few days (possibly 21) of care. You must be improving rapidly and significantly, and you must need skilled nursing care. Custodial care in a nursing home or assisted living facility is *not* covered.

I can give my assets away, let the government pay the bills, and guarantee my family's inheritance. The misconception persists that, by artificially impoverishing yourself, your care will be covered by government subsidy via Medicaid, a program for the medically indigent of any age. Aside from the questionable ethics of organizing your affairs in this manner, there are some very real arguments against this.

There is a *look-back period* of three years for direct gifting and five years for assets conveyed to Trusts. Also, some states aggressively pursue recapture of estate assets when a Medicaid recipient dies. If your motivation is to provide for your heirs, you may have your last wishes denied. If you have resources, you may be better served by purchasing long-term care coverage rather than relying on this government program.

End Note$

For more information, visit http://www.medicare.gov or http://www.senioranswers.org.

MARY A. BROOKS, CFP® (Colorado Springs, Colorado)

TIP 80 CHOOSING A PLACE TO LIVE DURING RETIREMENT

Q. Should I take any financial considerations into account when selecting where I will live during retirement?

A. For most of us, the change from an active work life to retirement also suggests a major change of lifestyle. We also can expect changes in our physical abilities as we age. As part of your retirement plans, you might consider moving to a new area or to a smaller, less demanding home or renovating your current home.

Following is a list of many things you should consider when choosing a home for your retirement. They are not listed in any particular order of importance, because everyone has different priorities. Research, think through, and discuss each.

The Community You Live In

- What size is the community? Does it have your preferred daily atmosphere?
- How available is public transportation, if and when you no longer drive?
- What is its proximity to airports, bus service, and train stations, if travel is in your retirement plans?
- Are community centers, activities, libraries, and theaters readily available?
- Is the community senior-friendly? What senior programs, educational programs, assisted-living facilities, and home health care agencies are in place; and how well-funded are they?
- Is it close to family and/or friends? Will family easily be able to visit you?
- What's the community's tax base?
- What's the median age? A youthful community may have more demands for school growth and funding issues. Will other services be sacrificed?
- Look at the crime statistics for the area. Has there been a significant change in the past five years?
- What's the weather like?
- How close is shopping for food, clothes, gasoline and auto repairs, pharmacy needs, household items, gifts, and more? How far do you want to travel for regular grocery needs?
- Do you have banking choices?
- Is there public and private mail and package delivery?
- How far do you have to travel for fun and entertainment outside your home?
- What is the distance to major highways?
- How large are nearby major cities, and how do they affect your community?
- What community groups are active in town?
- How far will you have to travel to worship? What is the spirit and health of the local place of worship you will most likely attend?
- What's the diversity of the community—ethnicity, income, and age?
- Are restaurants nearby?
- How available are the sporting activities that you enjoy?
- How far will you have to travel to engage in hobbies?
- How close are doctors, specialists, and hospitals?
- What long-term care facilities are in the area, and would you want to stay in any of them?
- Do you want ever to move again?
- What's of interest nearby when friends, family, and grandchildren stay with you?
- What is the fire department's rating?

- What's the availability of hotels and motels in the area?
- How close are dry cleaning, shoe repair, a hair stylist, an accountant, and other services?

Your Retirement Home

- What size of home do you require?
- Where will your guests stay?
- If you enjoy entertaining, what facilities do you want in the kitchen, dining area, and outside area?
- How much yard work do you want to do?
- How old is the home, roof, paint etc.?
- What is its proximity to many of the community items listed above?
- Where will the grandchildren play when they visit? Can they bicycle, skateboard, and roller-skate in the neighborhood?
- Is there space for storage, doing hobbies, etc.?
- How close are the nearest neighbors?

Good Books on Retirement and Retirement Planning

Here are a few books that can help you plan for a more secure retirement.

- *Retiring—A Smart and Easy Guide to an Enjoyable Retirement,* by Hope Egan and Barbara Wagner (Barnes and Noble Books)
- *Bankroll Your Future: How to Get the Most from Uncle Sam for Your Retirement Years—Social Security, Medicare, and Much More,* by Ellen Hoffman (Newmarket Press)
- *You've Lost It, Now What? How to Beat the Bear Market and Still Retire on Time,* by Jonathan Clements (Portfolio Books)
- *Retirement Bible,* by Lynn O'Shaughnessy (John Wiley and Sons)

MARY L. GIBSON, CFP® (San Juan Bautista, California)

Chapter

6

LIFE TRANSITIONS

TIP 81 YOUR FIRST JOB

Q. I'm about to start my first job. What can I do to make the most of my paycheck?

A. Like most people who have just accepted their first job, you're probably being bombarded with new challenges, commitments, opportunities, and intimidating questions. Making wise financial decisions when you enter the workforce can have a dramatic effect on your ability to reach your future financial goals.

Some of the issues to be concerned about include managing your new cash flow and debt, paying off education loans, developing savings and investment plans, and evaluating employee benefit programs.

Managing Your New Cash Flow and Debt

Now is the time to develop a budget. Without a budget and financial plan, it's all too easy for your earnings to wither away.

Take care of your needs first, then your savings, then the fun stuff. The budget probably will be a bit more difficult to manage than you originally thought, because despite the new source of income, you will have a slew of expenses.

An easy way to develop a simple budget is to calculate your monthly cash flow on a simple pad of paper or using a spreadsheet software program like Intuit's

Quicken (http://www.quicken.com), Microsoft Money (http://www.microsoft.com/money), or Mvelopes Personal (http://www.mvelopes.com).

Other budget tips include the following:

- Pay off credit card debt.
- Evaluate your spending habits and cut back on nonessentials.
- You may no longer be covered under your parents' insurance policy. Don't underestimate the need for adequate insurance.

Paying Off Education Loans

Typically, education loan repayments begin six months after graduation, so don't forget to include them in your initial cash flow worksheet. A few lenders, such as Sallie Mae, offer incentives for borrowers to pay on time or pay electronically. Additionally, interest paid on education loans may be deductible from income taxes if you meet an income test. Income limits, adjusted annually for inflation, are based on a modified version of the borrower's adjusted gross income (AGI). Talk to the IRS or your tax advisor to find out if you meet the income test.

Developing a Savings and Investment Plan

The first step in any financial plan is to ensure that you have an emergency fund with three to six months of living expenses readily available. To calculate how much you need, take your total monthly living expenses, subtract taxes and nonessential expenditures, then multiply the result by a number of months (usually three to six). This number is your goal for building a cash reserve.

Retirement Savings

Next on the agenda is your retirement savings. It is never too early to begin saving for retirement. One thing that we hear over and over again from clients is that they wished they would have started saving earlier—no matter what their age now.

Take full advantage of your retirement plan at work, because many employers offer payroll deduction plans where a specified amount is deducted from each paycheck. Put as much as you can into the retirement plan. At a minimum, it should be as much as your employer will match. Some companies, for example, contribute 50 cents for every dollar the employee contributes. That's an immediate 50 percent return on your investment.

Evaluating Employee Benefit Programs

Salary is only part of any total employment offer. Benefits are an important piece of a compensation package, and you should consider them carefully before accepting any new position. Fortunately, many employers offer benefit packages that include health, disability, and life insurance coverage.

When you read your company's benefits package, don't hesitate to ask the benefits administrator if you have any questions. Knowing how benefit programs work can help save money now and in the future.

TODD SHEPHERD, CPA/PFS, MBA (Leawood, Kansas)

TIP 82 GETTING MARRIED

Q. We're getting married. What are some of the financial issues that my spouse and I need to consider?

A. Marriage brings many changes in a couple's financial situation that will affect goals and objectives, personal property, assets, debts, retirement accounts, savings, taxes, and more. However, with proper planning and good communication, two people can combine their assets and live nearly as cheaply as one with a better quality of life and an increased standard of living.

Handling Bank Accounts

One of the first challenges for a couple is how to manage their checking accounts. The most common options include lumping everything together right away or keeping three separate checking accounts: his, hers, and ours. Whatever the agreement, it is critical for each person to have their own fun money to be used as each desires. If one spouse wants to hit the golf course and the other wants to run by the manicurist, the fun money provides freedom and independence without guilt.

Talking about Finances

Small financial problems often grow into larger ones, simply because some couples find it difficult to talk about money. But financial problems are the number one reason that couples argue and are the leading cause of divorce. Before marriage, many couples avoid the subject, believing that a partner is fiscally fit, only to find out that their partner is deep in debt or has other problems managing money.

Before and during your marriage, it is important to communicate openly about money on a regular basis and keep each other informed of the financial situation. As your financial discussions progress, you will get a good sense of each other's spending habits and freely share your dreams for the future. Many couples set aside time each week or each month for a financial discussion and reward themselves afterward with a dinner out or a movie.

Budgeting

Before you can make any financial decisions, you have to know the value of what you own, how much you owe, how much you bring in monthly after taxes, and where your money goes each month. To do that, start by collecting all your financial documents (bank and credit card statements, checkbooks, information on assets and debts, employer benefit packages, and so on). The next steps include the following:

- Put together a combined balance sheet listing all assets and debts.
- Set aside money for an emergency fund with three to six months of living expenses.
- Determine where the monthly cash flow goes and try to spot areas where spending can be reduced.
- Review your combined investment portfolios. Rebalancing may make good sense if your combined portfolio is overweighted in any particular asset class.
- Find ways to maximize contributions to your retirement funds.
- Obtain a copy of your credit report to see if any issues will affect your future borrowing power.
- Split up duties such as paying the bills, consolidating statements, and keeping tabs on your savings. Then assign responsibilities based on each person's strengths. Alternatively, you can assign duties to the spouse who needs to develop a particular skill, then have the other spouse provide coaching.

Changing Beneficiaries and Creating or Modifying Wills

When you get married, you will want to change the beneficiaries on your accounts like 401(k)s, IRAs, disability insurance, and life insurance. You also will need a Will so that your assets are disbursed properly if you die. If either of you have children from a previous marriage, a Will is especially important to ensure that they receive a stake in your estate.

Prenuptial Agreements

The topic of prenuptial agreements generally raises a few eyebrows. Many believe that developing a prenuptial agreement dooms a marriage. But a prenuptial agreement can be the right move when one spouse has more assets or earns much more than the other, has substantial debt, has children from a prior marriage who need to be protected in case of death or second divorce, owns part or all of a business, or is planning to go back to school (the prenuptial agreement can help ensure that the working spouse's contribution to the other spouse's education is properly rewarded).

Taxes

While some relief from the marriage penalty tax went into effect in 2003, a two-income couple with more than $120,000 of household income still owes more in taxes than two single people with the same total income. So prepare now to pay more to Uncle Sam come April 15.

When you marry, you have the choice of two filing statuses, married filing jointly or married filing separately. Discuss your situation with your tax and financial advisor to determine which situation works to your advantage. Usually, married filing jointly is the better option.

TODD SHEPHERD, CPA/PFS, MBA (Leawood, Kansas)

TIP 83 FINANCIAL PLANNING ISSUES FOR NONTRADITIONAL COUPLES

Q. Married people and their assets are automatically protected by hundreds of laws. How can unmarried couples—same-sex and opposite-sex couples—enjoy the same protections?

A. Before specifically answering your question, it is important to note that some of the issues described herein also are applicable in the case of any two unmarried people sharing ownership of assets.

Compared with married couples, unmarried partners face many legal limitations, including the fact that they do not have the automatic right to inherit each other's property; manage the other's financial assets should one become incapacitated, speak for one another in a medical crisis, and in some cases, visit the other in the hospital.

However, careful planning can protect your rights and ensure that your wishes are honored.

Ownership of Assets

Revocable Trusts can be extremely effective tools for unmarried couples as well as for single people. For estate tax purposes, you own the assets individually, but the Trust document specifies what happens to Trust property when you die, thus avoiding probate delays and related costs.

Life, Disability, and Health Insurance

You must find a life insurance company that will recognize a nonmarried partner as a beneficiary. Comprehensive disability and medical insurance is more important than ever for people who may not have family they can depend on for support. Long-term care insurance is important for unmarried couples, too, because Medicaid prohibits the healthy partner from living in the jointly owned home, unless they buy out the interest of the ill partner who requires Medicaid.

Homeowners and Auto Insurance

If an adult lives in a residence, and their name is not on the deed, they may not be covered by the homeowner's policy. They need to be added to the homeowner's policy, if possible, or get renter's insurance. If an auto insurance company will not issue joint coverage for an unmarried couple, the owner can be listed as the primary driver and the partner as an occasional driver on the policy.

Income Taxes

Maximize your deductions by arranging tax-deductible expenses so that the higher wage earner pays for the tax-deductible items and makes the charitable contributions, while the other claims the standard deduction. Also, when opening a joint investment account, consider whose Social Security number is listed as primary on the account. If all else is equal, use the Social Security number of the partner in the lower tax bracket. That person will report the income on their tax return at the lower rate.

Employer-Provided Benefits

More employers are offering domestic partner benefits to their unmarried employees. This includes health insurance and other benefits. However, the employer's contribution is taxable to the employee as additional income. Married employees pay no taxes on the benefits they receive.

Social Security Benefits from a Prior Marriage

If at any time you were legally married, check with the Social Security Administration (http://www.ssa.gov) to find out the benefits to which you may be entitled. If you were married for ten years or more, for example, you are entitled to your ex-spouse's retirement and government benefits if they are/were eligible to receive benefits. Plus, in the event of death, a surviving unmarried partner has no legal right to the deceased's Social Security benefits or pension, so financial planning is critical for nonmarried couples.

Gifting Limits and Other Asset Transfer Problems

One potentially huge landmine is the inadvertent gifting between unmarried partners. Married couples are allowed unlimited marital transfers, but unmarried people are not. When an unmarried couple wishes to transfer a large asset like a home from individual to joint ownership and avoid the gift tax, one strategy is to draft a document that spells out the terms of a gradual ownership transfer. To do this, consult an attorney experienced in estate planning or real estate transactions.

Other Legal Issues and Possible Solutions

Because federal laws do not recognize domestic partnerships, unmarried couples must take responsibility for many estate planning issues that married couples take for granted. Here are some other issues to consider.

- *Create a Living Will.* This document stipulates what kind of medical care you do or do not wish to receive if you become incapacitated.
- *Establish a Durable Power of Attorney for Health Care.* This gives your partner visitation rights, the power to make health care decisions, and the authority to hire and fire medical personnel. Your partner can even limit which next of kin may visit.
- *Establish a Durable Power of Attorney for Finances.* This allows you to name someone to manage your financial affairs if you are unable to do so. Without this document, one would have to ask a court for the authority to take over the financial affairs of an incapacitated partner.

- *Another valuable document might be a Domestic Partnership Agreement.* This describes how finances will be managed and defines each partner's obligations and duties to the other while living together. A *Written Property Agreement* is necessary if a home is owned together or any other large financial and emotional commitments are involved. In addition, a *Cohabitation or Living-Together Agreement* delineates who owns what, the sharing of expenses, and how assets and property would be divided if the relationship were to end.
- *When children are involved, attorneys recommend that unmarried couples sign an Acknowledgment of Parenthood, also known as a Paternity Statement or Parenting Agreement.* This document lists both parents on the birth certificate and is a written commitment stating the desire to parent together. It includes language that states the intention to continue coparenting, even if the relationship ends.
- *If you feel strongly about funeral arrangements, create a document expressing your wishes.* If no document exists, the next of kin has the right to make the funeral arrangements.
- *Establish a Domestic Partnership Agreement when implementing your estate and financial plans.* It's wise to consider the possibility that the relationship will have ended by the time either partner retires. A Domestic Partnership Agreement will ensure that you are as prepared as you can be for any foreseeable outcome.

End Note$

For more information on issues facing unmarried couples, consult the following resources:

- *4 Steps to Financial Security for Lesbian & Gay Couples,* by Harold Lustig (Random House Publication Group)
- Law for All (http://www.nolo.com)
- Lambda Legal Defense & Education (http://www.lambdalegal.org)
- Alternatives to Marriage Project (http://www.atmp.org)
- *Personal Financial Planning for Gays & Lesbians,* by Peter Berkery (Irwin Professional Publishing)
- *JK Lasser's Gay Finances in a Straight World,* by Peter Berkery (JK Lasser)

SHERYL GARRETT, CFP® (Shawnee Mission, Kansas)

TIP 84 STARTING A FAMILY

Q. We're thinking of starting a family. How much does it cost to raise a child, and what other important financial matters do we need to consider?

A. Without a doubt, a new arrival will impact significantly a family's financial situation. For example, the cumulative expenses for a child born in the Midwest in 2004 are estimated to reach more than $500,000 by the time that child graduates from college. The price tag for the first year of a baby's life alone could be $10,000, taking into account delivery, hospital stay, baby furniture, clothes, food, diapers, day care, toys, books, well-baby visits, and immunizations.

Consider Some Alternatives

Before you go out and buy everything that baby needs and then some, consult more experienced moms and dads for guidance. Is the item really necessary? Can you borrow, buy secondhand, or do without? Baby will not know the difference, and the $500 saved now turns into $1,500 or more when the grown baby heads off to college.

Start by developing a budget that includes things like day care, saving for college, the cost of creating or revising a Will, any changes in insurance coverage, and finally, any tax savings available for your new family. Here are some ideas for factoring these items into your new spending plan.

Day Care

Day care prices vary greatly and depend on many factors. Have a frank discussion with your spouse regarding your day care needs and family values as you determine the best option for your baby. Do a quick projection to determine how each option would affect your budget. If your employer offers a Flexible Spending Account (FSA), you can save hundreds of dollars in taxes each year by using it.

Education

The earlier you start saving for your child's education, the more time your money has to grow. The cost of a college education is one of the largest expenditures in raising children. Currently, it costs $10,000 per year to attend a public college if you factor in books, tuition, and room and board. For children born today, that amount will soar to more than $24,000, assuming a college-cost inflation rate of 5 percent. That's more than $96,000 for four years of education at a public college or university. Fortunately, several options are available that offer both tax-deferral and tax breaks.

Remember: Don't neglect your own retirement savings in favor of saving for college. There are plenty of funding sources available to help pay for college if your own savings fall short, but you're on your own for retirement.

Wills and Beneficiary Designations

If you die without a Will, your state will determine the distribution of your assets and the guardian for your children. With a Will, you choose. Every parent should make a Will, yet more than 70 percent of adults do not have one.

Choosing a legal guardian can be a daunting task. You must decide who will raise your child in your absence. Issues to consider include who shares your values, your education, your way of life, your religion, and your love for your child. Often, the answer to this question is a family member. But, before you name a guardian, find out if that person is willing to take on this responsibility. You also need to name a Trustee for your child's inheritance. One person can be both Guardian and Trustee, or you may choose to split these duties between two people you trust.

Check to ensure that the beneficiary designations on your investment accounts and insurance policies take your new baby's arrival into account and are consistent with your Will.

Insurance

When you have a child, you may need to increase your life insurance, disability insurance, and health insurance coverage.

Selecting the right policy and amount can buy you peace of mind that your family will be financially stable if you die. You have several options in the type of life insurance—term life, whole life, variable life, universal life, etc. However, a term life policy is typically the best for most young, middle-income families with children, because it has affordable premiums and can be purchased to cover a set period for the same rate.

It's also time to review your disability coverage. During your prime earning years, ages 35 to 65, you are more likely to become ill or injured and unable to work than you are to die. Disability insurance guarantees you a portion of your salary (usually 50 to 70 percent) if you cannot work.

Many health care plans have agreements with doctors, hospitals, and other facilities that offer favorable terms if you use these preferred providers. Become familiar with your health insurance coverage before you have your baby, so that you get the most out of your prenatal, maternity, and postnatal care. Knowing how to properly use your health care benefits can save you hundreds of dollars in medical costs. Fortunately, many health insurance plans have special coverage for babies that includes items like well-baby care. Read and understand your insurance documents so you know the procedure on when and how to add your baby to your policy.

Tax Breaks

Children generate some wonderful tax breaks. You can claim a deduction for your new baby on your income tax form in the form of a child tax credit. Also, you may qualify for a childcare credit and/or an adoption credit.

To smooth the tax issues, apply for a Social Security number for your child as soon after birth as possible. You'll need to file a form SS-5 with the Social Security Administration. Most hospitals assist you with this form after the birth of your baby.

Regardless of your filing status, you can claim a $1,000 (2003–2004) per child tax credit if your dependent child is a U.S. citizen or resident. However, the credit may be phased out for higher income families.

Also depending on your income level, you may be entitled to a 35 percent credit on up to $3,000 ($6,000 if you have two or more children) of your expenses for qualified child care while both you and your spouse work or look for work.

Those with higher income levels might opt to use an employer's Flexible Spending Account (FSA) for dependent care expenses, if available. Contributions of up to $5,000 are taken out of your salary before federal income taxes, Social Security taxes, and most state and local taxes. You end up paying fewer taxes and have more money available on payday.

In addition to the other applicable tax credits, the current law allows a tax credit up to $10,000 per child for qualifying adoption expenses. There are income limitations, however, and the tax credit phases out for higher income couples. Qualifying adoption expenses include court costs, attorney fees, adoption fees, travel expenses, and other expenses directly related to the legal adoption of an eligible child. If you adopt a U.S. child, you must claim the credit in the year after you incur the expense, or the year the adoption becomes final, whichever comes first. However, if you adopt a foreign child, the deduction can only be taken if and when the adoption is completed. Some employers also offer adoption-assistance programs, which can be used in conjunction with the adoption credit.

End Note$

For more information, check out the following Web sites:

- http://www.babycenter.com
- http://www.4woman.gov
- http://www.childrentoday.com
- http://www.parenthood.com/links.html

SHERI IANNETTA CUPO, CFP® (Morristown, New Jersey) and

TODD SHEPHERD, CPA/PFS, MBA (Leawood, Kansas)

TIP 85 HOW TO RAISE MONEYWISE KIDS

Q. How do I raise my kids to have good money habits?

A. As with teaching most family values, instilling good financial habits in your children is no simple task. It takes practice, responsibility, and patience. Yet it's worth the time and trouble because your children will reap rewards for life. Here are some basic ways that you can teach your kids good money-management skills.

Let Them Know How Much Things Cost

If an item costs $100, make your child understand how much time an average person has to work to earn enough money to pay for it. For example, it would take two full days of work for a minimum-wage worker to come up with the $100 to purchase the item.

Give Them an Allowance

Your child probably can handle an allowance by age five or six. Together, decide just what the allowance covers. The amount should cover the child's needs and include a little extra, so that not every penny is spent before they get it. That little extra will help them practice their decision-making skills.

Two Web sites with nifty educational tools can make it fun for your child to learn about how to manage an allowance. Money Savvy Generation (http://www.msgen.com) has a piggy bank with four slots for saving, spending, donating, and investing. Another site, http://www.moonjar.com, offers a money box for saving, spending, and sharing. Most experts agree that an allowance should not be linked to daily chores or grades. However, extra money for special jobs, such as cleaning out the garage, is fine.

Ask Them to Pay Half

Require your child to come up with half the amount for big-ticket items. They can save their allowance or do extra chores around the house to come up with the money. This helps your child understand the work-to-reward relationship and counteracts the desire for immediate gratification.

Open a Bank Account

A child can open an account for as little as $10. Some banks even have special programs for children to teach them about money and saving. Help your child make deposits and withdrawals, record the transactions, read the bank statement, and reconcile the account. Showing a child how the bank account balance grows is a great way to instill a desire to save. Want to really light their fire? Offer to match the amount that the child puts into a savings account earmarked for a long-term goal.

Identifying Needs versus Wants

Teach your kids about their needs versus their wants. Help your child understand the difference between the items they need to survive (food, housing, clothing) versus things that they want (a video game, a new CD, a doll). Discuss the idea of a *want* as something that we desire but do not need to live, while a *need* is something that we cannot live without.

Create a Budget

Help your child develop a simple plan for spending money. Have them write down the things that they need versus what they want, and help them calculate how long they will need to save to buy what they want. Explain that they may have to eliminate some of the wants if their allowance does not cover them. Or you could work out a plan where the child takes on extra household chores to earn the money to purchase the item. This approach will help instill the value of working to earn money and financial planning.

Give Them Responsibility and Let Them Make Mistakes

When you turn over their allowance to them, give your children full responsibility for their spending choices. Allow them to make their own decisions—and their own mistakes. When we spend money as adults, we must make choices, and not all our choices will be the right ones. Learning to live with the results of a poor money decision is a valuable lesson. As a parent, your direction should be available at all times and may be required in some instances. As your child grows older, think about giving them a monthly allowance rather than a weekly allowance. This helps them learn to budget money and make it last over a period of time.

TODD SHEPHERD, CPA/PFS, MBA (Leawood, Kansas)

TIP 86 PLANNING A SMOOTH TRANSITION TO A NEW CAREER

Q. I'm thinking about making a career change. What steps can I take to manage the financial aspects of this transition successfully?

A. If you are reading this, chances are you are about to embark on the fascinating, enriching, and sometimes frightening journey that a career change—whether self-imposed or involuntary—often represents. Career change also often results in a change in financial circumstances, whether temporary or permanent, large or small, up or down. Whatever the outcome, the transition will be smoother if you consider the financial implications of a job change before you make it.

Gather Information

First, familiarize yourself with your current benefits package and, if possible, your new one. For some, this will provide leverage when negotiating your new compensation package. But it's also an opportunity to take full advantage of your existing benefits package while you still can.

Pay It Forward

If you anticipate fewer comprehensive benefits in your new career, consider moving up elective visits, expenses, and procedures. For example, if you will no longer have vision benefits under your new employer's health plan, schedule your annual check-up before the transition. Fill ongoing prescriptions now rather than wait. Prepay your dependent care or health club expenses if possible.

Use It Before You Lose It

Check the balance on your Flexible Spending Account. If you contributed more than you spent, you will forfeit the balance when you leave the company. So spend it on qualifying expenses before you go. On the other hand, your employer must reimburse you for all eligible expenses through your date of termination (up to the annual amount you would have contributed), even if you have contributed less than the amount of those expenses.

Are You Playing It Close to the Vest?

With most retirement plans, the employer's contribution vests over a period of several years, but if you leave before being fully vested, you will lose some of these benefits. Therefore, if you're close to becoming more fully vested, consider changing the timing of your career switch accordingly.

Stay on a Roll

When you leave an employer, you can roll over your retirement plan to an IRA or to the new employer's plan, or you can keep it where it is (if allowed). You may also have the option to cash out. If you're not yet 59½, cashing out carries a 10 percent penalty *and* you'd owe income tax on the amount withdrawn. If you have borrowed from your retirement plan, the outstanding loan comes due immediately on termination. If you don't have the cash, the loan amount is considered an early withdrawal (subject to that same 10 percent penalty and income tax.) Generally, it is most advantageous to roll over your retirement account from your former employer to an IRA when you change jobs.

Stay Covered

If your new employer doesn't provide a health plan, consider purchasing the coverage offered by your previous employer for up to 18 months (per the Consolidated Omnibus Reconciliation Act of 1985, also known as COBRA). Investigate your health insurance options before changing jobs.

Get a Handle on Expenses

If you expect a significant decrease in income with your career change, get a handle on your expenses. If you haven't already done so, determine your monthly expenses and estimate how they will change. Do not forget nonreimbursed job training and relocation expenses, business start-up costs, and new commuting costs. If your decrease in income is permanent, decrease expenses accordingly. If the decrease is temporary, calculating your expenses will help you to save for interim cash needs.

Build a Cushion

Although it's always a good idea to have an emergency fund of at least three to six months of expenses, it's especially important if you're earning less. Consider beefing up your cash cushion if you're unsure how long the lean times will last.

Give Yourself Some Credit

In general, try to avoid taking on a lot of debt prior to your transition. But, if you need to purchase a big-ticket item and can make the required payments, it will be much easier to get a loan approved while you show a steady income. Also, consider securing a home equity line of credit now. That increases your available emergency funds, and you will only owe interest if you actually use the money.

Plan for Uncle Sam

Where possible, consider timing income and expenses to reduce your overall tax liability. For example, if you know that you're in a high tax bracket this year but will be in a lower one next year, incur tax-deductible expenses this year but defer income until next year. If you plan to sell securities held at a loss, do so while you have income against which to offset the loss.

Create a Disability Safety Net

If you're starting a business and not already covered by an employer or individual policy, consider purchasing disability insurance while still employed. Once you are in business for yourself, you generally have to show a year's track record of income before you become eligible to purchase disability insurance. Even if you have disability coverage from an employer, consider a supplemental policy to help cover you after you leave the company.

Keep Your Eye on Goals

Depending on the timing, a career change can have a significant impact on your ability to meet financial goals like retirement, college funding, and more. Consider working with a financial planner to determine the extent of the impact.

End Note$

While a career transition can dramatically change your financial situation, it is important to plan for and manage the impact where you can. Money, however, isn't the only factor in this important decision. Ultimately, few things in life are as satisfying as finding (or creating) personally and financially rewarding work. To successfully make the journey from where you are today to this destination, you must take into account personal goals and satisfaction, long-term opportunities for growth, and the effect on your family's lifestyle. Then apply a healthy dose of money smarts.

SHERRILL ST. GERMAIN, MBA (Hollis, New Hampshire)

TIP 87 HOW TO PROTECT YOURSELF IN TODAY'S UNCERTAIN JOB MARKET

Q. What should I do if I'm laid off or lose my job?

A. Losing your job can be a shock. Your boss may suddenly call you in and cut to the chase: "We are undergoing a restructuring and some positions have been eliminated," or, "The corporate office is closing," or, "You are no longer right for this position." It can happen so fast that you are numb.

One minute you're a valued employee, and the next minute you're out. Sometimes you are given only an hour or two to clean out your desk, say goodbye, and leave the building. When it happens that quickly, the details are a blur—severance, outplacement, exit interviews.

A little self-pity may be inevitable, but you would be wise to listen to the "Chairman of the Board," singer Frank Sinatra, who offers this piece of advice: "Each time I find myself flat on my face, I pick myself up and get back in the race. That's life . . ."

Here are some tips to help you through a tough transition.

Get Back in the Race as Soon as Possible

Don't be tempted to take a vacation or spend your severance. That might be OK if you're thinking of a career change and need time to prepare for it. But, if you like your profession and know you want to find another job in your field, it's best to get started right away. If you are like most people, then you need a job.

A Good Outplacement Firm Is Invaluable

If you're lucky, outplacement will be part of your severance package. If not, pay for it yourself. It's money well spent if it shortens the job search period by a month or two. Shop carefully for a firm. Meet with a few different outplacement companies, get references, and choose the one that feels right for you.

Remember that your primary *work* for a while is finding a job. It is helpful to establish a routine of going to the outplacement office every day. Your coach will keep you focused and motivated, and you will have a support group of people who are going through a similar experience.

Your Resume Is Your Calling Card

It's essential to develop a resume that highlights your accomplishments. With the help of your outplacement coach, you will see that you have done more good work than you ever really recognized before.

You also might consider creating business cards with an interesting slogan and your contact information; you could even add a line or two about your qualifications or personal mission.

Perfect Your Positioning Statement

The elevator speech is a brief and engaging statement about you and your unique abilities. Use it when meeting people or introducing yourself on the telephone. A positioning statement is longer—generally 30 to 60 seconds—and goes into slightly more detail. You'll want to develop a formal and informal version. Be creative when asked, "What do you do?" at social and business gatherings. Saying, "I'm between jobs," or "I just got laid off," is not an engaging statement. Try something more upbeat that expresses your personality: "I'm a computer programming wizard," and smile humbly. When asked who you work for, you could say, "I'm self-employed, but am always interested in talking with business owners who would like to increase company productivity and add to the bottom line." You might even add, "Why? Are you a business owner who fits this description?"

Network. Network. Network.

The reality is that most jobs are filled without ever being listed in the newspaper or online. Instead, it's about networking. Talk with friends, relatives, acquaintances, and business associates, and let them know that you're looking for a job. Ask them to keep you in mind as they routinely talk with their own network of people. If you ask for introductions to their contacts, be clear that your objective is to expand your network, not to ask for a job. That puts people at ease and makes them feel good to think that they can help even when they are not in a position to offer you a job.

As you meet new people, think of what benefits you may be able to offer them before you focus on what they can do for you. Remember that you are planting seeds, and seeds take some time to grow. Your chances of success are greater when you work from the inside out instead of the outside in.

Set Your Goals and Put Them in Writing

Writing down your objectives is a powerful tool. The human mind subconsciously seeks the things that it thinks about most. Once you have written down your goals, you will be compelled to reach them and usually will surpass them.

Aim at a Target

Most job seekers do the opposite and use the shotgun approach. It may seem counterintuitive, but the narrower your focus, the more likely it is that you will find a job soon. If you tell people that you will accept any job, anywhere, with any type of responsibilities, they may not know how to help you, even when they want to.

Brush Up Your Skills

If you're missing a credential or a degree and are close earning it, take the time to do so. In some situations, a certain credential can put you ahead of an applicant who does not have it.

Limit Your Spending

Figure out how many months of savings you have in reserve. The general guideline when looking for a job is that the search will take one month for every $10,000 in salary you have been earning.

Be Careful Accepting the First Job Offered

Being out of work is stressful. You may be tempted to accept an offer, even if the job is not perfect and the salary lower than you're used to. But it might be better to pass on it. On the other hand, if you are struggling financially and the stress is affecting your family, the relief of being employed again could outweigh the negative aspects of the position.

ROBERT BUBNOVICH (Irvine, California)

TIP 88 WHEN DIVORCE IS INEVITABLE

Q. What are my financial rights during and after divorce?

A. As soon as divorce comes up, your financial well-being is at risk. Below are several steps you can take to maintain some control over the situation. Whether—and when—you take all of the steps depends on how your household finances are organized, the possibility that your spouse may be taking some of the actions described, and the likelihood that your spouse will follow through with divorce proceedings.

Credit Issues

Check your credit report. Make sure you are aware of all requests for credit, purchases, or loans.

Notify creditors of your situation. Cancel joint credit accounts. Remove your name from the accounts, or have your spouse's name removed from the account if it will be your responsibility. For accounts that must be in both your names (utilities, mortgage, and the like) contact the creditor and ask to be notified directly if a payment is missed.

Establish credit in your name alone. If you haven't already done so, establish credit in your own name right away. That will help you build the good personal credit history you'll need to make major purchases or even to rent an apartment.

Open an individual bank account. Move an appropriate amount of your joint funds into your new personal account to prevent your spouse from withdrawing all of your funds without your knowledge.

Get copies of your past income tax returns. You will need copies for at least the last five years. Put them in a safe place. Also, get copies of other key financial information such as loan agreements, bank statements, brokerage statements, and creditor statements.

Understand the Legal Situation

Please understand that a divorce court's task is determining a property settlement that is fair and equitable to both spouses. However, the definition of *fair and equitable* is very much open to interpretation by the judge in most cases. Many people who live in community-property states are under the mistaken assumption that all marital property is divided 50/50 between the two spouses. This is not so. The judge has latitude to divide the property in an unequal fashion, depending on their own view of a fair and equitable settlement. Clearly, how your situation is presented to the judge can make a huge difference in the outcome of the property settlement.

Protect Yourself in a Number of Ways

When you realize that the divorce is inevitable, hire a competent attorney with significant divorce experience. You also may want to consider a collaborative divorce if you and your spouse are parting on good terms. This is a new dispute resolution model in which specially trained lawyers represent each side with the intent to find a win-win solution to the legitimate needs of both parties. If unsuccessful, the divorcing parties can go to court to determine the appropriate division of property. For more information, see http://www.collaborativedivorce.com.

Consider Your Standard of Living

Most likely, you won't be able to maintain your previous standard of living after the divorce, so start to prepare now by adjusting your budget accordingly. Make sure the financial projections for your budget consider the impact of inflation over time. If not, you may underestimate the share of property you will need to maintain your agreed-upon lifestyle.

Visit a Financial Professional

Strongly consider as part of your divorce team a financial professional who specializes in helping divorcing parties achieve an equitable financial settlement.

You may want your attorney actually to contract with the financial professional, because this may extend attorney-client privilege to conversations, memos, and work products of the financial professional. Make sure that your financial professional has the knowledge and skills specific to the financial aspects of divorce—for example, that they have earned the Certified Divorce Financial Analyst credential, administered by the Institute for Divorce Financial Analysts (http://www.institutedfa.com).

GLENN A. BISHOP, CDFA, CMA, MBA (Carrollton, Texas)

TIP 89 DIVORCE AND YOUR MONEY

Q. How can I protect my financial interests during divorce?

A. Going through divorce is a very stressful experience. You might often feel a desire to rush and get it over with, but you have to stay rational and make some very important financial decisions. They will impact your life for many years to come.

Key Issues

A few of the issues that you must address include the following:

- How to divide property
- What is considered separate and what is marital property
- What will happen to the house
- How to determine the need for alimony
- How much child support you need—or your spouse can afford to pay
- Who gets custody of the kids
- The value of your spouse's pension or retirement plan
- Who is responsible for the credit card debt
- How you divide your investment portfolio
- The value of your spouse's business
- Whether you get any Social Security benefits if you never worked outside the home

To emerge from this "money crazy time" as a winner, you must hire the right professional help and develop a financially focused attitude. What you keep matters, not what you get. Your main objective should be to get an equitable, fair property division, not necessarily a 50/50 split.

Some Helpful Tips

Try to settle out of court. If you go to court, the divorce will take longer and cost more, and a complete stranger, the judge, will have wide discretion in making decisions affecting your financial future.

Secure your financial well-being. Do your homework. If you're not comfortable handling financial issues, engage a qualified financial professional for help.

The moment you realize that the marriage is over, start protecting your financial interests as detailed in Tip 88. And don't forget to take inventory (including photos) of the contents of your joint safe-deposit box. If you're afraid that your spouse will empty it, get a restraining order from the court and give a copy to the bank.

Prepare for the Settlement

Create net worth and cash flow statements. Hire qualified professionals to appraise your assets and evaluate the tax consequences and risks of keeping or giving up certain property. Women usually have an emotional attachment to the house and want to keep it, while men hate to give up their pensions and/or investments. Make sure that you understand all costs attached to the assets you want to keep, and determine if you will have enough liquid assets to cover those costs. The worst thing would be to get the house, only to find that you can't afford to keep it.

Make a list of all the items you want the settlement agreement to cover. Chances are that you won't get everything you want, but you can negotiate toward a goal.

Before negotiating, make sure you know where you stand financially. Don't act on an offer or counteroffer until after evaluating its tax and financial consequences. Consider trading property interests of similar value. Decisions about alimony and child support should be made only *after* the property division is finished.

Review all your financial papers (wills, retirement accounts, IRAs, and insurance). After the property division settlement is finalized and the divorce is official, make sure that the beneficiary designations are updated to reflect your desires.

Consider hiring a Certified Financial Planner™ professional who charges by the hour to work with you and your attorney. If you never have been involved in managing your finances, you may be a bit overwhelmed. Expect to pay $100 to $200 an hour for a CFP® practitioner's services.

IANKA TOCHEVA, CFP® (Salem, Massachusetts)

TIP 90 DETERMINING FAIR AND EQUITABLE DIVISION OF ASSETS

Q. Our divorce is now inevitable. What is the best way to divide property and income?

A. It is up to the court to determine a fair and equitable division of property, so put forth your best efforts to ensure that you receive your fair share of property and future income. Below are a few considerations in the division of property.

Pensions

A nonworking spouse typically is entitled to a portion of the pension of a working spouse. The portion of that pension fairly attributable to a nonworking spouse is based on the present value of the future pension, adjusted by the ratio of years worked while married to total years worked. Consult an experienced financial professional, such as a Certified Divorce Financial Analyst, to determine this value and the right documentation for the court and employer. To ensure that the spouse receives a fair share of the pension, the court can issue a Qualified Domestic Relations Order (QDRO), which legally divides the pension into two pieces, with each piece owned by the respective ex-spouse. Without the QDRO executed correctly, the ex-spouse likely will lose all rights to the pension.

Property

Always look at the value of property after any tax implications. Often, property divisions fail to consider tax implications, leaving one spouse with unrealized tax liabilities and less property as a result. For example, if a spouse receives stocks with a low cost basis that have significantly appreciated, significant capital gains taxes will be due when they're sold. Also, consider the expected future tax brackets of each party; it may be more advantageous for one spouse to receive a piece of property at a particular value than it would be for the other spouse, simply because of tax considerations.

Effective tax planning actually can increase the size of the pie to be divided.

Family Business

If a family business is involved, bring in an independent business appraiser to value it.

Any transfer of property incident to a divorce is tax-free, assuming both spouses are U.S. citizens. However, the divorce transfer must either

- occur within one year of the divorce, or
- be pursuant to the divorce decree and occur not more than six years after the divorce.

Alimony

Alimony, sometimes called maintenance, is taxable to the recipient and tax deductible for the payer, while child support is neither deductible by the paying spouse nor taxable to the receiving spouse. To be classified as alimony, the payments must meet the following requirements:

- They are paid via cash, check, or money order.
- They are based on a written court order or separation agreement.
- The couple may not agree that payments do not receive alimony tax treatment.
- Ex-spouses may not reside in the same household.
- Ex-spouses may not file a joint tax return.
- No portion of the proposed alimony payment may be considered child support.

Even though the transfer payments are called alimony in the court order, if they are structured incorrectly, the IRS will identify them as child support payments or a transfer of property.

Health Insurance

Don't overlook the cost of health insurance after a divorce and do factor it into your budget. Once the divorce is final, you're no longer covered under a spouse's health insurance plan. One option is COBRA, a federal law that says an ex-spouse is entitled to health insurance coverage through COBRA for 36 months after the divorce is finalized. The ex-spouse must pay the insurance premium, and this may be expensive. The ex-spouse also needs to be in a position to have replacement insurance once the 36 months expires.

Social Security

An ex-spouse is entitled to Social Security benefits based on the earnings of the prior spouse, if the following is true:

- The higher-earning ex-spouse is entitled to receive Social Security benefits.
- They were married for ten years or more before the divorce became final.
- The lower-earning ex-spouse is not married.
- The lower-earning ex-spouse is age 62 or over.
- The lower-earning ex-spouse is not entitled to a Social Security retirement benefit that equals or exceeds one-half of the higher-earning ex-spouse's benefit.

The higher-earning ex-spouse doesn't have to be retired, either, for the lower-earning ex-spouse to begin receiving retirement benefits. For more information, see the Social Security Web site (http://www.ssa.gov).

Tax Returns

When filing your income tax return, marital status is determined on the last day of the tax year. For example, if your divorce is final on December 30, you're not eligible to file a joint income tax return for that year. However, you may qualify for head-of-household status, which can reduce your income tax if the following is true:

- You are not married at the end of the year or have lived apart from your spouse for the last six months of the year.
- You pay more than half of the costs to maintain the household.
- A child who qualifies as a dependent lives with you for more than half the year.

Alimony counts as earned income and therefore can be contributed to an IRA. Child support does not count as earned income and cannot be contributed to an IRA.

Maintaining Good Credit

Continue to monitor your credit history status on an annual basis to ensure that there's no incorrect information or unlawful activity by someone else.

GLENN A. BISHOP, CDFA, CMA, MBA (Carrollton, Texas)

TIP 91 VIATICAL SETTLEMENTS CAN HELP THE TERMINALLY ILL, BUT WEIGH ALL YOUR OPTIONS FIRST

Q. I have just learned that I am terminally ill. My doctor expects me to live another 6 to 12 months. What options do I have to pay my medical bills and replace my income now that I can no longer work?

A. If you have life insurance and have been diagnosed as terminally ill, one option may be to sell the policy to a viatical settlement provider.

What Is a Viatical Settlement?

When you sell your life insurance policy to a viatical settlement company, in exchange for all the rights and obligations under your life insurance policy, you receive a lump-sum cash payment that is a percentage of the face value of your policy (usually 40 to 85 percent). The settlement company then can sell the policy to a third party who buys it as an investment. The investor makes money on the difference between the policy's face value and the amount you will receive.

The investor continues to pay the premiums on your policy until you die and the policy benefits are paid to the investor.

In general, the amount you will receive if you are *terminally ill* is not subject to federal income tax. If the diagnosis were *chronically ill*, then the settlement also would not be subject to federal income tax, as long as you use the funds to pay for long-term care services.

Eligibility for Viatical Settlements

Each viatical settlement company sets its own rules for determining which life insurance policies it will buy. Most viatical companies will require the following:

- You have owned your policy for at least two years.
- Your current beneficiary signs a release or a waiver.
- You are terminally ill (some companies require a life expectancy of two years or less, while others may buy your policy even if your life expectancy is four years).
- You sign a release allowing the viatical settlement provider access to your medical records.

If your employer provides your life insurance policy, purchasers will want to know if it can be converted into an individual policy or otherwise be guaranteed to remain in force.

How to Choose a Viatical Settlement Provider

In most states, the viatical settlement providers must be registered or licensed by the department of insurance to do business. Some states forbid the practice of selling viatical settlements. The National Association of Insurance Commissioners' Web site (http://www.naic.org/state_contacts/sid_websites.htm) can help you find licensed settlement providers in your area. You can also find out if there are any complaints or fraud cases pending against a viatical settlement company.

Here are a few things to keep in mind if you're shopping for a viatical settlement.

- Contact two or three viatical settlement companies and compare their discounts. Generally speaking, the shorter your life expectancy, the greater percentage of the face value of the policy you should receive.
- Check with your state insurance department to see if viatical settlement companies and their brokers must be licensed and if they are in good standing with your state's insurance commission.
- Do not fall for high-pressure sales tactics and too-good-to-be-true promises. Make sure that the viatical settlement company has the money for your payout readily available. Insist that the company set up an escrow account with a reputable, independent, third-party financial institution to deposit the funds used for your offer. Do not sign any paperwork until the money is in the escrow account. Insist on a timely payment. Once the life insurance company has completed its work, you should get your money in two to three business days from the escrow agent.
- Ask about privacy. Potential investors can make a decision about your viatical case without your name and personal information.
- Consult an attorney to discuss possible probate and estate considerations.

Alternatives to a Viatical Settlement

Viatical settlement transactions require time. They can also be complex legal and financial matters. Your physician as well as the insurance company and your financial advisors will all be getting involved. Sometimes the entire process can run up to four months or longer.

You may wish to consider these options.

- Use any accumulated cash value already in the life insurance policy (if it is a whole life, universal life, or variable life policy).

- Borrow money from the original beneficiary of your life policy. They will get the money that they lend you back when they receive the death benefit.
- Some life insurance companies offer "accelerated death benefits" directly to you in return for increased premium payments or a reduced final death benefit to the original beneficiary.
- Sell other financial assets, such as equity investments, or liquidate retirement accounts. While this approach may sound drastic, when you do the math, you may find that you come out further ahead with this strategy.

While you will have a lot of things weighing heavily on your mind right now—and you may feel as if you do not have the energy to focus on financial matters—you should take the proper amount of time to educate yourself regarding all your options. The choices that you make about your life insurance benefits can affect the people you love. Before you make any decisions about a viatical settlement, talk it over with your family and friends. Also, talk to a reliable third party who has no financial stake in your decision such as a lawyer, an accountant, or a financial planner.

PATRICK VAN NICE, CFP® (West Des Moines, Iowa)

TIP 92 MANAGING AN INHERITANCE OR OTHER LUMP SUM

Q. My mother has passed away and willed my siblings and me $125,000 each. I have never had this much extra money in my life. What should I do with it?

A. The time to start planning is when you first know about the inheritance. An inheritance is usually a once-in-a-lifetime opportunity. Use the opportunity to improve your financial picture. Whether you have inherited money or won the lottery, you will be faced with some big decisions. Initially, your first response will probably be: "What can I buy, or what should I pay off?" Do not react to that first response. Take some time to think about what is really important to you.

Possible Pitfalls

Squandering the money. Forget the Alaskan family cruise, kitchen remodel, or house full of new furniture. Three months later, you'd be left with $25,000, having squandered the opportunity for a potential early retirement.

Delusions of wealth. You inherit the $125,000 and decide to quit your job or jump to a wealthier lifestyle. A few months later, you discover you cannot sustain your new lifestyle. You've just missed the opportunity for a better life.

Debt drag. Paying off debt, especially credit cards, with the $125,000 can leave you in deeper trouble. That's because, if you clean up your credit but don't change your spending habits, you will be right back into debt again, dipping into the inheritance over and over until it's gone.

Avoiding investment responsibilities. Just because your father held the $125,000 in stock for years and your mother didn't do anything with it, either, doesn't mean that these investments are right for you. Investments held by an older person are not always appropriate for a younger person and may need to be repositioned. Do so, or you risk the opportunity to fully maximize the investments for your personal objectives.

Not considering future value. What could that $125,000 be worth if you invested it? It depends on your rate of return. The following table shows some examples.

Watch an Inheritance Grow!

Return on Investment	10 years	20 years
5%	$203,611	$331,662
6%	$245,894	$483,711
7%	$295,920	$700,551

What Should You Do?

After notification of an inheritance, distribution generally takes time. Use that extra time to prepare or update your financial plan.

First, list your goals and dreams. Rate them by order of importance, and ask yourself if having money helps accomplish them.

It may be in your best interest to hire a third party, such as a financial advisor, to help you work through this self-examination process. The third party can give you guidance and also provide you with a reality check.

Here are some additional thoughts on how to approach your inheritance. Let's assume that you are working, raising a family, and carrying typical family debts and obligations.

How to Properly Manage an Inheritance

On a $50,000 inheritance, consider paying off credit cards first, then investing the remainder of these funds for your retirement. Your life won't change much, but you will feel more relaxed. Remember: Watch your spending. You don't want to end up in debt again. If you're itching to buy something or want to have some fast fun, spend 5 percent of the inheritance on that.

On a $250,000 inheritance, you may be able to afford a few extras, like a family vacation or eating out more often, while preserving most of the money for your retirement fund. Consider paying off your credit card debts and your house only if you can control your spending. Control the urge to purchase new vehicles, furniture, and other wish list items. They may make your life more comfortable but will not add to your long-term financial picture. Do not quit your job unless you also have significant investments outside of the inheritance.

On a $1 million inheritance, you might be able to quit working, depending on your age; make a career change; or increase your standard of living. Larger inheritances usually come with a team of advisors to help you out. Still, it's up to you to evaluate whether that inherited team is right for you.

COLLEEN M. MILLER, CPA, JD, CFP® (Windsor, Colorado)

TIP 93 FINAL ARRANGEMENTS—PREPARING YOUR FAMILY

Q. How can I make my funeral easier for my family?

A. The best way to ease your family's stress level in the event of your death is to prearrange as much as possible. Go to the local funeral home, sign a contract with the details, and provide enough money to pay for your funeral.

Like most people, you probably haven't thought much about arrangements for your death. But if you don't know what you want, how can your family possibly know?

You Can't Be Too Prepared

Consider visiting a helpful Web site, http://www.funeralplan.com/funeralplan/preneed/personalplan.html. It has an online worksheet for planning a funeral. Fill it out, and discuss it with your family. Help them fill out one as well.

Then, completed worksheet in hand, visit providers and compare prices. Consider signing a preneed contract that outlines all the details of the services you desire and locks in current prices. This can spare your family at least part of the ordeal.

End Note$

Following are some helpful books to check out:

- *Widowed: Beginning Again Personally and Financially,* by Sharon Trusty and Barry Corkern (August House Publishing, 1999)
- *The Widow's Resource,* by Julie Calligaro (Women's Source Books, 1997)
- *Suddenly Single: Money Skills for Divorcees and Widows,* by Kerry Hannon (Wiley, 1998)

SHERYL GARRETT, CFP® (Shawnee Mission, Kansas)

TIP 94 FINAL ARRANGEMENTS—COSTS FOR FUNERAL SERVICES AND GOODS

Q. What is the average cost of a funeral? How can I control the costs?

A. The average cost for funeral-related services in the United States is approximately $6,200, according to the funeral industry. The good news is that you can comparison shop. The bad news is that the funeral will cost more than you planned.

Federal regulations, specifically the Funeral Rule, set minimum standards for state laws governing fair-trade practices in the funeral industry. For information about the rule, visit the Federal Trade Commission Web site (http://www.ftc.gov/bcp/conline/pubs/buspubs/funeral.htm).

The Most Important Provision

Funeral providers must provide a general price list to anyone who asks, in person, about funeral goods, services, and the prices of such goods and services. It must be a copy you can keep, and the list allows you to comparison shop from one provider to another. The list must be offered at the beginning of any face-to-face discussion on the following topics:

- The type of funeral or disposition of remains
- The goods and services that the particular provider offers
- The provider's prices for goods and services

The only exception to this rule is if the provider is transporting the deceased and only asks for permission to embalm (then no general price list is required to be provided). The provider must, however, disclose if embalming is required by law—it usually is not required.

Services Performed by Funeral Providers

Funeral providers, in general, obtain all the funeral goods you require: flowers, prayer cards, flags, etc. They generally advance monies to subcontractors for these goods (or they pay after the fact) and bill you in one large invoice.

Funeral services include the following:

- Services used to care for and prepare bodies for burial, cremation, or other final disposition
- Services used to arrange, supervise, or conduct the funeral ceremony or final disposition of human remains

In addition, many funeral directors perform personal and financial services such as helping you file forms, notify the Veterans Administration and Social Security Administration, or make reservations for a family dinner at a local restaurant. Funeral directors also obtain the necessary copies of death certificates (but be careful—you may be able to do this more cheaply on your own if you need many copies). Ask potential providers what other services they might be able to provide and for what price.

SHERYL GARRETT, CFP® (Shawnee Mission, Kansas)

Chapter

7

INVESTING

TIP 95 INVESTMENT MISTAKES TO AVOID

Q. I have heard about conflicts of interest on Wall Street and about people who lost their life savings on bad investments. What advice can you offer about avoiding investing pitfalls?

A. This question is very important. The following tips should help you avoid the most common mistakes that people make with their investments.

Mistake 1: Not Diversifying

To safeguard against problems should the industry or a specific company run into economic problems, don't keep more than about 10 percent of your total investments in any one stock, including your employer's stock.

Don't put all your eggs in one basket. For most people, true diversification means investing in mutual funds, not individual stocks, and in spreading your money across various asset classes: stocks, bonds, international investments, and real estate (including Real Estate Investment Trusts, a primary residence, and investment property).

Mistake 2: Not Controlling Costs

Unnecessary costs reduce investment returns. Do your own research on no-load, low-cost investment vehicles, or get advice from a fee-only financial advisor.

Mistake 3: Paying Too Much Attention to Short-Term Results

Which would you prefer: to know where the stock market will be in six months or six years? The smartest investors choose the longer-term outlook. Don't let the day-to-day market fluctuations mesmerize you; avoid the urge to buy "hot" stocks, last year's winning mutual fund, or this year's trendy sector fund; and don't expect some investment guru's newsletter to help you time the market's ups and downs. Last year's hero may become this year's embarrassment. Unfortunately, this happens frequently.

Fluctuations in market value—including periodic bear markets—are a normal part of equity investing. Time in the market, not market timing, is one key to long-term investment success.

Mistake 4: Not Sticking to Your Plan

If you have a well-thought-out, long-term plan, don't get discouraged and abandon it after a market decline. You will lose out. You and/or your advisor should monitor your results on a quarterly and annual basis, but investment decisions should be made in a rational, unemotional way.

Once you have made your portfolio decisions and set your asset allocation, stay the course until your goals and/or personal situation change. If the allocation percentages get out of balance, rebalance your holdings to bring the portfolio back to its proper weightings.

Mistake 5: Ignoring Tax Consequences

Some investments (usually actively managed funds or investments that would generate capital gains taxes) are best sheltered in tax-advantaged accounts like 401(k)s and IRAs. Other tax-efficient investments, like index mutual funds and municipal bonds, can be held in taxable accounts. However, don't pay too much in account or policy costs just to defer taxes on the gains within these investments; for example, you do just that when you buy a high-cost variable annuity.

Mistake 6: Ignoring Investment History

Although history does not necessarily repeat itself, there are patterns worth watching. The run-up, then collapse, of the Internet and technology bubble was just the most recent in a long line of boom/bust cycles. Studying historical trends can help you understand market cycles and volatility.

Mistake 7: Allowing Emotion to Rule

Investing is about discipline—having a well-researched plan and sticking to it through thick and thin. Get-rich-quick or hit-it-big schemes are for casinos, not your investments.

Mistake 8: Not Protecting against Change in the Current Economic Climate

Interest rates, investment values, and inflation rates can change fairly quickly. While trade-offs are inevitable (risk/reward equations), a sound financial plan should seek to protect your principal and enhance your real rate of return throughout various economic conditions. Depending on individual circumstances and personal objectives, a diversified portfolio might include stocks and stock mutual funds, bonds and bond mutual funds, domestic and international equities, real estate and real estate investment trusts, and natural resources. When one investment zigs, the others may zag.

Mistake 9: Not Saving Enough for Retirement

Your retirement may last for 35 to 40 years. You can't depend on Social Security, so you need to build a substantial nest egg that takes into account variables like taxes, inflation, and exorbitant health care costs, to name a few.

The amount you need to save on a systematic basis will depend on your age, your expected life span, the current market value of your assets, and your personal goals and objectives. While younger individuals may be able to fund a comfortable retirement by starting early and saving approximately 10 percent of their gross annual income, older individuals who need to catch up on retirement savings may need to bank 50 percent or more of their take-home pay.

Also, be sure to take advantage of 401(k), 403(b), and other employer-sponsored retirement plans, especially if your employer matches your contributions. Other tax-advantaged accounts like IRAs and Roth IRAs can play a role in building a sound retirement plan. The self-employed have other specialized retirement planning options available. Don't overlook or underutilize these tax-advantaged, wealth-building tools.

ROGER STREIT, MBA (Montclair, New Jersey)

TIP 96 GETTING INTO THE SAVING HABIT

Q. I have a good job, but I do not know where the money goes. I never have anything left at the end of the month. How can I save anything?

A. It seems impossible for some folks to save money. The problem is legitimate when paying for basics like food, clothing, and shelter takes every penny. But most people truly can save if they remove the emotional and psychological roadblocks. All it takes is a change in actions and attitudes. Forget negative thoughts such as, "I'm not smart enough to learn about money," or, "I deserve it now; I do not want to wait." They're an excuse to procrastinate.

The Good News

Fortunately, most limiting thoughts aren't true but result simply from lack of confidence and knowledge. With knowledge comes understanding and power to make things happen. Small successes give way to big successes, and you begin to save more and more. Eventually, you save enough to achieve your dreams.

Where to Begin

Begin with some basic rules of saving. Start small to achieve those small successes and learn that you really can do it. Then build up to bigger things.

- *Make a realistic budget.* Work hard to stay within this budget. In a family, everyone needs to participate in setting it up, then hold weekly or monthly progress meetings. Reward yourselves with a little something special for making it work.
- *Spend less than you earn.* Doing so will create short-term, if not permanent, changes in your lifestyle. Commit to the changes and learn the difference between something you need versus something you want.
- *Set savings targets.* Create a savings plan. Start simply to build your confidence. Determine a realistic amount for a specific time period, and have a goal in mind for your savings.

- *Make savings automatic.* Arrange for your bank, credit union, and/or mutual fund automatically to deduct a specific amount from your checking account each month. Also, sign up for automatic payroll deductions.
- *Think of savings accounts as untouchable except for targeted goals.* Don't use them for anything except true emergencies. Stick to your budget, savings plan, and goals.

MARY L. GIBSON, CFP® (San Juan Bautista, California)

TIP 97 THE SOONER YOU BEGIN SAVING AND INVESTING, THE WEALTHIER YOU CAN BE

Q. I have many important, long-term goals I want to work toward. What's the value of investing early?

A. This is a great question, one that more people would do well to ask. To illustrate the value of investing early, here is a true story. As with so many things, historical events can also teach us much about investing success.

A Lesson from the Dutch Colonists and American Indians

Back in the 1620s, Dutch colonists settled in an area of the New World that they called New Netherlands. On May 6, 1626, the newly appointed director of The Dutch West Indies Company, Peter Minuit, convened the chiefs of several nearby Indian tribes to buy the island that today is Manhattan. The Indians relinquished portions of the island to the colonists in exchange for cloth, hatchets, and other trinkets valued at about $24. Thus, one of the major bargains in history was made. Today, the 14,000 acres of Manhattan are worth approximately $51 billion. Sounds like a fortune, until you realize that, hypothetically, if the Indians had invested that $24 at 6 percent, today it would be worth $83 billion. That's a whopping $32 billion more than the land at today's market value. That's the value of long-term investing.

A Lesson from Twins

Consider Debbie and Tom, fraternal twins and recent high school graduates. Debbie works part-time while attending college and saves $2,000 a year, which she invests in her Individual Retirement Account. She does that every year until she is 25 years old, for a total investment of $14,000.

Her brother, Tom, meanwhile, also works and attends school, but he doesn't start investing in an IRA until he's 25. Then he faithfully invests $2,000 a year for the next 40 years for a total investment of $80,000.

Both Debbie and Tom's accounts earn 10 percent per year. At age 65, Tom has $893,704 while Debbie has $930,641. Yet Debbie only invested $14,000 while Tom invested $80,000. The value of starting early is obvious.

If Debbie had started investing $2,000 per year at age 14 to 19, that $10,000 IRA investment would be worth $1,174,600 when she turned 65. Wherever you are in saving for your future, it's never too late to start—but the sooner, the better.

DAVID R. DELEEUW (Kalamazoo, Michigan)

TIP 98 INVESTING EARLY PAYS OFF—HOW TO MEASURE YOUR INVESTMENTS' REAL RATE OF RETURN

Q. Please help me determine how long it will take my $500 to grow to $1,000. I want to make a deposit and then leave my money alone until it has doubled in value. Also, how can I measure my rate of return if I also factor in inflation and taxes?

A. Here are three useful concepts help determine the required rate of return on your money to accomplish your objectives. The first is The Rule of 72; the second, Real Rate of return, and the third, Tax-Adjusted Returns. The Rule of 72 is easy to figure out, but the other two are a bit more complicated, so you may want to check with a financial advisor for help.

Rule of 72

Compound interest is the greatest mathematical discovery of all time.

—ALBERT EINSTEIN

The Rule of 72 is related to the powerful concept of compound interest and is a simple way to tell how long it will take your money to double in value. Simply divide 72 by an interest rate to determine the number of years it will take your money to double. For example, assume you earn a 6 percent real rate of return on your money. How long will it take for $500 to grow to $1,000?

72 ÷ 6 percent = 12 years

Based on the Rule of 72, here's a look at how long it will take to double your money, depending on the interest rate that an investment earns.

Interest rate	Years to double money
1%	72.0
2	36.0
3	24.0
4	18.0
5	14.0
6	12.0
7	10.3
8	9.0
9	8.0
10	7.2
11	6.5
12	6.0
13	5.5
14	5.1
15	4.8

Real Rate of Return (Adjusted for Inflation) and Tax-Adjusted Return

Inflation eats away at your purchasing power, so your investments must work hard and smart. The real returns on your investments are the earnings that exceed the rate of inflation. An investment with a low rate of return actually could have no real growth or even negative growth after adjusting for inflation and taxes. Or the after-tax yield on a municipal bond could be higher than that of a corporate bond, even though the corporate bond carries a higher stated rate of return. Smart investors know that it's not what you make but what you keep that makes the difference. Only after taxes, inflation, and other investment costs have been subtracted, can you ascertain your real rate of return.

PATRICK VAN NICE, CFP® (West Des Moines, Iowa)

TIP 99 FUNDING AN INVESTMENT PROGRAM THAT'S RIGHT FOR YOUR POCKETBOOK

Q. Because I don't have a lot of money to invest, I don't meet the account minimums set by many brokerages and investment firms. How can I start my investment program?

A. Options abound for starting an investment program with limited funds (usually less than $1,000).

Direct Stock Purchases and DRIPS

Direct stock purchases and dividend reinvestment plans are an excellent method to invest in individual stocks with little up-front money. More than 1,200 companies allow small, monthly purchases of their stock directly with no commission costs. In addition, your dividends can be reinvested without charge. Among those companies: Intel, Pepsi, Johnson & Johnson, Texaco, Chevron, Proctor & Gamble, Exxon, and McDonalds.

To find out more, you can call the Direct Stock Purchase Plan Clearinghouse (800-774-4117) or visit its Web site (http://www.dripinvestor.com). The primary disadvantage with direct stock purchase plans, however, is the lack of diversity in your portfolio; so be sure to diversify your holdings in other ways.

Mutual Funds

Mutual funds are pooled investments that can provide instant diversification. Many fund companies also offer low-cost investing; however, most funds have minimum initial purchase requirements of $500 to $1,000 and up. Those minimums usually are lower for shares purchased for your IRA ($250 and up) or through automatic investment plans ($25 a month and up).

A few sources to help you find low-cost mutual funds include the following:

- *Money* magazine (http://www.moneymag.com). Use the search tool, then click on Mutual Funds.
- *Mutual Funds Investors Center* (http://www.mfea.com). You can screen for "funds for less than $50."

Company-Sponsored Plans

A great way to invest painlessly and inexpensively and build tax-deferred wealth is through company-sponsored plans like 401(k)s. For the self-employed and very small businesses, SEPs and SIMPLEs are popular. Mutual funds are the investment vehicle of choice in most plans, thus adding a measure of safety through diversification. In addition, because you are investing a percentage of your pay, you can invest as little as 1 percent.

Discount Brokerages

Specialized low-cost discount brokerages offer another option for starting with less than $100. Two such companies are ShareBuilder (http://www.sharebuilder.com) and BUYandHOLD (http://www.buyandhold.com). Most discount brokerages have lots of options for mutual fund investors, including No-Transaction-Fee (NTF) funds. Keep in mind, though, that the fees to purchase mutual funds that are not part of the broker's NTF program often range from about $15 per trade to more than $100, depending on the size of the investment. One company that has no transaction fees, provides access to all the funds on its platform, and charges a minimal annual custodial fee is FTJ Fund Choice (http://www.ftjfundchoice.com).

While you may feel as if investing little bits of money is not worth the bother, doing so, carefully and over time, can add up. Everyone must start somewhere, so get started now.

MAHLON EDWARDS, AAMS (Las Vegas, Nevada)

TIP 100 USING BENCHMARKS CAN HELP YOU EVALUATE PORTFOLIO PERFORMANCE

Q. I am investing regularly. How do I know if I am getting good results?

A. Successful investing requires an evaluation of the performance of your investments every six to twelve months. You should do this to make sure your investment strategy is on track. Too often this evaluation boils down to a simple, "If my portfolio is up, then I'm doing well, and if it's down, then I'm disappointed." A more reliable, objective way to measure your returns is to use benchmarks.

Definitions of Benchmark

The word *benchmark* was originally used to describe a mark a surveyor made to indicate a specific height above sea level. In the language of investing, a benchmark has come to mean an index or average against which a group of other securities can be compared. An *index,* then, is usually a group of individual securities that have been selected to stand as a proxy for a whole category of securities (for instance, international securities or large-cap domestic).

Common Benchmarks for Stocks

The idea to use an index as a benchmark is not new. In fact, it was for this purpose that Charles Dow developed the Dow Jones Industrial Average (DJIA) in 1896. At that time, what has become the DJIA was comprised of 12 of the biggest companies in the United States. Today, it includes 30 of the largest and most influential blue-chip companies in the country and is the most widely recognized financial index in the world. You will often hear it referred to as "The Market" in the media. While well known, the Dow Jones has a shortcoming in that it includes only 30 of the thousands of public companies in America.

The Standard and Poor's 500 Index (also referred to as the S&P 500) is becoming more popular as the benchmark of choice for the U.S. stock market. It includes the 500 most widely held companies and covers all major industries in the economy, including transportation and utilities, which are absent from the DJIA. Its 500 companies represent about 70 percent of the U.S. market, and its performance is considered to be a solid barometer of overall market performance.

The growing interest in technology and other high-growth companies has resulted in more attention for an index that was created in 1971, The Nasdaq Composite Index. Unlike the DJIA or the S&P 500, this index includes all of the more than 4,000 companies that trade on the Nasdaq exchange. Because these companies tend to be more speculative and risky, the index tends to be more volatile than the other broad indexes.

While these three indexes may be the best known and most widely followed, there are many others: The Wilshire 5000 and the Russell 2000, for example. The Wilshire 5000, which despite its name contains over 6,500 stocks traded in the United States, is sometimes considered a "total market index." The Russell 2000, on the other hand, focuses on small-cap companies and thus includes only those firms with market capitalizations of no more than $550 million. There are many more: Foreign and regional stock indexes, sector indexes, and—okay, you get the picture.

Steps to Assess Performance of Your Portfolio

- Determine your long-term financial goals, such as paying for a college education for your kids, or funding your retirement.
- Carefully evaluate your tolerance for risk.
- Allocate your assets.
- Identify an index that has a close correlation to each asset class of your investment portfolio.
- Assume that the best you will do over time is what the market does over the same period. Eighty percent of the efforts to beat the market fail.

- At least once a year, measure the returns on your portfolio against those of the index that most accurately reflects its components. If the performance is as good as or better than the benchmark, you are on track. If the performance falls short of the benchmark, consider changing the investments that correspond to that asset class.

Simplify the Investment Process with Index Funds

Mutual funds that have been designed to mimic the performance of an asset class are called *index funds.* For instance, if you want to invest in large-cap U.S. stocks, instead of picking individual companies, buy an index mutual fund that holds the same stocks as the S&P 500.

Mistakes to Avoid

- *Be careful not to use a benchmark that does not correlate to a particular asset class in your portfolio.* Using a small-cap index such as the Russell 2000 to assess your returns from a portfolio comprised of the large-cap stocks such as GE, Microsoft, Proctor & Gamble, Boeing, Wal-Mart, Coca-Cola, Merck, Amgen, and 3M—or a large-cap balanced mutual fund—will tell you little and will likely mislead you because the historical performance of large-cap stocks is quite different from that of small-cap stocks. Instead, measure this group of large-cap value and growth stocks against the S&P 500 Index.
- *Watch the highs and the lows.* If your mid-cap value fund is returning 9.3 percent over the past 12 months, but your mid-cap value benchmark is up 11.1 percent, it is not time for you to be celebrating. You may want to make a change if the returns of your mid-cap assets keep lagging behind the benchmark. Conversely, if your mid-cap value fund is returning 17.1 percent over the past 12 months, and you mid-cap value benchmark is only up 5.1 percent, you should check the underlying sectors and industries that the mutual fund manager is investing in. Overperformance like this is usually due to what is called *style drifting*—which, in this case, may mean that the manager could be investing in growth stocks—something you may or may not want in your portfolio at that time and in that weighting.

End Note$

Most major metropolitan newspapers have a finance section where they print daily, quarterly, and/or year-to-date index performance. *USA Today, The*

Wall Street Journal, Barrons, Investors' Business Daily, and other financial dailies are also a good resource.

In addition, here are some Web sites you may wish to visit for benchmark information:

- http://www.factset.com/www_23.asp
- http://www.morningstar.com
- http://www.lipperweb.com/daily.shtml
- http://www.russell.com/ww/indexes/default.asp

JOHN GODDARD (Seattle, Washington)

TIP 101 PORTFOLIO DESIGN CAN REDUCE VOLATILITY AND RISK

Q. What is asset allocation, and how can it make me a better investor?

A. Asset allocation is the process of determining which asset classes (stocks, real estate, bonds, cash, and more) should be represented, and in what proportions, in your investment portfolio. It's a critical part of the financial planning process but often is ignored in favor of sexier stock picking or a broker's hot tip-du-jour.

Importance of Asset Allocation

Research shows that more than 90 percent of the variation in investment returns among pension plan portfolios comes from the choice and weighting of asset classes, not from stock selection or market timing.

Asset allocation is rooted in the principles of modern portfolio theory, which de-emphasizes individual security analysis and selection, instead focusing on how broad asset classes perform and how closely their long-term returns correlate with each other. If the returns of a particular asset class zig when those of others zag, including it in a portfolio can help reduce volatility and improve returns over time.

Factors in Asset Allocation Decisions

Figuring out your portfolio's asset allocation depends on your unique circumstances like age, time horizon, financial goals, and tolerance for investment risk. Allocation decisions also can be influenced by more transitory factors like market valuations, interest rates, and economic conditions. A portfolio's asset mix will change over time, too, as circumstances change.

Maintaining Allocations with Periodic Review and Rebalancing

Review your portfolio's allocation and rebalance it, if necessary, on a regular basis, usually annually. Wherever possible, rebalance with tax consequences in mind.

End Note$

At its core, asset allocation involves developing a formal investment strategy to achieve your financial objectives. It plays a critical role in your financial plan and provides a framework in which to make objective, unemotional portfolio decisions. It may not be the way to immediate, exceptional returns, but it is the proven way toward long-term wealth accumulation.

ANDY CLAYBROOK, CPA/PFS, CFP® (Franklin, Tennessee), **BRYAN TOTRI,** CFP® (Roswell, Georgia), and **STEVEN YOUNG,** CFP® (Springfield, Missouri)

TIP 102 ASSET ALLOCATION PRINCIPLES AND INVESTING FUNDAMENTALS

Q. I'm ready to start investing. How do I decide how to allocate my portfolio?

A. Taking time now to put together your investment strategy can help you avoid mistakes and move forward with greater confidence.

To determine the right portfolio mix for you, start by asking three questions.

1. How long is my investment horizon?
2. What is my tolerance for risk?
3. What are my financial objectives?

Time Horizon

Your investment time horizon, or when the money will be needed, is important because of the risk or volatility of equities (stocks). Over the longer term, investors generally can assume more risk and thus allocate more of a portfolio to stocks. Here's a potential guideline for an investor's maximum equity exposure.

Time Horizon	Maximum Equity Allocation
0–3 years	0%
4–5 years	20
6 years	30
7 years	40
8 years	50
9 years	60
10 years	70
11+ years	80

Risk Tolerance

Risk tolerance is how you feel and react when the value of your investments declines. For example, let's assume that you have allocated 70 percent of your portfolio to stocks and regularly add to your account. This year, you watched the bear market take 30 percent of your stocks' value. Can you continue to invest the new dollars needed to maintain your 70 percent allocation to equities, while at the same time watching the value of your portfolio go down? Over longer periods of time (10 to 20 years), history has shown that stocks outperform all other asset classes, so a well-thought-out investment plan can help you stay the course during the market's ups and downs. You want to avoid making emotionally based decisions that will hurt your portfolio's performance over the long run. Here's a guideline to help you determine the right percentage of equity exposure for you based on your risk tolerance.

Maximum Tolerable Loss	Maximum Equity Exposure
5%	20%
10	30
15	40
20	50
25	60
30	70
35	80
40	90
50	100

If you factor the tolerable loss in with the investment time horizon that we discussed above, the lower of the two percentages should be your portfolio's equity allocation.

Financial Objectives

Finally, what are your financial objectives, and how much potential risk will you likely need to take on to reach them? Sometimes, the amount of money you need drives the amount of risk or equity exposure you will take on. For example, if, based on the number of years to retirement, you need an 8 percent return on your investment, roughly 60 percent of your portfolio should be allocated to equities. Would you still be able to sleep at night while taking this kind of risk with your money?

If the risk to achieve the return is more than you can stomach, but you don't want to reduce your retirement spending plan, the options are to increase your savings or delay your retirement date (or some combination of the two) to make up for the lower expected return that comes with taking less risk. The other alternative would be to accept a reduced retirement income.

The following table shows historical (1926–2000) annualized returns for a portfolio composed of various percentages of equities and treasuries.

Portfolio Allocations % Equities/% Treasuries	Return
80/20	8.87%
70/30	8.28
60/40	7.92
50/50	7.24
40/60	6.70
30/70	6.00
20/80	5.31

Here's a look at the historical returns of the S&P 500 and Treasury bills over five-year periods since 1972.

5-Year Period	**S&P 500**	**T-Bills**
1998–2002	–0.6%	4.2%
1993–1997	20.2	4.6
1988–1992	15.9	6.3
1983–1987	16.5	7.6
1978–1982	14.0	10.8
1972–1977	4.9	5.8

SOURCE: Ibbotson Associates

End Note$

Over the long term, returns on volatile assets like stocks can average out, even though considerable swings may occur over the short term. If you develop a good game plan and stick with it, you have the potential to be rewarded.

KAREN F. NORMAN, CFP® (Troy, Michigan)

TIP 103 TRYING TO TIME THE MARKET CAN BE HAZARDOUS TO YOUR PORTFOLIO'S HEALTH

Q. A friend says they have had great returns over the past year because they know how to get in and out of the market. Is this an investment strategy I should follow?

A. Over the years, "proven strategies to time the market" have been more numerous than sightings of Elvis. Unfortunately, both are myths based on little more than the hopes of investors (and fans).

Market Timing

Market timing involves moving in and out of stocks based on some measurement of whether current prices are too high or too low. It can also refer to the shifting of assets to various sectors of the market based on predictions of future, short-term market performance. The increased volatility of the stock market in the last several years has generated a renewed interest in anticipating when the market has hit bottom or top.

Lessons from History

Despite all the hype and the plethora of strategies out there, market timing's record of success is dismal. The behavior of the market, after all, is the market-timer's greatest foe. Much of the return from equities comes from rallies when investors least expect them, so you can't afford to be out of the market, even for a short time. You can't actually invest in a stock index, but let's take a hypothetical look at what would have happened if you had invested in the S&P 500 over the 15-year period ended December 31, 2002. If you had stayed fully invested for the entire time, your investment would have gained 9.34 percent. If you had pulled out of the market briefly, missing just ten of the best-performing days, your investment gains drop to 4.29 percent. If you missed out on the 20 best days, you come away with just 0.47 percent growth; and if you missed the best 40 days, your investment actually lost 5.34 percent. (Source: Fact Set Research Systems. All figures show annualized returns, from December 31, 1992, to December 31, 2002.)

End Note$

Rather than wasting time and money with market-timing strategies, the prudent investor applies solid asset allocation principles to achieve long-term goals. "Buy and hold" may not be the most exciting investment strategy, but it is certainly the only one that has stood the test of time.

BRUCE BRINKMAN, CFP® (Rockford, Illinois)

TIP 104 PORTFOLIO BASICS—UNDERSTANDING GROWTH AND VALUE INVESTMENTS

Q. To build a portfolio of stocks, which style is better: value or growth?

A. The growth versus value debate is one of the longest-running on Wall Street. The prevailing logic—and myth—pitched to unsuspecting buyers is that glamorous growth stocks produce higher returns than unglamorous value stocks. History shows, however, that value stocks have delivered consistently higher returns to investors over time, with less fluctuation than growth stocks

Analysis of the Cost of Capital

One way to explain why value investments are perceived as risky is the concept of cost of capital. Imagine that you're a banker and your job is to make a loan to two companies, one of which is considered a good risk and the other not so good, perhaps because it's newer and less established, in a depressed business environment, or even has defaulted in the past.

Now translate that example to buying stocks. A value stock is priced low relative to its intrinsic value. The company could have a great balance sheet but be in a slow growth sector or going through a cyclical challenge. Nonetheless, it's perceived as a riskier investment, so its stock is priced lower to compensate for that extra perceived risk. The lower purchase price offers the opportunity for a greater gain if the company performs well despite the perception that it might not. This extra risk is the reason that value stocks are expected to generate higher returns over time.

Value Stocks Fluctuate Less and Produce Higher Returns over Time

Along with higher returns, value stocks fluctuate less than growth stocks. Adding value stocks to your portfolio should reduce the overall fluctuation in your portfolio and increase your expected return over time. Keep in mind that value stocks will not always outperform growth stocks, nor will value stocks always fluctuate less. There will be periods, sometimes long ones, when growth stocks will dominate the market and value stocks will look like losers.

Because no one knows in advance when value will outperform growth, also keep growth stocks in your portfolio. A combination of both will help smooth your returns over time.

JOHN CARRIG, CFA®, CFP® (Dearfield Beach, Florida)

TIP 105 UNDERSTANDING INVESTMENT PHILOSOPHIES—ACTIVE AND PASSIVE

Q. Should I consider index investing?

A. Investors have two basic alternatives: active and passive investing. Active investing involves trying to beat the market. Passive investing doesn't, instead relying on approximating the market's investment returns.

How Index Funds Work

Index funds are passive investments, because they seek a market return on your investment instead of trying to outperform the market. Index funds attempt to replicate the securities and structure of a market benchmark, like the S&P 500 or the Wilshire 5000 index. Stock index funds own all the publicly traded companies that make up a particular stock market index, so a manager need make no specific stock selections. Index funds are judged on how closely their performance matches their target benchmark. Trading fees, management fees, and inflows and outflows of cash in the fund generally cause the difference in performance between an index fund and its benchmark. This difference should be .25 percent or lower.

Index funds achieve higher returns than the vast majority of actively managed funds that try to beat a benchmark. Why? The first reason that active managers consistently underperform the stock market average is because the stock market is already very efficient; therefore, one is less likely to find the winners much before anyone else on a consistent basis.

Another reason is because the costs of managing an index or asset class fund are far lower than the costs of actively managing a mutual fund. For example, the cost of the Vanguard S&P 500 index fund is .18 percent per year compared with the 1.29 percent average annual cost of a no-load, large-cap blend mutual fund, whose typical benchmark is the S&P 500 Index.

Active versus Passive Management

Every year, mutual fund managers become stars, mostly by chance. A great majority of these rising stars quickly become falling stars as the market runs in another direction. Mark Hulbert's *The Hulbert Financial Digest* tracked the performance of the Morningstar five-star funds for the period 1993–2000. For that eight-year period, the total return (pretax) on those top-rated funds averaged 106 percent, while during the same period, the stock market, as measured by the Wilshire 5000 Equity Index (a measure of the total stock market's performance), had a 222 percent total return. In addition, the Hulbert study found that, while underperforming the market, the top-rated funds also carried more than 25 percent greater risk than the market.

No academic evidence suggests that any system of selecting actively managed mutual funds works. Numerous academic studies have shown that past performance is not helpful in predicting future performance. That's why the Securities and Exchange Commission requires a warning/disclaimer whenever an investment advisor or investment company discloses past performance figures to the public. However, when you review the charts and historical trends, two conclusive facts emerge. First, mutual funds that will beat the market next year cannot be identified in advance. Second, mutual funds with lower fees have a greater likelihood of beating mutual funds with high fees. Both of these factors bode well for adopting an indexing investment approach.

Performance Comparisons

The best way to prove that index funds outperform actively managed mutual funds is to review actual historical returns. In 1976, the Vanguard 500 Index Fund became the first index fund available to the general public. If you had invested $10,000 in the Vanguard S&P 500 Index fund, it would have grown to $162,531 in 20 years, which is more than 50 percent greater than the average actively managed equity mutual fund, which would have grown to only $106,998 during the same period (assuming all interest and capital gains were reinvested).

In addition to providing the potential for superior earnings, an investment in index funds saves time and reduces stress.

For any indexing strategy to be effective, however, it takes the right mix of index funds and patience.

Equity Index Funds

If you've decided to adopt a passive investment strategy with a portion of your money, you can use either indexed mutual funds or Exchange Traded Funds (ETFs). The low turnover of both makes them tax efficient and an excellent choice for tax-conscious investors. To understand how tax-efficiency can help you, consider that the after-tax performance of nearly all categories of actively managed U.S. equity funds has been 3 percent less than the pretax return.

Investors who want the greatest breadth of stocks in the U.S. market should consider an index benchmarked to the Wilshire 5000. Some examples of low-cost index funds benchmarked to the Wilshire 5000 (with their ticker symbol and the minimum required initial investment) include the following:

- Vanguard Total Stock Market Index (VTSMX), $3,000
- Fidelity Spartan Total Market (FSTMX), $15,000
- Schwab Total Stock Market (SWTIX), $2,500
- Vanguard Total Stock VIPERS (VTI), no minimum initial investment

Index funds of all kinds exist for more specific U.S. stock indexes. However, sector funds substantially increase risk and are generally not recommended for most investors.

International Index Funds

International index funds are made up of stocks, the companies of which are headquartered outside the United States. Global funds invest in both international stocks and U.S. stocks. The most often quoted international index is the Morgan Stanley Capital International Europe/Australasia/Far East index, known as the MSCI EAFE® Index. It's made up of about 1,000 large companies from 21 developed markets.

Some low-cost index funds benchmarked to the MSCI EAFE (with their ticker symbol and their minimum initial investment) include the following:

- Vanguard Developed Markets (VDMIX), $3,000
- Fidelity Spartan International Index (FSIIX), $15,000

- Dreyfus International Stock Index (DIISX), $2,500
- Schwab International Index (SWINX), $2,500
- iShares MSCI EAFE (EFA), no minimum initial investment

Index funds also exist for emerging markets and for individual countries. However, most investors may not want to buy individual country funds because of the high risk involved.

Bond Index Funds

Using bond index funds helps create a diversified portfolio and can lower risk without greatly impacting returns. Unlike stock index funds, which own all the stocks in the benchmark they match, bond index funds cannot match a benchmark like the Lehman Aggregate Bond Index. This index tracks more than 6,000 bonds, and these bonds are not actively traded. For this reason, bond index managers use sampling to create a bond portfolio with the same characteristics as the index they try to match. Bond index funds also provide the investor the advantage of minimal fees. A popular fund is the Vanguard Total Bond Index Fund, which invests in about 600 bonds and is benchmarked to the Lehman Aggregate Bond Index.

End Note$

Index funds can help you design and implement an appropriate portfolio based on your risk tolerance and long-term objectives. If you believe markets are efficient, consider index funds. If not, try actively managed funds. The key is to consider what will happen in each case if you are wrong. If you bet that the market is efficient, and it isn't, you do not give up much. You still get the above-average returns of an index portfolio. But, if you bet that markets are not efficient, and they are, you risk having your portfolio badly underperform the markets.

KAREN F. NORMAN CFP® (Troy, Michigan)

TIP 106 MUTUAL FUND FEES AND EXPENSES

Q. I'm confused by all the different mutual fund fees. What are those fees on the various kinds of mutual funds?

A. Mutual fund expenses are described in various terms. Here's a look at a few of the most common.

Mutual Fund Terminology

Sales charges. Also called loads, these charges are applied to your mutual fund at the time of purchase, in the form a of a front-end load, or when you sell the fund, in the form of a deferred sales charge or back-end load. Either way, they compensate the advisor, planner, stockbroker, or salesperson. One common back-end load is the contingent deferred sales charge that applies for the first few years, then phases out. Mutual funds with no sales commissions are called no-load funds.

Management fees. Both load and no-load funds have ongoing expenses, called annual fund operating expenses, that are paid by the investors. Management and investment advisory fees pay for managers and employees of the mutual fund company. A component of fund operating expenses, they average 1 percent annually.

Administrative costs. Also part of annual fund operating expenses, these fees are for record keeping, mailing, and customer service costs and usually range from .2 percent to .4 percent.

Marketing and distribution costs. Known as 12b-1 fees, these range from .25 percent to 1 percent. No-load funds cannot have a 12b-1 fee in excess of 0.25 percent. The advisor/planner/stockbroker/salesperson who recommended this fund to you also receives a portion of those fees, in most cases.

How Fees Affect Returns on Mutual Funds

Mutual fund fees can have an enormous effect on returns over time. In exchange for these fees, an investor gets professional management and security-selection expertise, as well as accounting and administrative services. Each investor must decide if the cost is acceptable for the benefits provided.

Look for a less expensive fund with comparable returns. All things being equal, the fund with the lower expense ratio will provide a greater total return. For example, suppose you invest $100,000 in two similar large-cap domestic equity funds. Fund A has a 1.25 percent expense ratio, and Fund B .75 percent. If both earn 8 percent annually for 30 years, cumulative expenses for Fund A total $111,033 and Fund B $73,113. That is a difference of nearly $38,000, or one-third less than Fund A.

End Note$

In the long run, expense ratios matter a great deal. In general, low-cost funds have beaten high-cost funds by substantial margins over long periods, regardless of which part of the market they targeted. When you see a huge difference in similar funds' returns, one fund is probably taking more risk or employing a different strategy. Does it make sense to pay an above-average expense ratio for that? Only if you think the fund's manager can keep generating returns that compensate you for the extra risk and the extra costs.

MAHLON EDWARDS, AAMS (Las Vegas, Nevada)

TIP 107 UNDERSTANDING FUND SHARE CLASSES CAN HELP MANAGE INVESTING EXPENSES

Q. What are the different share classes for mutual funds, and what should I know about each share class?

A. Different share classes have different expenses beyond commissions. If you buy from a broker or financial planner who charges a commission, the most common share classes are A, B, or C shares.

Most Common Share Classes

- *Class A shares.* These can carry an initial sales commission from 0 percent, if purchased from a discount broker, to 5.75 percent if purchased from a full-service broker. Even if purchased commission-free, these shares may carry 12b-1 fees of .25 percent to provide ongoing compensation to your broker. Breakpoints or reduced commissions may be possible, depending on how much you invest into a family of mutual funds and over what time frame.
- *Class B shares.* These carry no apparent initial brokerage commission and generally a 1 percent annual 12b-1 fee. However, if the shares are sold in the first six years or so, there's a 5 percent back-end commission that gradually phases out each year. It's sometimes possible to avoid the back-end load during those six years if the proceeds of the sale are reinvested in shares in the same mutual fund family. There are no breakpoints on B shares.

- The B shares convert to Class A shares after six to eight years, and the 12b-1 fees drop accordingly.
- *Class C shares.* Although you pay no initial commission, you pay a 1 percent annual 12b-1 fee as long as you own the shares. There is no back-end commission, unless you sell the C shares in less than a year; then you might be charged a 1 percent commission. There are no breakpoints on C shares.

No-Load Mutual Funds and Other Considerations

Discount brokers such as Ameritrade (http://www.ameritrade.com), Charles Schwab & Co., Inc. (http://www.schwab.com), or TD Waterhouse Investor Services Inc. (http://www.tdwaterhouse.com) are limited on the B share funds they'll work with and generally do not deal with C shares—something else to consider.

Also, keep in mind that some funds start out as no-load funds, but due to mergers and/or acquisitions of mutual fund companies, they may actually become a load fund with A, B, and/or C shares. In that case, the original no-load shares become Z shares.

If you own Z shares of a mutual fund and make additional investments into that fund, generally you will continue to purchase the Z shares, so you would not pay a commission.

Other Fees and Restrictions

Vanguard is a no-load mutual fund family with very low expense ratios, but a few of its funds have minimum holding periods with penalty fees, if you sell before the required holding period ends.

Approximately one half of all mutual funds available are no-load funds.

Transfer of Funds

Some classes of fund shares, like B and C, are not transferable to another broker. If you invest in Class B or Class C shares with one broker and later decide you want to transfer your account to another broker, generally you will have to liquidate those shares rather than transfer them in-kind. This might force you either to leave your account with a broker you don't like or to liquidate a mutual fund investment unfavorably. Class A shares, on the other hand, are transferable, except for proprietary funds. Proprietary funds are only available through a particular broker and, once purchased, must remain with that broker or be sold.

Institutional Shares

One share class that is listed in the prospectus but is not available for you to purchase through a traditional broker is institutional shares. These are reserved for investment advisors and large institutions like pension funds, foundations, and employer-sponsored retirement savings plans. They carry much lower ongoing fees than other share classes.

In many employer-sponsored savings plans, you purchase institutional shares, usually classified as Class I shares. You have no choice in the share class purchased through an employer-sponsored savings plan.

Making the Best Share Class Decisions

Exercise your right to choose the share class when making individual mutual fund investment decisions. The most expensive share class is B, with its 1 percent annual 12b-1 fee and a back-end commission. Individual investors should avoid this class. The National Association of Securities Dealers (http://www.nasd.org) even issued a warning to investors about the costs associated with the purchase of B shares.

ROSEMARY O. DANIELSON, CFP® (Shawnee Mission, Kansas)

TIP 108 EXCHANGE TRADED FUNDS

Q. What are Exchange Traded Funds? Should I have some in my portfolio?

A. First offered in January 1993, Exchange Traded Funds (ETFs) are one of the newer investment products. These are similar to conventional mutual funds in that they provide investors an easy and affordable way to invest in a diversified group of securities. But, while mutual funds only can be bought or sold at the price at the end of each trading day, ETFs can be traded throughout the day, bought on margin, or sold short. Short selling and/or buying on margin may not be allowed in some accounts, specifically IRA accounts. In addition, only experienced investors with a stomach for risk should leverage their portfolios to buy investments on margin.

Pros and Cons

Some of the most popular, best-known ETFs include the following:

- *Spiders (SPDR).* A fund that tracks the S&P 500 Index.
- *Diamonds (DIA).* A pooled investment designed to provide results corresponding to price and yield performance, before fees and expenses, of the Dow Jones Industrial Average.
- *Qubes (QQQ).* A pooled investment designed to provide investment results that mirror the price and yield performance of the Nasdaq–100 Index.
- *iShares.* Like the Nasdaq Biotechnology Index Fund (IBB), which tracks the Nasdaq Biotechnology Index throughout the trading day, these follow a specialized index.
- *Boulders (BLDRS).* Baskets of listed depository receipts sponsored by and listed on the Nasdaq.

ETFs are attractive in that they can provide either broad or focused market exposure. They have low management fees and are tax-efficient investment vehicles. Because EFTs do not have to issue or redeem stocks when individual investors place buy or sell orders, they can minimize capital gains-type transactions. ETFs are designed to track a static benchmark, therefore they have fewer trades and lower turnover in their portfolios, so capital gains occur less frequently.

But ETFs also carry buy/sell commissions that can add up over time, especially if the funds are bought or sold frequently, and negate their low-cost benefits.

Bond ETFs

The easiest, most economical, and lowest-risk method for participating in the bond market is with fixed-income Exchange Traded Funds or baskets of bonds, similar to mutual funds.

Three of the newer bond ETFs are short-term (one-year to three-year maturity, SHY), intermediate-term (maturity of seven to ten years, IEF), and 20-year term (TLT). All three invest only in U.S. Treasuries, so they carry no credit or default risk.

Among the advantages are the following:

- When individual bonds are bought or sold from a broker, there is a spread between the buy and sell price, which can be costly. Bond ETFs don't have a spread.

- Annual expense ratio for a bond ETF is around .15 percent, compared with .40 percent for an average index bond fund and 1 percent for a managed bond fund.
- Bond ETFs pay monthly dividends, as opposed to individual bonds, which generally pay twice a year.

Among the disadvantages of bond ETFs are the following:

- As with other types of ETFs, you pay buy/sell commissions.
- As with other bond investments, when interest rates rise, the value declines.

DAVID R. DELEEUW, MBA, CFS (Kalamazoo, Michigan)

TIP 109 PROS AND CONS OF MUTUAL FUNDS VERSUS INDIVIDUAL SECURITIES

Q. Which is better: investing in mutual funds or in individual securities?

A. It depends. Let's look at the differences first. The most common individual securities are stocks (which represent partial ownership of a company) and bonds (in which you are essentially lending money to a company or government entity). With individual securities, you make the purchase directly, typically through a securities broker (or you can do it on your own through a self-serve discount broker). When you invest in a mutual fund, a fund manager makes the specific investment decisions for you.

With that background, here are advantages and disadvantages of both and the factors that may affect your decision.

Mutual Funds

The advantages include easy diversification; professional security selection, management, and monitoring; and the fact that abundant research and information are available to investors about mutual funds. Among the disadvantages of mutual funds is that the investor still has to make the asset allocation decisions and choose from thousands of funds. The investor must weigh the different management expenses, multiple share classes, and fee structures, and understand that fund managers or investment strategies can change unexpectedly. With mutual funds, the investor has less control over decisions affecting tax consequences, and there may be quarterly performance pressures that can influence manager decisions.

Individual Securities

The advantages of stocks include making it easier to tailor investment decisions to individual needs, making it easier to focus an investment strategy, giving you the ability to buy and hold versus trade, having no ongoing management fees, and giving you better control of taxes. The disadvantages of individual securities include the fact that the investor still has to make asset allocation decisions to achieve proper diversification; owning and monitoring individual securities is time consuming; research is difficult, time consuming, or costly; individual investors often can't access research or interpret it as well as fund managers; and transaction costs add up.

Factors That Affect Your Decisions

Research. Finding a mutual fund is relatively easy due to all the independent research available. Good resources are Morningstar (http://www.morningstar.com) and Value Line (http://www.valueline.com). But don't chase past performance. That approach generally results in a buy-high, sell-low outcome. Some investors opt for index funds instead. Vanguard (http://www.vanguard.com) and TIAA-CREF (http://www.tiaacref.com) are good sources.

Costs. Brokerage commissions to buy and sell individual securities as well as mutual funds can be costly compared with buying and holding onto individual securities for the long term. These expenses vary and directly affect your return.

Asset allocation and diversification. Mutual funds make it easier to diversify your holdings and, therefore, can be excellent vehicles, particularly for smaller accounts. A particular mutual fund may be diversified within its particular investment category or objective, but it is still your job to assemble a portfolio of mutual funds that is diversified among the various asset classes.

Investment control and taxes. Mutual fund investors have less control over investment and tax issues than do investors in individual securities. Mutual funds are required to distribute income and realized capital gains each year. Capital gains distributions often occur toward the end of the year and can be fairly large, depending on the particular fund and circumstances. If you purchase shares in a fund in a taxable account just before a distribution, you are buying a taxable distribution, and that's not good. This problem can be managed by concentrating on tax-efficient funds and buying index funds, but such options reduce, not eliminate, the problem.

Investors in individual securities have better control over the timing of capital gains. Capital gains distributions are extremely rare, and the company's dividend policy is, for the most part, known when the security is purchased and remains fairly constant.

Which Option to Choose and When

Individual securities may be suitable if you

- do your own research.
- have sufficient amounts to be able to diversify your investments.
- want more control over investments.
- need to manage taxes carefully.

Mutual funds may work better if you

- have a small amount to invest.
- want an easier way to research the investments and diversify on your own.
- are investing within a tax-deferred account.
- prefer a fund manager who selects and manages the securities.
- are not very concerned about control and tax issues.
- do what's necessary to manage the tax and expense issues.

RICH CHAMBERS, CFP® (Menlo Park, California) and **BRAD BOND,** CFP® (Murrysville, Pennsylvania)

TIP 110 WHEN INVESTING IN REAL ESTATE MAKES SENSE

Q. I've seen various infomercials on TV, and a friend is talking to me about the benefits of investing in real estate. When should real estate be a part of my investment portfolio?

A. Relatively high returns and low correlation with other major asset classes are good reasons to include real estate in your portfolio.

Historical Returns

Real estate historically has better returns than bonds but less than stocks. A study by a respected magazine shows that the compound annual return for residential real estate from 1980 to 2001 was 5.11 percent, compared with 11.09 percent for the S&P 500. However, returns can be enhanced by the use of leverage via a mortgage.

Consider a $100,000 property producing $10,000 per year in income, with $5,000 in annual costs. If you bought the property in an all-cash deal and sold it five years later for $128,300 (a 5.11 percent increase), the total return for the period would be 9.67 percent. But if you use leverage and take out an $80,000 mortgage at 7 percent for 30 years, the overall return increases to 16.67 percent.

Of course, leverage is a double-edged sword. If, for example, the above property doesn't increase in value, then total return for the all-cash sale would be 5 percent and for the mortgaged sale only 2.1 percent.

Characteristics and Risks of Real Estate Transactions

Characteristics of real estate transactions include the fact that they are complex transactions with high buying and selling costs, they involve large amounts of money, they have high ownership costs, buyers often have incomplete and imperfect information about the property and market, and each property is subject to many state and federal regulations.

Among the risks of investing in real estate are inflation, which erodes purchasing power so that returns could be less than the rate of inflation; physical risks like flood, fire, and more; business/market risks; liquidity risk; political/regulatory risks; financial risk; and valuation risk when, for example, a poor appraisal leads to an inflated purchase price.

Is a Direct Real Estate Investment for You?

If you answer yes to the following questions, direct ownership of real estate may be the right investment for you.

- Do you have the dollars available for a down payment? Typically, you need 20 to 30 percent down on an investment property.
- Do you have the time and knowledge to find the right property?
- Do you have the time, ability, and the long-term interest to manage the property after you buy it?

Indirect Ownership of Real Estate

Real estate also can be part of your portfolio through indirect methods such as buying shares of publicly traded companies that develop or manage real estate; buying shares of mutual funds that own, develop, or manage real estate; investing in companies that supply the real estate industry; and buying into a real estate limited partnership.

- *Real Estate Limited Partnerships.* With a RELP, investors pool their money to buy property, making you a limited partner. A manager, the general partner, purchases, manages, and eventually sells the property, returning to the investors their pro rata share of the profits. RELPs are not publicly traded, the management fees are high, and historical performance has been mediocre. For most investors, RELPs should only be an option after all the basics have been covered.
- *Real Estate Investment Trusts.* A REIT is a pool of properties and mortgages, or a combination of both, that's publicly traded—just like stocks. For more information, visit the National Association of Real Estate Investment Trusts' Web site (http://www.nareit.com). Also, see the next tip in this book.
- *REIT mutual funds.* Several mutual fund families offer real estate-oriented funds. Some of the well-known companies that offer real estate funds include Fidelity, Van Kampen, PBHG, Vanguard, and American Century.
- *Stocks of related companies.* A third option is to purchase stocks of real estate-related companies like homebuilders, paper companies, or building-supply manufacturers.

ED POWELL, CFP® (Columbia, South Carolina)

TIP 111 HOW TO ADD REAL ESTATE TO YOUR PORTFOLIO USING REITS

Q. I want to add real estate investments to my portfolio. Are there different kinds of REITs, and what should I look at when investing in a REIT?

A Several kinds of Real Estate Investment Trusts are available, each with different considerations.

Types of REITs

First, not all REITs own real estate. A REIT, for example, could hold mortgages backed by real estate. Thornburg Mortgage, Inc. (NYSE: TMA) is one of several residential mortgage lenders structured as a REIT to allow earnings to pass to shareholders without paying federal or state income tax at the corporate level. It would not give a portfolio real estate exposure.

A mutual fund with a portfolio of REITs could be a better alternative than buying a few individual REITs.

Some REIT Considerations

External forces like the economy and more affect REITs. For example, tourism dropped after the events of September 11, and so did the value of hotel REITs. Some other issues include the following:

- How diversified are your real estate holdings in terms of the number and location of properties?
- How much debt/leverage does the REIT carry on its portfolio of properties? This can affect a REIT's ability to service the debt on the properties during hard economic times.
- What's the cap rate on the properties the REIT buys into its portfolio? That can affect the rate of return on the investment properties.
- What's the quality of properties in the REIT's portfolio?

When Mutual Funds and Nontraded REITs Make Sense

Both a mutual fund that owns REITs and a REIT index fund are available through regular mutual fund companies or Exchange Traded Funds (ETFs). The expense ratio of both typically mirrors that of actively managed and index funds, although the ETF expenses tend to be much lower.

Nontraded REITs also are available, though they're hard to find. These REITs do not trade on stock exchanges, and, therefore, share prices more directly relate to the value of the real estate. Atlanta-based Wells Real Estate Funds, Inc. (http://www.wellsref.com) is one of the limited number of nontraded REITs available today.

End Note$

If you're considering one of these nontraded REITs, remember that due diligence is especially important, because this investment is not liquid. Expenses can be higher, and nontraded REITs must be purchased from a registered investment advisor or broker. Weigh costs and opportunities carefully.

ROSEMARY O. DANIELSON, CFP® (Shawnee Mission, Kansas)

TIP 112 UNDERSTANDING EMPLOYEE STOCK OPTIONS

Q. My company has granted me several stock options. What are stock options, and what do I need to know about them?

A. Companies routinely grant employee stock options as a way to give employees equity ownership, increase key employee retention, and improve productivity. Essentially, a stock option allows the employee to purchase a certain number of shares of company stock for a specific price during a specific period of time. If the company does well and the stock price increases, the stock options grow in value. Conversely, if the company does poorly, stock-option values drop and eventually become worthless.

Types of Stock Options

Three main types of employee stock options are available: Incentive Stock Options (ISO), Nonqualified Stock Options (NQO), and Section 423 Employee Stock Purchase Plan (ESPP) Options. Because ESPPs will be covered in greater detail in the next tip, this discussion will be limited to ISOs and NQOs.

Important Terms to Know

- *Stock option grant.* This is a right issued by a corporation to an individual or entity to purchase a certain number of shares of company stock at a stated price within a specific period of time. Employees who remain with a company for a long time may have numerous grants.
- *Strike price.* This is the price, per share, at which an option can be exercised (also called exercise price).
- *Stock option exercise.* This is the decision to purchase the shares of a particular stock option grant.
- *Spread or bargain element.* This is the difference between the strike price and the fair market value of the stock on the date of exercise. Depending on the type of stock option and how it is exercised, the spread is taxed at either capital gains tax rates or ordinary income tax rates.
- *Qualifying and nonqualifying disposition.* Related to the exercise of ISO, a qualifying disposition of ISO stock receives preferential capital gains tax treatment.

Incentive Stock Options (ISOs)

ISOs, also known as statutory stock options, grant an employee the option to purchase stock at some point in the future at a specific price (known as the strike price). ISOs must meet certain requirements, including the following:

- The option must be granted to an employee (independent contractors and nonemployee directors are not eligible). An employee who leaves the company while holding active stock options must exercise them within three months.
- The grant period is ten years, so an ISO granted on September 15, 2003, must be exercised by September 15, 2013.
- The strike price must be equal to or higher than the fair market value of the underlying stock on the date of the grant.
- The employee cannot own more than 10 percent of the company at the time of the grant.
- The ISO grant is not transferable, with an exception for the death of the option holder.
- The value of all grants (number of shares × strike price) in a single year cannot exceed $100,000.

Many companies require employees to wait two years prior to exercising an ISO grant, so a grant provided on September 15, 2003, would become fully exercisable on September 15, 2005.

Taxing incentive stock options. Typically, there are no tax implications for the exercise of ISOs. Taxes are due after exercise when the stock is sold. For the best tax advantage, the sale of ISO stock must be a qualifying disposition. This means that the employee sold the stock either two years after the initial grant or one year after exercise, whichever is later. A qualifying disposition results in the gain or spread (the difference between the strike price and the sales price) and all future appreciation being taxed at capital gains tax rates. A disqualifying disposition, which occurs when a sale does not meet the qualifying disposition test, results in the spread being taxed at ordinary income tax rates. Because capital gains tax rates are generally lower than ordinary income tax rates, a qualifying disposition of ISO stock is preferred.

Nonqualified Stock Options

Companies use a variety of NQOs when they want to avoid the stringent qualification standards for ISOs. But, in general, NQOs are similar to ISOs. Each grant gives the employee the right to purchase a certain number of shares at a given price for a specified period of time. NQOs are often subject to vesting schedules, meaning that only a portion of the grant is available at the end of a particular time period.

Taxation of nonqualified stock options. The main difference between ISOs and NQOs is their respective tax treatment. With ISOs, there is usually no taxable event until the ISO shares are sold. With NQOs, the exercise of the option creates a taxable event even if the shares are held for a long time afterward. When an NQO is exercised, the spread is treated as compensation income and subject to ordinary income taxes. There is no need to worry about qualifying and disqualifying dispositions, because these ISO rules do not apply.

PHIL DYER, CFP® (Timonium, Maryland)

TIP 113 UNDERSTANDING YOUR EMPLOYER'S STOCK PURCHASE PLAN

Q. Should I participate in my employer's optional stock purchase plan?

A. Many publicly traded companies now offer employees an opportunity to purchase shares of company stock through payroll deduction, often at a discount on the actual fair market value of the stock. These programs are distinct from the nonqualified or incentive stock options that you might receive from an employer, but very similar tax laws apply.

How an Employer Stock Purchase Plan (ESPP) Works

The exact terms of ESPPs vary, but in general, here's how they operate.

- An individual enrolls in employer's ESPP account.
- The employee defers a percentage of gross salary from each paycheck into a personal ESPP fund account. The IRS limits the annual stock purchases under an ESPP to $25,000.
- After-tax cash contributions accumulate over a predetermined offering period (frequently three to six months).
- At the end of the offering period, the cash accumulated in your ESPP account is used to purchase your employer's stock.
- The purchase price is often discounted from the fair market value of the stock, often by 15 percent.
- Stock is deposited in a brokerage account in your name, usually a couple of days after the actual purchase.

Before Investing in an ESPP . . .

While the discount makes this a compelling benefit, participation is not a given. There are a number of competing interests for your cash, including funding your employer's retirement plan. Can your cash flow accommodate deferring income to an ESPP, too?

Diversification of your financial interest. Before buying into an ESPP, look closely at how your existing financial interests are tied into your employer. Do you have a 401(k) with company stock already? Be careful that you aren't too dependent on how the company and its stock perform. Remember: Your paycheck is tied to the success of the stock, too.

Weigh tax realities. Shares purchased in an ESPP are taxed differently from shares purchased in a taxable, brokerage account. The only up-front taxation is on the deferred salary that's used to buy the shares. When the ESPP shares are sold, a portion is treated as ordinary income and a portion as a capital gain (or loss), depending on how long you owned the shares and whether the stock appreciated.

Before you sell ESPP shares, consider the tax implications. Sometimes it makes sense to delay a sale to qualify for a more favorable tax treatment.

End Note$

If you want to go for profits while minimizing your risk in the ESPP, participate in the plan to the maximum extent that your cash flow allows, then sell the shares as soon as possible after the end of the purchase period. It's that simple.

ERIC RABBANIAN, JD, CFP®, MBA (Austin, Texas) and **RICH CHAMBERS,** CFP® (Menlo Park, California)

TIP 114 FIXED-INCOME INVESTING—UNDERSTANDING YOUR OPTIONS

Q. Why should I invest in fixed-income securities, and what are my options?

A. Fixed-income securities offer interest payments at regular intervals and act as a hedge against the relative volatility of stocks, real estate, and commodities. For investors who want to save for specific goals such as buying a home, funding children's college education, or living off their earnings, a portfolio should have a substantial fixed-income allocation.

Types of Fixed-Income Securities

The list of fixed-income investments is endless. Here's a look at a few.

Certificates of deposit. These usually offer higher rates of return than savings accounts and bank money market accounts, they're FDIC insured for a $100,000 per account, and they are available at any bank. Check your local bank's rates against benchmarks at Bank of America (http://www.bankofamerica.com) or Bankrate.com (http://www.bankrate.com).

Money market mutual funds. Money market funds generally consist of short-term Treasury and other securities with the highest credit ratings. Interest rates are higher than on savings accounts but less than for CDs and bonds. Most mutual fund companies, including Vanguard (http://www.vanguard.com), offer the option. Also, check out a few of the mutual fund superstores (http://www.schwab.com and http://www.ameritrade.com).

Fixed-income annuities. An annuity is a contract issued by an insurance company that's funded by the purchaser either in a lump sum (a single premium annuity) or over a period of time. The annuity returns the investment and any earnings to the owner at a later date.

Contributions are on an after-tax basis (unless the annuity is in a qualified plan or IRA, which is generally not the best decision; see the index for more information on the pros and cons of annuities). Interest on the contributions accumulates tax-deferred until the money is paid out.

Traditional fixed annuity contracts offer an initial, guaranteed rate of return for a limited period of time. After that, the issuer can change the rate; however, you always will be offered a minimum guaranteed rate for the life of the contract.

Sources for annuity purchases include most life insurance companies and some mutual fund companies. Look for a contract with low costs, good guarantees, and a solid rating.

Learn more about annuities at http://www.annuityshopper.com.

Bonds. There are four basic types of bonds, generally classified by the issuer of debt.

1. *Government bonds or Treasuries.* Issued by the U.S. Treasury and backed by the full faith and credit of the U.S. government, their earnings are exempt from state and local taxes. Various types of Treasuries include Treasury bills, Treasury notes, Treasury bonds, and inflation-indexed notes. Maturities range from three months (T-bills) to 30 years (T-bonds). The

Treasury also issues savings bonds. The most common are Series EE/E, Series HH/H, and Series I. You can purchase Treasuries through the TreasuryDirect program (visit http://www.treasurydirect.gov).

2. *Government agencies and government-sponsored entities (GSEs).* Agency and GSE bonds are issued by federally related institutions, which were specifically created by Congress to fund loans to homeowners, students, and farmers. Some of the well-known agencies and GSEs are Government National Mortgage Association (Ginnie Mae), Federal National Mortgage Association (Fannie Mae), and Student Loan Marketing Association (Sallie Mae). Agency bonds have the backing of the full faith and credit of the U.S. government. The government has a moral obligation (but does not fully guarantee) to repay the interest and principal on GSE issues. Earnings may be free from state and local tax. Agency and GSEs bonds are generally available only through bond brokers.
3. *Corporate bonds.* These are debt obligations issued by U.S. and foreign corporations. Unlike stockholders, bondholders are not owners of the issuing corporations but creditors who receive periodic, fixed-interest payments and return of principal at maturity. Bondholders do not benefit in the growth of a company (like stock shareholders do). The length of maturity and investment grade determines interest. Debt rating agencies (Standard & Poor's, Fitch and Moody's) assign credit ratings to corporate bonds based on the company's ability to repay its loans. Interest earned on corporate bonds is taxable at the federal, state, and local level.
4. *Municipal bonds.* Issued by states, counties, cities, and other local governments to fund public projects, the two most common types are general obligation (GO) bonds and revenue bonds. GO bonds are backed by the taxing authority of the issuing state or local government. Revenue bonds are supported by income generated from the facilities that the bonds were issued to fund (e.g., bridges, tunnels, and sports stadiums). Interest on municipal bonds is exempt from federal income tax. State and local taxes generally are exempted to residents of the state or locale.

Preferred stock. Many investors mistakenly believe that preferred shares are the same as common shares, just with higher dividends. Preferred stock is a hybrid between a stock and a bond. Preferred shareholders have priority rights to assets and dividends over common shareholders, but not over bondholders, in case of liquidation. Dividends are generally fixed and have a higher yield than bonds issued by the same corporation. Investing in preferred stock funds is a good way to diversify and reduce risk. Preferred stocks, and their caveats, vary. Check with your advisor before investing.

Real Estate Investment Trusts. A REIT is a specialized equity that allows investors to own a portion of a group of real estate properties. See the index to learn more about real estate investments.

Risks with Fixed-Income Securities

- *Interest rate risk.* This is the hardest concept for investors to understand. Bond prices move in the opposite direction from interest rates. When interest rates rise, bond prices fall; when interest rates go down, bond prices rise. Bonds with shorter maturities are less susceptible to interest rate risk. Conversely, longer-term bonds offer higher yields but also have greater potential for larger price swings.
- *Purchasing power.* Returns on your fixed-income investments may not keep pace with inflation and increasing prices. If they don't, you risk outliving your money.
- *Reinvestment risk.* If interest rates drop dramatically over time, you risk the possibility that you will have to reinvest your money at a lower rate of return than your current yield.
- *Default risk.* Will your bond issuer be able to make its payments on time? The degree of this risk depends on the type of bond you own and the borrower's financial health. U.S. Treasuries are considered to have virtually no credit risk (often referred to as the risk-free rate); junk bonds have the highest.

Individual Bonds versus Bond Mutual Funds and Bond Exchange Traded Funds

The main advantage of investing in bond mutual funds and bond Exchange Traded Funds (ETFs) is the opportunity to diversify your portfolio with limited capital. You also get professional research and management, and because dividends are paid monthly, your cash flow is instantly managed.

The biggest disadvantage for bond funds is that they do not have a fixed maturity, so neither your principal nor interest is guaranteed.

Taxable versus tax-advantaged account. If possible, allocate investments with tax-exempt or tax-deferred earnings into taxable accounts. Buy your fixed-income investments that are taxable on the federal, state, and local levels for qualified accounts such as 401(k) and IRAs.

Appreciation versus income stream. If your objective is a steady income stream, buying bonds or bond funds with a short-term to intermediate-term range is the more suitable choice.

Reduce reinvestment risk with a laddered bond portfolio. Buying bonds or bond funds with various maturity dates creates a laddered bond portfolio. Each rung is a bond with a different maturity date, from one year to ten years in the future. When the one-year bond matures, the money is reinvested into a ten-year issue, and so on. This locks in a range of yields and somewhat protects you from interest rate volatility.

Fees and expenses. Fees and expenses can be reduced considerably by buying bond index funds and Exchange Traded bond funds.

End Note$

For more information, visit the following Web sites:

- http://www.bondsonline.com
- http://www.treasurydirect.gov
- http://www.publicdebt.treas.gov
- http://www.bloomberg.com
- http://www.quantumonline.com
- http://www.municipalbonds.com
- http://www.vanguard.com

JOHN P. CARRIG, CFP®, CFA® (Dearfield Beach, Florida)

TIP 115 PROTECTION AGAINST INFLATION—TIPS AND SERIES I BONDS

Q. Why should I invest in inflation protection securities, and what are my options?

A. In a prolonged investment cycle of declining interest rates and low inflation, traditional, fixed-income investments historically have produced considerably above-average returns. As we have experienced in the equity market, cycles change. At some time in the future, an environment of higher interest rates and inflation will reduce the real returns of fixed-income investments. Inflation-protected bonds are the exception. They hedge against the erosion of inflation. Two securities offered by the government that are specifically designed to eliminate the risk of inflation are Treasury Inflation Protections (TIPS) and Series I Savings Bonds.

Treasury Inflation Protection Securities (TIPS)

First issued in January 1997, TIPS are a relatively new investment vehicle and not as widely traded as other Treasury issues. TIPS offer the investor a hedge against inflation, because their principal value is adjusted to reflect changes in the consumer price index (CPI). Interest is calculated using the adjusted principal amount and paid semiannually.

Available directly from the Treasury. TIPS are auctioned, as ten-year notes, quarterly by the U.S. Treasury. TreasuryDirect (http://www.treasurdirect.gov) has no fee transactions and allows the direct debiting of your bank account. Bonds are available in denominations of $1,000 and multiples thereof. Investors can invest up to $5 million at one auction. TIPS also can be bought through a bank or broker; however, you probably will be required to maintain an account and pay commission.

TIPS tax considerations. TIPS are exempt from state and local income taxes but subject to federal income taxes. Interest and any gains when the principal grows are considered reportable income and taxable in that year. TIPS work best in tax-advantaged accounts that allow tax deferral.

TIPS principal protection. If the inflation-adjusted principal amount at maturity is less than the principal amount at issuance, the original principal amount is paid. Even in a deflationary period, the original principal is guaranteed. Prices of TIPS will rise and fall with the rise and fall of interest rates, just like ordinary bonds (although probably not as much).

Series I Bonds

The U.S. Treasury issues another type of inflation-adjusted security called a Series I savings bond. They are sold at face value in denominations ranging from $50 to $10,000. Interest is paid according to an earnings rate that is partly fixed and partly adjusted for inflation. Interest is earned for up to 30 years.

Availability of Series I bonds. Up to $30,000 per year per Social Security number may be invested. Series I savings bonds may be bought directly at http://www.treasurydirect.gov (which accepts credit cards), from commercial banks, or through payroll savings plans.

Bond tax considerations. Interest earnings are exempt from state and local taxes. Federal taxes can be deferred up to 30 years (maximum holding period) or when redeemed. Investors must hold Series I savings bonds for 12 months to receive original investment and earnings. If redeemed within five years, three months of interest is forfeited. Similar to Series EE bonds, Series I savings bonds can be used for college tuition and fees. (There is additional information about this in Chapter 4 on college planning.) Up to 100 percent of interest is exempt from federal taxes, depending on certain eligibility requirements. Check with your financial advisor or accountant for more details.

I Bonds at a Glance.

- *Minimum purchase.* $25 through TreasuryDirect.
- *Maximum purchase.* $30,000 per person per year.
- *Denominations.* Any amount of $25 or more when buying through TreasuryDirect.
- *Purchase method.* Electronic debit from your checking or savings account.
- *Interest.* Fixed rate of return plus a semiannual inflation rate based on CPI-U, added monthly and paid when the bond is cashed.
- *Interest-earning period.* 30 years.
- *Minimum ownership.* 12 months.
- *Early redemption penalty.* Forfeit three most recent months' interest if cashed before five years.

JOHN P. CARRIG, CFP®, CFA® (Dearfield Beach, Florida)

TIP 116 FIXED-INCOME INVESTING WHEN INTEREST RATES ARE LOW

Q. What do people who depend on fixed income do in a low-interest environment?

A. When dropping interest rates cut into your income, you need to review your long-term approach to find ways to create more cash flow.

To ensure that you will not outlive your nest egg, you must think through your options and carefully calculate the possibilities. You would be wise to ask a competent financial advisor to double-check your calculations and provide a second opinion on your course of action.

Here is a closer look at a few of your options.

Option 1: Do Nothing

If you continue to withdraw the same income, hoping that rates will go up over time, you will start depleting your original capital base and, very possibly, outlive your money.

Option 2: Reallocate a Portion of Your Portfolio, Withdraw the Same Amount

If you don't mind some fluctuation in your portfolio, reallocating a portion of it to solid equity investments, then systematically withdrawing the same amount in proportion to the new allocation can work. You can help avoid depleting your portfolio by diversifying into asset classes that historically have provided a higher return than fixed-income investments.

The downside is that you could get a lower or even a negative return, and your portfolio might not last as long. However, if you end up achieving your required return or better return, your capital may last indefinitely, or you might even be able to give yourself a raise.

Option 3: Split Solution

Do nothing different with half of your portfolio and reallocate the other half. Continue to take the same income but only from the half in fixed-income investments. Let the other half grow.

Although this strategy is a combination the first two, it may provide greater mental comfort, because it offers security and growth potential. The hope is that by the time one half is depleted, the other half that was left to grow will be worth the original amount.

For the portion left to grow, you may also consider investing in individual stocks, bonds, REITS, or ETFs, in which case opening a discount brokerage account would make sense.

GELEG W. KYARSIP, CFP® (Seattle, Washington)

TIP 117 MAKING A DIFFERENCE—SPEND AND INVEST YOUR MONEY BASED ON YOUR VALUES

Q. I want to invest in and support companies that share my values. How can I find those companies?

A. Where you spend and invest your money really does make a difference. For example, throughout the 1970s and 1980s, U.S. investors pulled hundreds of billions of dollars out of South Africa to protest that country's systematic oppression of black people by the white minority. With his country's economy devastated, Prime Minister F.W. de Klerk had no choice but to end oppression and work toward democracy. This type of investing is called socially responsible or values-based investing.

Values-Based Investing Options

With the world's increasing concern about pollution and environmental conservation; war and terrorism; human and animal rights; the effects of alcohol, tobacco, and gambling; religious issues; and other issues, many people pay attention to where their money goes. The options for socially responsible investors have grown, too. Currently, there are more than 100 socially screened mutual funds.

However, the decision about how much of a portfolio should be socially screened is a personal one. Some funds screen for single issues like tobacco manufacturing, while others consider a range of issues like the environment, weapons production, nuclear versus alternative energy, product safety and quality, fair employment practices, and community investment.

Socially Responsible Mutual Funds

Some socially responsible mutual fund companies include Citizens Funds, Domini, Green Century Funds, and Walden Asset Management. For more information on these funds, the various screening criteria, and socially responsible investing in general, visit the following Web sites:

- Co-op America (http://www.coopamerica.org)
- SocialFunds (http://www.socialfunds.com)
- Social Investment Forum (http://www.socialinvest.org)

Methods of Socially Responsible Investing

Socially responsible investing can be done in four ways: exclusive screening, inclusive screening, community investing, and shareholder activism.

1. *Exclusive screening.* With this method, you opt not to invest in companies with disagreeable policies, practices, or products. The most popular

exclusive screen is tobacco manufacturing. If you feel strongly about not promoting or profiting from the tobacco industry, you wouldn't want to own shares of Philip Morris, RJ Reynolds, and other manufacturers.

2. *Inclusive screening.* With this approach, you seek to invest in companies that you feel are doing positive things. For instance, Xerox has developed the Green Machine document-center product line as part of its Zero Landfill initiative. All Green Machine parts can be reused or rebuilt into other products, thereby eliminating them from the waste stream.
3. *Community investing.* This avenue helps make affordable loans available in areas overlooked by most lenders. Such loans help people buy homes, start small businesses, and renovate neglected neighborhoods. Two sources of community investing information are the Coalition of Community Development Financial Institutions (http://www.cdfi.org) and the National Federation of Community Development Credit Unions (http://www.natfed.org).
4. *Shareholder activism.* This involves owning shares of socially irresponsible companies. Because each share equals a vote, if you get enough shares, you can have a lot of pull within a company. For example, in 1999, shareholder pressure led Home Depot to stop selling old-growth lumber and instead seek sustainable sources of wood.

End Note$

The bottom line, of course, is how well socially responsible investments perform. Quite well, actually. For example, the Domini 400 Social Index (DSI 400) gained an annualized return of 9.13 percent over the ten-year period ending March 31, 2003. Over the same period, the S&P 500 gained 8.54 percent. The DSI 400 is a socially responsible stock index modeled on the S&P 500 but with companies involved in alcohol, tobacco, gambling, nuclear power, and military weapons removed. Companies also were evaluated on their environmental impact, employee relations, and diversity policies. About half of the S&P 500 companies passed the screening process. Another 150 companies were added to mirror the various industries represented in the overall stock market.

SHERYL GARRETT, CFP® (Shawnee, Kansas) and **MADELINE MOORE,** CFP® (Portland, Oregon)

TIP 118 USING A DISCOUNT BROKER

Q. When should I use a discount broker?

A. That depends on your situation. Let's first look at a bit of history.

History of Discount Brokerages

Before 1973, commissions on stock trades were set by the New York Stock Exchange and were quite high compared with what we're accustomed to today. Once commissions were deregulated, the Charles Schwabs of the world emerged, offering low-cost, no-frills, no-advice execution of trades.

As discount firms evolved, they began offering other services like stock quotes over automated phone systems and no-load mutual funds. The advent of the Internet in the 1990s led to further enhancements for getting information to investors. With quotes, news, research, and information so readily available that the execution of trades became a commodity, so both discount firms and full-service firms had to justify their fees and add value for what they charged. Today, some discount firms offer advice, and some full-service firms discount commissions and fees.

Many discount and full-service brokerage companies want their employees to be perceived as financial planners or financial advisors, which may or may not be warranted based on the employee's education, background, and experience. It is up to you to determine what you're paying for and whether you're getting your money's worth.

When to Use a Discount Broker

Following are some typical situations:

- If you already have decided to buy or sell a particular stock, using a discount broker will keep more money in your pocket.
- If you're an experienced investor and make your own investment decisions, a discounter makes sense.
- If you don't want the hassle of tracking your stock certificates or you have mutual funds at several different fund families, a discount broker can provide the convenience of consolidating your investments in one place.
- If you use a fee-only financial planner to help with your investment decisions, a discount broker is ideal to place trades.

Discount brokers generally do not give advice; however, in recent years, some have started to recommend specific investments. Before purchasing any investments, make sure you know with whom you are dealing and the reasons for their recommendations. Sales representatives may be under pressure to make a sales quota or steer you toward a particular product.

At a minimum, you should visit at length on the telephone or actually sit down and talk with anyone who might give you investment advice. Make sure that they are interested in your situation, know your circumstances, and have your best interests at heart.

End Note$

The primary reason to use discount brokers is to save on commission costs while consolidating your investment assets. You can shop around based on price, but also take a look at other services they may offer, such as market information and research. If you do need advice, seek competent help and realize that, although professional advice can be cost-effective (e.g., hourly, fee-only; project-based; or flat-fee services), you will have to pay for it. When you do the math and consider the options, you likely will find that paying for independent advice to assist you in making decisions and then implementing them through a discount brokerage makes a ton of sense.

Here is a list of discount brokerages to research. Be sure that you compare their brokerage commission and fee schedules as well as their services. Or ask an independent financial advisor for their recommendation.

- http://www.ameritrade.com
- http://www.brownco.com
- http://www.fidelity.com
- http://www.schwab.com
- http://www.scottrade.com
- http://www.vanguard.com
- http://www.waterhouse.com

JAMES J. PASZTOR JR. CFP® (Greensboro, North Carolina)

TIP 119 IMPROVE YOUR KNOWLEDGE OF INVESTING—TAP INTO THE WEB

Q. I want to use the Internet to find investment information. Can you suggest Web sites that would help?

A. You are wise to use the Internet for your search for information. The Web has become a treasure trove of information that covers all facets of investing. However, whether you are reading a publication or online advice or talking to someone in person or on the phone, you need to be sure you are getting reliable information. Just because information has been published (or said) doesn't mean it's so. The following assortment of investment sites will address the questions that a beginning, intermediate, or advanced investor might ask.

Comprehensive Sites: All Levels of Experience

- CNBC on MSN Money (http://www.moneycentral.msn.com), free
- CBS MarketWatch (http://www.cbsmarketwatch.com), free
- Morningstar (http://www.morningstar.com), free with subscription required for advanced information
- The Motley Fool (http://www.fool.com), free

Investment Terminology

- Investor Words (http://www.investorwords.com), free

Mutual Funds

- Morningstar (http://www.morningstar.com) free with subscription required for advanced information
- CNBC (http://www.moneycentral.msn.com) free
- Quicken (http://www.quicken.com/investments/mutualfunds), free

Stocks—Intermediate and Advanced Experience Levels

- Multex Investor (http://www.multexinvestor.com), free with registration required for detailed information
- Smart Money (http://www.smartmoney.com), free
- Thomson Financial (http://www.thomsonfn.com), free

Risk Assessment

- Risk Grades (http://www.riskgrades.com), free with registration required for features

Financial Data on Companies

- SEC Filings (http://www.freeedgar.com), free with registration required

Stock Offerings to the Public

- Hoovers IPO Central (http://www.hoovers.com/global/ipoc/index.xhtml), free

Earnings Estimates

- CNBC at MSN Money (http://www.investor.msn.com), free
- Thomson Financial Network (http://www.thomsonfn.com), free

Real Estate Investment Trusts

- Invest in REITs (http://www.investinreits.com), free
- REIT Net (http://www.reitnet.com), free with subscription required for advanced features

Technical Analysis/Charts

- Ask Charts (http://www.askchart.com), free with registration required
- Big Charts (http://www.bigcharts.com), free

Exchange Traded Funds

- Nasdaq (http://quotes.nasdaq.com/asp/investmentproducts.asp), free
- American Stock Exchange (http://www.amex.com), free. This is the primary exchange for ETFs.
- iShares (http://www.ishares.com), free. This site lists both domestic and foreign ETFs.

Options

- Chicago Board Options Exchange (http://www.cboe.com), free

International Stocks

- ADR.com (http://www.adr.com), free
- Global-Investor (http://www.global-investor.com), free

Bonds and Fixed Income

- Bonds Online (http://www.bondsonline.com), free. This site lists corporate, municipal, and Treasury bonds.

- Investing in Bonds (http://www.investinginbonds.com), free. This educational site can help you learn about bonds.
- TreasuryDirect (http://www.treasurydirect.gov), free. This site is educational and offers direct access to purchase U.S. Treasury obligations.

Additional Financial Links

- Momentum Resource Center (http://www.momentumcd.com), free

End Note$

The main problem with using the Internet for investment advice is that the volume of data often creates more confusion than solutions. A basic knowledge of investing can help you distinguish inaccurate and just plain wrong information. Happy surfing.

LARRY T. AYERS, CFP® (Greenville, South Carolina)

TIP 120 SOFTWARE AND WEB SITES FOR PORTFOLIO TRACKING

Q. How can I effectively track and monitor my portfolio?

A. Plenty of good, free Web sites and software can help you track your portfolio. The Web site that's right for you depends on what information you want about your investments.

Web Site Functionality

Web sites can help you

- track the current value of your portfolio.
- get the latest news related to your investments.
- monitor your investment allocations, style, and risk.
- combine multiple accounts to get an overall picture.

Start with the information that's available on your brokerage firm's Web site. This site always will be the most automated and up-to-date source of portfolio valuation. However, if you need more information or have more than one investment account and need an overall picture, consider using some other sites. Also, consider Morningstar (http://www.morningstar.com), Quicken (http://www.quicken.com), and MSN Money (http://www.moneycentral.msn.com). All of the features are free unless otherwise noted.

Analysis of Your Portfolio

Periodically check the following aspects of your portfolio:

- *Asset allocation.* How much is in stocks, bonds, and cash.
- *Style diversification.* How much of your stocks are in small, medium, and large companies (capitalization) as well as whether those stocks are considered value or growth stocks.
- *Sector diversification.* How much of your stocks are in different sectors of the economy (examples of sectors are health care, energy, and financial services).
- *International exposure.* What portion of your portfolio is invested in other countries.
- *Expenses and fees associated with your mutual funds.*
- *Performance of each position relative to its peers.*

The best Web site overall to accomplish the above tasks is Morningstar.com. By using its Instant X-Ray® feature, you can obtain a complete analysis of your portfolio with great charts. MSN Money (http://www.moneycentral.msn.com) and Quicken.com, in addition to offering good analysis tools, offer the automatic update feature if you have multiple accounts.

Automatic updates. Both MSN Money and Quicken.com let you create portfolios and keep them current with data electronically transferred from certain brokerage firms. However, setting up permissions with your brokerage firms and your portfolio tracking software does require multiple steps. In the end, you may find it easier to manually enter your investment data, then update it yourself as needed.

Once your portfolio is set up, these Web sites automatically update the current price for stocks and mutual funds, so you always have the current value for your portfolio as well as performance data for different time periods. MSN Money gives you the ability to enter stock splits and dividends. Quicken.com automatically pops up a window telling you about a stock split or dividend, with your choices spelled out.

What about Bonds and Cash?

The bad news is that Web sites, in some cases, cannot accept a portfolio entry for bonds, CDs, or cash and cannot update the current market value. The good news is that both Quicken.com and MSN Money provide features to handle this. Quicken.com allows entries for cash and bonds. You have to update manually the market value of the bonds you enter via Quicken.com, but it does recognize them as bonds when doing asset allocation analysis. MSN Money allows entries for cash, bonds, CDs, and other types of investments. As with Quicken.com, you have to manually update the market value, but the asset allocation analysis reflects these asset categories.

Morningstar.com allows the entry of cash, stocks, and mutual funds only; however, you can approximate individual bond positions using a proxy. A proxy is a stand-in or substitute, and for individual bonds, a bond mutual fund proxy may be used. You might use a general-purpose bond fund like Vanguard's Total Bond Market Index Fund (VBMFX) to represent your individual bond positions. This approach will ensure that your asset allocation analysis reflects the correct proportion of bonds.

CHARLES TURNER (Highlands Ranch, Colorado)

Chapter

8

TAX ISSUES

TIP 121 CAFETERIA PLANS—AN EMPLOYEE BENEFIT OFTEN OVERLOOKED

Q. My company offers a cafeteria plan as an employee benefit. What is it, and how will it help me?

A. A cafeteria plan enables you to customize your employee benefits package to better meet your individual needs. Most cafeteria plans include a flexible spending account (FSA), in which you can set aside pretax dollars to pay for eligible benefits that. It's a win-win situation for you and your employer. You win because you save money by paying for just the benefits you need with untaxed dollars, and your employer has a satisfied employee and less payroll taxes to pay.

How a Flexible Spending Account Works

At the beginning of the year, you fill out a form telling your employer the amount of pretax money to be deducted from your paycheck and placed in your individual FSA. Then, as you pay for benefits during the year, your employer periodically distributes those pretax dollars from the account to you. The FSA reimbursements show up as a nontaxable amount on your paycheck, or the plan may write you a separate check. Each employer has a detailed reimbursement procedure in place.

Another way the program sometimes works is for your employer to specify a certain bonus amount (say $1,000) and allow you either to put it into your FSA for reimbursement or to take the cash. If it goes into the FSA, it works as described above and is tax-advantaged. If you take the cash, however, the entire amount is taxable.

Allowable Benefits

The following are some of the most common benefits available in a cafeteria plan.

Medical expenses. This includes health and dental insurance—the employee portion of premiums, copayments, deductibles, and other out-of-pocket expenses; medical and dental copays; prescription drugs; vision care, glasses, and contacts; chiropractic care; orthodontic care; and many additional medical expenses, including certain equipment and therapies if deemed medically necessary.

As a general rule, any health care expense you could deduct on your federal income tax is eligible for reimbursement from your Health Care FSA. In 2003, even over-the-counter remedies such as aspirin and cold medicine became acceptable for FSA reimbursement. So, if you are nearing year-end and have a hunch that you have not yet used all of your FSA withholdings, do a quick calculation and accelerate any qualified expenses that you can into the current tax year. If you do not use it, you lose it. Stocking up on bandages, antacids, and eye drops at tax-advantaged prices makes sense.

Dependent care. This includes eligible dependent care expenses such as qualified day care centers for children (up to age 13) or disabled adults as well as care inside your home. You must be paying for a dependent's day care so that you can work. In addition, if you are married, your spouse must work, attend school full-time at least five months each year, or be disabled.

Group insurance. This can include group term life insurance (with some exceptions) as well as disability insurance.

Adoption assistance. This varies by employer plan.

Expenses Not Allowed

A cafeteria plan cannot reimburse for use of athletic facilities, educational assistance, meals, transportation, or employee discounts. Your benefits department can let you know what is and is not allowed.

Tax Savings from FSA Benefits

The table below shows the actual tax savings from using $1,000 of FSA Benefits.

	Federal Tax Bracket					
	10%	15%	25%	28%	33%	38%
Federal tax	$100.00	$150.00	$250.00	$280.00	$330.00	$350.00
State tax (assume 5%)	50.00	50.00	50.00	50.00	50.00	50.00
Social Security and Medicare (7.65%)*	76.50	76.50	76.50	76.50	76.50	76.50
Total tax savings	**$226.50**	**$276.50**	**$376.50**	**$406.50**	**$456.50**	**$476.50**

*Individuals in higher tax brackets may not owe the full Social Security portion of their payroll tax.

The Catch

There is, of course, a catch with an FSA. It's the old "use it or lose it." If you don't use the full amount of money you put aside in the FSA during a calendar year, you lose it at year-end. If this is your first year using the FSA strategy, you might want to be conservative with the amount you put in, but do review the list of acceptable expenses and think carefully about how you might maximize your cash flow by using your FSA wisely. Let Uncle Sam subsidize the medicines, health care, childcare, and other out-of-pocket costs that you will incur anyway. The tax savings can add up to real money in your checkbook.

End Note$

Read your plan carefully to understand the exact benefits available to you. Create a budget for expected expenses during the upcoming year and determine the amount you want your employer to set aside. Then start saving. It is a win-win for everyone involved.

KEN DOWNER, CPA (Prior Lake, Minnesota)

TIP 122 STRATEGIES FOR MANAGING TAXES ON YOUR INVESTMENTS

Q. What can I do to minimize the taxes I pay on my investments?

A. The benefit you gain from an investment is measured not just by how much you earn on it, but, ultimately, by how much of those earnings you keep. Thus, taxes are a critical element of successful investing. While taxes should not drive your investment decisions, their impact on your investment earnings can be minimized. Depending on your objectives, your income level, and whether you intend to itemize deductions, the ideas that follow can help you do just that.

Invest for the Long Term

When you sell securities, you must pay taxes on any capital gains (the increase in value since the shares were first purchased and any capital gain on which taxes have not been paid). The length of time you held the shares makes a big difference in the taxes owed. For example, if you sell an investment you held for 12 months or less, you pay your ordinary income tax rate on any gains. These rates are the same as your normal tax bracket for 2004, which can be 35 percent, 33 percent, 28 percent, 25 percent, 15 percent, or 10 percent. In contrast, if you held the investment for more than 12 months, you would qualify for the reduced capital gains rate: 15 percent for those in the tax brackets of 25 percent or more, 5 percent for those in the 10 and 15 percent tax brackets.

Contribute the Maximum to Tax-Advantaged Accounts

Retirement plans. Plans like 401(k)s, 403(b)s, and traditional IRAs (as well as SEP-IRA, SIMPLE, and Keogh plans for the self-employed) offer multiple benefits for investors.

Because the accounts are funded with pretax dollars, you pay lower taxes now (during the years in which you contribute) and no taxes on the earnings until funds are withdrawn. As an added bonus, some employers match a portion of your contributions to the retirement plan. It's essentially "free money." Take it.

Contributions to a Roth IRA, on the other hand, are made with after-tax money, but that money grows tax-free and can be withdrawn tax-free once the account has been open more than five years and you are over age 59½. The advantages of Roth IRAs are numerous; next to the retirement plan your employer may offer you, a Roth IRA may be the very best wealth-building vehicle available. There are, however, some income limitations, and not everyone qualifies to open a Roth IRA. (Check the index to find tips that contain additional Roth IRA information. Also be sure to read Chapter 5.)

Education accounts. Consider using 529 Plans and education savings accounts to help save for education expenses. Withdrawals from these accounts are tax-free if used for qualified higher-education expenses. (The index will guide you to much more information about education accounts.)

Tax-exempt securities. Consider how you can reduce taxes on investments in your taxable accounts. One way is to select tax-exempt securities, if they fit your investment objective. Such investments include the following:

- *State and local municipal bonds and bond funds.* Interest on these is exempt from federal income tax and state tax in the state where the bond is issued. Typically, these investments are best suited for those in high tax brackets, but to know for sure if your tax-exempt investment comes out ahead, compare the tax-equivalent yield of your investment to the yields of the taxable investments available.

  For example, let's compare a municipal bond paying 2.2 percent (tax-free) with an equivalent corporate bond yielding 3.0 percent. Converting the tax-free yield into a decimal you get .0022. Divide that number by .75 (1.0 minus the tax rate of .25), and you will get a tax-equivalent yield of 2.93 percent. Therefore, all else being equal, the taxable bond at 3 percent will provide a slightly higher after-tax return then a tax-free bond. For this example, we did not take into account state income tax.

  Tax-equivalent yield = Tax-exempt yield ÷ (1 – your tax bracket)

- *U.S. Treasury securities.* Interest on Treasury securities is exempt from state, but not federal, income taxes. Investors who live in states with high income tax rates, but who are not necessarily in a high federal income tax bracket, may want to consider such investments to reduce their state income tax liability.
- *Series E and EE savings bonds.* Unless you elect to report the interest annually, the interest on Series E and Series EE bonds is deferred until the year in which you redeem the bond or until it reaches maturity.

Invest in Tax-Efficient Securities in Taxable Accounts

Investors should consider these alternatives for implementing a tax-efficient equity portfolio. Each offers a degree of control over the timing of capital gains and losses (like individual stocks) while facilitating diversification (like mutual funds).

Exchange Traded Funds. ETFs are similar to index mutual funds but are traded on an exchange (like a stock), not redeemed (like a mutual fund). Thus, ETFs escape the capital gains that mutual funds face when selling stocks to redeem shares; but, like mutual funds, annualized gains on ETFs must be recognized when the investment is sold.

Folios and wrap accounts. A folio is a basket of securities that investors prebuild or customize to their investment objectives. With folios, the investor, not a fund manager, executes trades, therefore controlling the timing of capital gains. With wrap accounts, the investor pays a financial professional to manage a portfolio that meets his investment objectives, which can include tax efficiency.

Smart Giving

If you own securities that have increased in value since their initial purchase, consider donating them instead of giving cash. A gift of appreciated securities offers a double benefit. For those who itemize deductions, there's a tax deduction for the securities' full fair-market value, and no capital gains tax is due. Because the charity can sell the security without paying taxes on the gains, it receives the same benefit as if you had donated cash. It truly is a win-win situation.

Conversely, it is not tax-smart to donate securities held at a loss. By selling first and then donating the cash proceeds, you capture the capital loss (which can be used to offset income), and the charity ends up with the same benefit.

SHERRILL ST. GERMAIN, MBA (Hollis, New Hampshire) and
KRISTINE A. MCKINLEY, CFP®, CPA (Lee's Summit, Missouri)

TIP 123 TAX STRATEGIES FOR MUTUAL FUNDS

Q. How can I reduce taxes on my mutual fund investments?

A. Mutual funds must distribute their capital gains and dividend income to investors at least once per year. These distributions are subject to income taxes, whether taken in cash or reinvested into the fund. Even in a down market, do not assume that your fund will not have capital gains to distribute. Capital gains result from stocks (or bonds) being sold at a profit, which means that, even if your mutual fund posted a loss, you still could be hit with a capital gains distribution.

Here are some strategies to reduce the tax liability from your mutual fund investments.

Invest in Tax-Efficient Mutual Funds

Depending on how they are managed, some mutual funds generate a larger tax bill than others, so it pays to consider tax efficiency when choosing funds. To reduce tax liability, consider investing in a tax-managed fund or an index fund.

Tax-managed funds are those in which the fund manager takes steps to reduce capital gains distributions throughout the year by reducing the number of trades in the fund and/or by offsetting gains with losses before the end of the year.

Index funds are inherently tax-efficient, because they are designed to track a benchmark (like the S&P 500). Benchmarks are baskets of selected stocks pooled together to represent the broad stock market or a specific segment of the market. Because the makeup of the baskets does not change regularly, the stocks therefore aren't traded frequently, and the fund doesn't realize capital gains on the sale of appreciated stocks in the portfolio.

Invest in Tax-Exempt Municipal Bond Funds

As with individual state and local municipal bonds, the interest earned on municipal bond funds is exempt from both federal and state income tax in the state in which the bonds originated. Thus, investors in high income tax brackets reap the tax benefits of municipal bonds, while also benefiting from the diversity, lower investment minimums, and professional management of mutual funds.

Time Your Investments Carefully

If you invest in a mutual fund late in the year and that fund has realized significant capital gains that year, you may be purchasing a tax liability. To avoid this, review funds for the estimated dates and amounts of capital gains distributions before you invest, and purchase after the capital gains distributions have taken place. You can usually get information about expected capital gains distributions by calling the mutual fund company or visiting them online.

Harvest Tax Losses

Before the end of each year, inventory capital gains distributions that you have or expect to receive. If you have significant capital gains, consider selling an investment at a loss to offset some of those gains. You may even wish to consider this strategy in a down market where you do not have capital gains. This strategy is called *harvesting tax losses.* You may repurchase the same positions that you sold after 31 days, or you may purchase similar investments right away.

Identify Which Shares You Are Selling

The IRS allows you to determine which shares you are selling when you sell a portion of your stock or mutual fund holdings. The shares you specify will determine your tax liability. You may choose from the following methods when determining which shares to sell: first in, first out; average cost; and specific identification. If you do not choose a method, the IRS assumes that the shares sold were the first shares you purchased. A note of caution, however: This method usually results in realizing the greatest tax liability in the near term. The average cost method is the simplest to use, and it may help balance your tax liability by averaging the purchase cost over all of your shares. The specific identification method gives you the greatest control over matching your shares sold; however, it is also the most time-consuming method, and good record keeping is a must. Whichever method you choose, you must continue to use.

Keep Good Records

To correctly identify which shares to sell takes good records. Each time you make a mutual fund purchase, keep track of the date of purchase, number of shares, and price paid for all original and subsequent shares purchased. Also, keep track of all shares that were reinvested (dividend and capital gains distributions should be automatically reinvested in most cases). These distributions are taxed in the year received. If reinvested to buy more shares, these distributions, should be added to the cost basis of your investment. This will avoid double taxation when the shares are eventually sold.

If you own individual stocks, keep records of stock splits, spin-offs, and mergers so that later you have the historical information to accurately assess the capital gains/loss implications of selling. The easiest way to do this is with a software program like Quicken or Money and by using financial Web sites like Yahoo and your brokerage firm's.

KRISTINE A. MCKINLEY, CFP®, CPA (Lee's Summit, Missouri), and

SHERRILL ST. GERMAIN, MBA (Hollis, New Hampshire)

TIP 124 HOW TO CALCULATE THE COST BASIS OF YOUR MUTUAL FUNDS

Q. I sold some shares of a mutual fund that I bought ten years ago. How do I figure out the cost basis to complete my tax return?

A. Generally, if you sell shares of a fund in which you did not reinvest the dividends, all you need are the purchase and sale trade confirmations or equivalent information. However, if you sold shares of a mutual fund in which you had dividends and capital gains reinvested, reporting the sale gets more involved.

Calculation Methods

If all the shares of a fund are sold, your basis is the total cost of all purchases plus reinvested dividends and capital gains. If only a portion of the shares are sold, you can use one of three main methods to calculate the cost basis of mutual fund shares when reinvesting dividends: average cost; first in, first out; and specific identification.

1. Average cost. This method can be used if you purchased shares at various times and varying prices. But, once you start using it, you can't switch to another method until the entire investment is liquidated. Generally, this is the easiest way to calculate the cost basis.

To compute your cost basis, add the total cost of all shares purchased (including reinvested dividends and capital gains), then divide by the total number of shares you owned at the time of the sale. The result will be your average cost per share. Multiply the average cost per share by the number of shares sold and subtract that number from the total sale proceeds. If the result is positive, you have a capital gain. In determining whether it is a long-term or short-term capital gain or loss, treat it as having sold your oldest shares first.

2. Double category. First, divide your shares into those held long term (more than 12 months) and short term (12 months or less). Then do a separate calculation for each category as above. This will give you the average cost basis of shares on a long-term and short-term basis; you report those separately on your tax return.

3. First in, first out (FIFO). The IRS assumes you are using this method. It is pretty simple with funds that do not reinvest dividends or capital gains distributions. However, it can be tough to calculate when reinvesting. The first shares purchased are considered to be the first shares sold.

Specific Identification

This helps you determine your gain or loss by designating a specific purchase or lot of shares as the ones sold. You must notify your broker or discount brokerage firm of the specific shares you are selling and get confirmation of that sale in writing as proof of your actual intent to sell those specific shares.

End Note$

You can save yourself and/or your accountant some trouble by setting up a spreadsheet of all your funds and individual stocks and their cost. Do this now to make tax time a little easier. At a minimum, retain copies of all the investment statements and trade confirmations on your personally held securities.

JASON M. MORLEY, CPA (Bohemia, New York)

TIP 125 COMMON MISTAKES IN UTILIZING TAX DEDUCTIONS

Q. How can I avoid making mistakes when I take deductions for tax purposes?

A. The time to begin planning for taxes is well before the end of the calendar year. The earlier you begin your tax strategy, the more successfully you will achieve your objectives and maximize your deductions. That said, here are a few common mistakes that easily can be avoided when filing your income taxes.

Think Smart When Claiming Dependents

Do not file as single if you qualify to file as head of household. You will have lower taxes with the latter filing status. If your ex-spouse claims your child as a dependent on their tax return, but the child lives with you, then you probably still can file as head of household. A custodial parent who has given an ex-spouse the right to claim a child as a dependent still has the right to claim head of household status, the earned income credit, and dependent care credit. However, whoever claims the dependency exemption also should claim the child tax credit.

Also, if you can claim a parent, grandparent, nephew, niece, brother, or sister as a dependent on your tax return, you probably can file as head of household.

If you just had a baby, you need to get a Social Security number for the child before filing your tax return. The IRS will not allow you to claim a dependency exemption, child tax credit, or earned income credit without a valid Social Security number.

Charitable Contributions Are Tax Deductible

Millions of Americans fail to claim the full value of their charitable donations each year. If you donate old clothes, furniture, appliances, and other items to a favorite charity, claim the charitable contribution deduction for the fair market value of the donated items. Those deductions mount up. Consider Jack, who was in the 25 percent marginal tax bracket. He donated $600 in clothing and household items to the Salvation Army, which in turn gave him $150 in tax savings ($600 × 25 percent) on his federal income tax return. Be sure that you get a written receipt from the charity for donations of $250 or more; the rule applies whether you are donating cash (or by check) or goods.

H&R Block (http://www.hrblock.com) offers DeductionPro, a software application, to help folks value their charitable donations. The $20 program helps put fair market values on the most commonly donated household items, including clothing, baby accessories, linens, furniture, household appliances, and more. *It's Deductible: Turning Donations into Dollars* (http://www.itsdeductible.com) from Intuit is another program, also $20, that includes guidance in tracking other miscellaneous expenses.

Bunching Deductions Is a Good Idea

To get the most deductions on your income tax return, bunch deductions into one year to ensure that you exceed the minimum requirements. Only those medical expenses in excess of 7.5 percent of your adjusted gross income, and only those miscellaneous itemized deductions in excess of 2 percent of your AGI, can be deducted.

To be successful with bunching deductions, your plans must be well developed long before tax-filing day arrives. As the end of the year nears, if you see that you're nearing the limits, look for other expenses that could be bunched into the current year, hence sending you over the threshold.

Make Your Credit Card and Car Payments Tax Deductible

Convert nondeductible interest expenses on credit cards and automobile loans into tax-deductible home mortgage interest. Interest on a home equity loan or a line of credit up to $100,000 is deductible on Schedule A of the 1040, no matter how you use the money. One note of caution: Look at loan fees and compare interest rates to decide if it makes sense to convert nondeductible loans into deductible home equity loans.

Keeping Good Records Is Essential

Don't exaggerate expenses to rack up deductions; if you're ever audited, you will need to be able to prove your valid deductions.

Be sure your tax return line items match the 1099s you receive from your broker, employer, or investment company. The IRS receives a copy of all 1099s, so they can match what's on your tax return with what's on the 1099s. Avoid discrepancies.

End Note$

Useful Web sites include the following:

- The IRS (http://www.irs.gov) offers valuable information on everything from answers to commonly asked questions to tax tips, how to e-file, how to get copies of forms, and much more.
- Bankrate.com (http://www.bankrate.com) also offers a wealth of free information.

TODD SHEPHERD, CPA, MBA (Leawood, Kansas)

TIP 126 WORRY LESS ABOUT AN IRS AUDIT—PREPARATION IS THE KEY

Q. I lay awake at night worrying about an IRS audit. I panic every time I get a letter with IRS letterhead. What can I do to relieve my anxiety and find peace of mind regarding my taxes?

A. Let's say that you receive a notice from the IRS in the mail today. From what you've described, your first response would be dread, worry, or procrastination. Following is another perspective that provides a few ideas for planning, so that if you ever are audited, you will be ready and experience less stress.

A Word about IRS Notices in General

An IRS notice is often of no consequence. If you do receive one that says you owe additional tax, most likely it's the result of an IRS error, not yours. Many times, these issues can be resolved with a phone call. Check out the facts first. Don't just blindly pay the amount requested.

Get Organized So You Don't Have to Dread an Audit

Facts, in the form of written documentation, are your friend. You can avoid, or at least reduce, the trauma of an IRS audit just by being prepared. The most efficient way to do that is when your return is prepared—not three years later when you suddenly receive a notice in the mail requesting information from the past.

- Keep records of payment (ledgers, check stubs, check copies, invoices) and all other pertinent records with your tax returns.
- Have receipts for charitable contributions, both cash and noncash. Contributions in amounts of $250 or more at any one time require written acknowledgment from the charitable entity stating that you received no tangible benefit for your contribution. These statements need to be dated and in your possession at the time your return is filed to make your contribution deductible.
- Noncash contributions (like appreciated stock or personal goods) require signed receipts from the charitable entity. If the amounts are more than $500, IRS Form 8283 must be completed, showing the date of contribution, the entity, the entity's address, the date the item was acquired, the cost of the item, the fair market value being claimed, and the method used to determine fair market value. (Not filing this form or filling it out improperly could prompt an inquiry.)
- For sales of property, it is important to have credible documentation of the cost basis for that property. That can be difficult to find when it involves gifts received from relatives long ago. (If you give property as a gift, include the documentation for the recipient's files.) If you must file a gift tax return, the information will be on that return, so just give the individual a copy of the return.

How Long to Keep Certain Records

Being prepared also means keeping records for an adequate time. Tax returns, financial statements, corporate stock, corporate records and minutes, and real estate records should be retained permanently. Other records should be maintained to support your tax returns for at least the time that you could possibly be audited. That's usually seven years. This would apply to such things as bank statements and canceled checks (pertinent to the tax return), mileage, travel and entertainment records, other receipts, and acknowledgments. Other records should be retained for as long as you own the property plus seven years.

This includes asset and depreciation records, home purchase and improvement records, and investment records.

Ensuring a Correct Tax Return

A simple, although sometimes time-consuming, way to gain peace of mind with your income tax filings is to check your information and your return carefully. Here's a starting list.

- Be sure that names and Social Security numbers on the return match each individual's Social Security card (particularly important for newly married individuals).
- Have correct Social Security numbers or identification numbers for child-care providers.
- Make sure that the alimony deducted for one spouse is the same amount as alimony reported for the other spouse.
- Are the estimated payments entered in the correct amounts?
- Are all items entered on the correct line?

What to Do If You're Audited

No doubt about it, an IRS audit is a hassle. But, if you're prepared and approach the audit in a professional manner, it most likely will be resolved satisfactorily.

Here is the recommended approach.

- Respond promptly to the notice as requested.
- Plan to approach the audit with a professional at your side or representing you.
- Have ready all the documentation you organized and placed with your tax return copy once it was filed.
- Pull only the documents requested and no more.
- Remember that IRS agents are people with homes and family, just like you. Be courteous and treat them as you would like to be treated.
- Respond to direct questions but volunteer no more information.
- Do not sign anything without reviewing it carefully and getting the opinion of a tax professional as to its ramifications.

End Note$

Additional information about keeping good records and avoiding audits is available at http://www.finance.cch.com/text/c60s05d070.asp. The information, calculators, and resources there are provided by CCH Incorporated (http://www.finance.cch.com) and Meara King (http://www.mearaking.com).

CONNIE K. NEWBY, CPA/PFS, CFP® (Greensboro, North Carolina)

TIP 127 FAILURE TO FILE TAX RETURNS CAN CREATE BIG TROUBLE

Q. I have not filed my federal income taxes for several years. What's the best way to come clean?

A. Most likely, you've had a traumatic event in your life such as loss of employment, divorce, or family sickness. This is can be devastating all by itself. Or, you may have experienced a sudden increase in income; the income spike may have resulted in an unexpected and large amount of taxes due. When an individual cannot pay the taxes due, they may become so disconcerted that they don't file a tax return. When a tax year is missed and nothing bad happens, the next year is skipped, etc. The illusion that nothing happens, however, creates a false sense of security.

What the IRS May Do

Often, the first indication that the IRS is aware of your nonfiling is a levy on your wages. This might, in fact, be your first wake-up call. You may have moved and forgotten to send a change of address to the IRS (the IRS, by law, sends any notices to the taxpayer's last known address). To complicate matters, after six months, the post office will no longer forward your mail, so you are unaware that the IRS is trying to reach you. However, the IRS has a current W-2 or 1099 form provided by your employer (W-2) and/or customer (1099). The IRS may use that information to garnish your wages.

If you own a business with a sizeable amount of cash transactions and are a nonfiler, the IRS may already have accumulated a large amount of information on you. For instance, they may be aware of real estate, cars, trucks, boats, airplanes, RVs, bank accounts, cash transactions reported to the IRS, 1098 interest paid on residential housing, where you live, spouse's employer, or any transfer of assets.

Reasons to File Tax Returns Promptly

- Interest and penalties will accrue from the due date on the amount of tax due.
- After three years, a refund due will not be paid to you.
- Any earned income credits or child tax credits will be lost.
- The statute of limitations on collections will not start until a tax return is filed and the tax assessed. Many times, the IRS will file a return for the taxpayer called an SFR (a service filed return). This SFR is filed with the category "taxpayer single" and no itemization deductions. This results in the highest tax possible. Also, the statute does not run on an SFR return.

What to Do Now

- *Consult a qualified tax attorney if there is any reason to believe that the IRS would consider your nonfiling as willful—this could be considered fraud.* A tax attorney will have attorney/client privilege, and any information you share with your attorney (provided they do not prepare your delinquent tax returns) cannot be revealed to the IRS. Your attorney can then hire a qualified tax preparer to prepare the delinquent tax returns.
- *Get the tax returns prepared.* If you do not have any of your W-2s or 1099s, you can get this information from the IRS. If you file voluntarily before the IRS contacts you, just file for the last six years. Otherwise, file all the years that the IRS requests. Be sure that the returns are accurate and all income is reported. There is no statute of limitations on a fraudulent return, and even an amended fraudulent return is still considered fraudulent.
- *If the IRS decides to examine your delinquent returns, do not attend the examination.* Hire an Enrolled Agent, a CPA, or an attorney who practices representation of taxpayers before the IRS. If the IRS summons you to appear, you must appear but you do not have to testify. The IRS might intimidate you if you go to an examination alone; this could be serious and injurious to your tax situation.
- *Always request an abatement of any penalties if there is reasonable cause.* Such cause might include continued unemployment, divorce, drug addiction, or serious medical problems.

Settling Up

After your delinquent tax returns have been processed and the tax assessed, there are only five ways to settle a collection issue.

1. Pay the tax in full.
2. Enter into an installment agreement.
3. File bankruptcy and discharge the taxes.
4. Get the taxes owed classified as currently noncollectable.
5. Do an "offer in compromise" and settle the tax debt for less than full value.

End Note$

It is better to stay current on filing your tax returns, even if you cannot pay your taxes due all at once. Please note that the information in this article applies only to personal income taxes—not corporate, partnership, Trust, or employment taxes.

JIM TAYLOR, EA (Lubbock, Texas)

Chapter

9

ESTATE PLANNING

TIP 128 ESTATE PLANNING BASICS—THE PRIMARY DOCUMENTS

Q. Do I really need a Will? What about other estate planning strategies?

A. In a word: Yes. Or, more accurately, you need one or more of a series of legal documents that will protect you and your heirs in the event of your death or disability.

Myths

Let's start with some of the myths that many people use as excuses for not having a Will.

- I don't have children.
- I don't have enough assets.
- All of my assets are in retirement accounts with designated beneficiaries.
- It's too expensive to have a Will prepared.

Realities

Each of the myths has a reality associated with it.

- No children? Okay, but you still have assets to pass on to other heirs or charitable causes.
- No assets or all your assets in designated retirement accounts? That's OK, too, but you still may have minor children for whom you need to provide guardianship, and it is likely some assets like vehicles, collectibles, and employer-provided life insurance do not have designated beneficiaries.
- It's too expensive. Simple Wills can be prepared professionally for a few hundred dollars. Do-it-yourself options also are available using forms and software. One caution: If you go it on your own, be sure that any online form or information that you use adheres to the laws in your state. A possible resource comes from Quicken and Nolo (http://www.nolo.com), that have teamed to offer a highly rated Will Maker Program (includes a Trust Maker module and a book on Estate Planning, written by attorneys in plain English) priced at about $60.

Family History

Your family structure also plays an important role in the need for a Will.

Almost all single or married people need a Will. However, it is even more important for anyone who has remarried to consider preparing a Will (or revising an existing one), especially if either spouse has children from a prior relationship. That's because intestate (the term used to refer to dying without a Will) laws dictate disposition of assets and guardianships for minor children.

A common myth is that someone who is unmarried and has no children doesn't need a Will. But a Will also ensures the ultimate disposition of financial assets, even personal mementos.

Every state has a generic will for residents who die intestate. It's written for the masses, and you may not like the choices that would be carried out on your behalf.

Revocable Living Trusts

A document that functions much like a Will is a Revocable Living Trust (Inter Vivos Trust). You contribute some, or all, of your assets to the Trust while you are alive. Because it's revocable, you may change its provisions or even revoke the Trust anytime, for any reason, during your life. The two main benefits are the avoidance of the probate process and costs and to provide instructions to others during a period of incapacity (as opposed to only after death, as with a Will). While it is a very useful estate tool, it is not needed for all individuals. You should learn more about the benefits of a Trust and the costs of establishing one, then determine if it's right for you.

Other Significant Documents

Even if you have a Will, that's not enough to be prepared properly. For most people, the odds of becoming medically or mentally incapacitated are actually higher than the odds of dying. So you also need a series of ancillary documents that address incapacity and other issues short of death. These include a financial power of attorney and medical care documents.

Power of attorney. Financial power of attorney, or durable power of attorney for finance, provides for the appointment of someone to make financial decisions for you. This power may go into effect immediately on signing the document, or it may be delayed until an event occurs that triggers the power or until you are unable to manage your own financial affairs. This delayed activation is known as *a springing power.*

The power of attorney can include specific provisions allowing for financial activities that may otherwise cease if you become incapacitated, like a tax-free gifting program. Having this document eliminates the need for your family to petition the court to appoint a financial guardian or conservator.

As with all financial and legal decisions affecting your life, it is important to consider carefully to whom you give this power. Once in force, the individual with the power of attorney will be able to represent you in your financial affairs at any time. You also should consult with an attorney for rules that may be specific to your state of residence or domicile.

Medical documents. Medical care documents generally include the following:

- A directive to physicians, sometimes known as a Living Will, tells medical personnel what, if any, means of artificial life support you would want and under what circumstances, in the event of your medical incapacity.
- Durable Power of Attorney for Healthcare names someone to make medical decisions on your behalf if you can't.

You can save much headache—and additional needless heartache—by doing your basic estate planning now.

BRYAN CLINTSMAN, CFP® (South Lake, Texas) and

ALAN M. SCHAPIRE, CFP®, CPA/PFS (Media, Pennsylvania)

TIP 129 USING TRUSTS TO PRESERVE YOUR ASSETS

Q. Where can my spouse and I get a general understanding of the types of Trusts that are available, in terms we can understand?

A. It is important that you, your spouse, and, ultimately, your beneficiaries understand some basic terminology about Trusts. Then you can make an educated decision as to whether a Trust(s) is right for you. Trusts are highly flexible estate planning tools that may be designed to provide benefits based on your specific circumstances.

Trusts can be set up to provide for a spouse or other beneficiaries in a specific manner, support a favorite charity on a tax-advantaged basis, reduce taxes, or protect assets from creditors. The benefits of different types of Trusts vary, but let's start with the basics.

What Is a Trust?

A Trust is a legal entity like a corporation. It has its own tax ID and pays its own taxes, just like a corporation. It is established by a legal document, called the Trust agreement, that's prepared by a lawyer. The Trust agreement defines how the Trust operates, things it is and isn't allowed to do (such as distribute income to a certain person). The person who creates the Trust is called the grantor or settlor. The funds in the Trust are the Trust Corpus. The manager of the Trust is the Trustee. There may be one or several Trustees.

Current Estate Tax Environment

The estate tax exemption is $1.5 million (in 2004), gradually increasing to $3.5 million by 2009. Essentially, that exemption is the amount of money from your estate that is free of transfer tax (either during life or at death). Any money given away beyond that amount is taxed at the estate tax rate, currently 50 percent, dropping to 45 percent by 2009.

Because tax laws are changing, it's best to focus on the provisions in place today and understand that changes likely will occur in the future.

Trusts Commonly Used for Estate Planning

Revocable living trust. Established during your lifetime, this Trust is revocable and under your control—that is, subject to termination or amendment at any time for any reason by you. Note, however, that the assets of any trust you control still are subject to income taxes and are reported under your Social Security number. A primary advantage of this kind of Trust is that assets placed in it are passed to your heirs without going through probate. Probate is the sometimes lengthy and costly court-supervised process whereby your property is legally retitled into your heirs' names. The national average cost of probate is 6 to 10 percent of the value of the estate.

Other benefits of this trust include the following:

- Estate assets are more immediately accessible to your heirs, because they are not tied up in the probate process.
- You have more control over specifically how assets will transfer to heirs.
- The trust provides direction if you are medically or physically unable to manage your own financial affairs while living.
- It maintains privacy as to the ultimate disposition of your assets.
- Real estate titles held in another state are more easily transferred.

It is important to remember that a Trust document is valid only when set up correctly. Unfortunately, many people misunderstand how Living Trusts work, or they fail to complete the set-up process. It's imperative that, once the Trust document is established, your assets are retitled so that the Trust becomes the asset owner. You still will control the assets, though the Trust becomes the legal owner. If assets are not retitled, your heirs may end up in probate to retitle them, especially when dealing with real estate.

Marital Trusts and Marital Deduction Rules

First, let's look at the unlimited marital deduction, which entitles spouses to leave each other an unlimited amount of property estate tax free. It's a terrific savings for your estate, if used correctly. Unfortunately, many couples lose an estate tax exemption when the first spouse dies by transferring all assets to the surviving spouse. Proper estate planning should be done so that you and your spouse each receive your own estate tax exemption. Leaving everything to your spouse because there is no estate tax at the first death will guarantee the loss of the first exemption. With that in mind, let's discuss ways to provide maximum estate tax relief for you and your spouse.

Marital trust. A Marital Trust can be either revocable or irrevocable and is created for the benefit of the surviving spouse. You may leave 100 percent of your assets to your surviving spouse and avoid current estate taxation with use of the unlimited marital deduction. The spouse must be a U.S. citizen to qualify. So why use a Marital Trust?

- It provides income to the surviving spouse for life.
- It gives the spouse discretion to access Trust principal.
- It allows the spouse the discretion to direct assets to anyone they choose (a general power of appointment).
- It avoids probate costs and lengthy delays.
- It provides for a successor Trustee if the spouse no longer can handle financial affairs.

Credit Shelter Trust

Otherwise known as a Bypass or Family Trust, this is one of the most important Trusts in estate planning. Its purpose is to take advantage of the applicable estate tax exemption, thereby reducing the estate taxes due when you and your spouse die. Proper structuring should allow all principal to pass to your heirs without estate taxes at the death of the surviving spouse. That's because the amount transferred into the Credit Shelter Trust typically will be equal to the estate tax exemption (unified credit) amount. Because those amounts are changing, language may need to be added to a new or existing Credit Shelter Trust to specify an amount, a percentage, or some other formula for determining the value of assets placed in the Trust.

Credit Shelter Trusts do the following:

- Avoid probate costs and lengthy delays.
- Provide income to the surviving spouse for life.
- Give the spouse discretion to access Trust principal for specified needs (including health, maintenance, education, and support).
- Allow for a nonspousal trustee, which may protect the spouse in event of incapacity.
- Have the estate remainder go to heirs, bypassing estate taxation on the surviving spouse's estate.
- Often, the Marital Trust is used in conjunction with the Credit Shelter Trust.

Qualified Terminal Interest Property Trust (QTIP)

A QTIP lets you decide ultimately who will receive your assets after both you and your spouse die. As multiple marriages during a lifetime become more prevalent, it may be important to provide for other beneficiaries, possibly children from a previous marriage. The QTIP fulfills this need. When you leave assets in a QTIP, they are included in your estate because of the marital deduction, and your surviving spouse would be entitled to all of the Trust income during their lifetime. Ultimately, on the death of the surviving spouse, the Trust assets then pass to the beneficiaries designated by the first spouse to die. In essence, this Trust lets the decedent control the ultimate disposition of assets to beneficiaries of their choice (typically children from a previous marriage).

A QTIP requires that

- all income from the Trust is paid to the surviving spouse for life.
- the surviving spouse does not have the power to change the beneficiaries named by the decedent.

It qualifies for the marital deduction. Therefore, the assets eventually will be included in the surviving spouse's estate.

Irrevocable Life Insurance Trust (ILIT)

An insurance policy on your life is not subject to income tax when you die; however, it is subject to estate tax, because the policy proceeds become part of your estate. If your beneficiary is your spouse, of course no taxes will be paid because of the unlimited marital deduction. Setting up an Irrevocable Life Insurance Trust can eliminate the tax burden on subsequent heirs.

This Trust can hold many types of property and has specific provisions for holding insurance. Current insurance policies can be transferred to an ILIT. Often, however, a new policy is purchased directly by the ILIT. The reason: If you transfer an existing policy to an ILIT, you must live at least three years beyond the transfer date, or the insurance is included in your estate and taxed accordingly. If you are considering a large insurance purchase, do not purchase the policy without first consulting an estate planning advisor. It may be best to set up an ILIT first, then have it purchase the policy. Failure to plan properly for your insurance benefits could cost your heirs substantial amounts of money.

Charitable Trust

Several types of Charitable Trusts are available, depending on your needs and circumstances. When you make a gift to a Charitable Remainder Trust (CRT), for example, you receive a current income tax deduction for the present value of the future remainder interest to the charity. Typically, highly appreciated assets are placed in a CRT, enabling the donor to avoid paying capital gains taxes yet still receive income from the Trust each year until death, at which time the remainder goes to the charity.

A Charitable Lead Trust (CLT) provides an income stream to a designated charity first, and at the expiration of the Trust, the remainder reverts to you or your heirs. CLTs usually are done in a Will and a Revocable Living Trust, so they are funded at death (they rarely are established during life).

Grantor Retained Interest Trust

With Grantor Retained Interest Trusts (GRIT), appreciating assets may be removed from your estate, reducing the estate tax liability while allowing you to retain some benefits of ownership while you are alive. Although a GRIT does not eliminate income taxes, when executed properly, it can help reduce estate tax liability. With a GRIT, assets are transferred to a Trust and heirs named to receive the assets at the end of a stated term—typically your lifetime. The transfer of the asset represents a gift valued at fair market value on the date of the transfer less your retained interest. The key to this Trust is that your retained interest lowers the value of the taxable gift.

Qualified Personal Residence Trust

A Qualified Personal Residence Trust (QPRT) is a type of Grantor Retained Interest Trust designed primarily for homes. Your residence is placed in the Trust, but you continue to live there for the term of the Trust. At the end of the term, the home becomes the property of your heirs. QPRTs are suitable if you own one or two appreciating homes and would like to enjoy these homes, keep them in your family, and ultimately reduce estate taxes.

As you can see, many estate planning strategies involving Trusts are available. Consult with a qualified estate planning attorney or financial planner to determine if any of these strategies make sense for you.

CAROLANNE M. CHAVANNE, CFP® (Laguna Niguel, California)

TIP 130 BLENDED FAMILIES—WHY ESTATE PLANNING IS CRITICAL

Q. I'm planning to remarry soon. Both my new spouse and I have children from our previous marriages. How can we plan correctly what to do with our money and property now that everything is more complicated?

A. Your situation is common today. Financial planning for your new marriage is more complex than the first time you were married, if you have more money saved, either of you have debts or less-than-perfect credit, or your children and new family members have competing interests in your property. You may want to take the following steps to prevent potential conflicts and ensure that your future financial relationship stays healthy.

A Heart-to-Heart Talk about Money

Talk with your intended about how you both handle money. Is one of you a spender and the other a saver? Have you talked about each of your financial goals? Are you being open about any past money problems? One of you may have ended your first marriage because of financial troubles. You both should sit down and lay all your cards on the table. Show the debts each of you owes. It's also a good idea to order credit reports and determine what, if any, blemishes are on your credit histories. It's better to disclose all this up front, even if you may feel a little embarrassed.

Consider a Prenuptial Agreement

A prenuptial agreement is a contract written and signed before the marriage that spells out the rights, obligations, and duties that each of you will have during the marriage. Prenuptial agreements can be a healthy result of having that honest conversation about finances. A prenuptial is a good idea if you have substantial assets or children to protect. The goal is to identify what assets and liabilities each partner brings to the marriage and to determine how those assets brought into the marriage and those acquired during the marriage will be divided, if necessary. This could help avoid the trauma should the unthinkable happen and your new marriage ends.

Consider Keeping Your Credit Separate

If one of you has damaged credit or has previously declared bankruptcy, you may want to consider keeping the finances in your new marriage separate. This complicates matters, but it could help later if your new family faces financial hardship. The other spouse's credit would not be affected because it has been kept separate. Also, should your new marriage end in divorce, with separate credit, each of you would be liable only for the debts and obligations you individually have. If one of you has been burned in your previous marriage and has had to pay your ex-spouse's debts, keeping your credit separate this time around might sound like a pretty good idea.

Review How Your Assets Are Titled

For you and your new spouse, any property you acquire after getting married can be owned as joint tenants with right of survivorship. This allows property to pass directly to the surviving spouse should one of you die. Both of you also should look at your current life insurance policies and retirement accounts (like a 401(k) or an IRA) to update your beneficiaries. If you want to name someone other than your new spouse as the primary beneficiary(s) of your qualified retirement plan assets, you need your spouse's written permission to do so.

Update Your Wills and Trusts

Be sure to update your Will so it clearly spells out your goals. It is also a good idea to make sure that everyone concerned knows your wishes. If your children feel slighted, they might challenge your Will after your death. Also, if you want your stepchildren (who may have no legal rights to your estate) to have part of your inheritance, use your Will to spell out your wishes for them.

Trusts can be useful in dictating the way you want your assets disposed. You can attach strings to how your money is used and managed. For example, you might want a Trust to make sure your children eventually inherit your home but also to allow your current spouse to live in it during their lifetime.

Your Children's Needs versus Your New Spouse's Needs

When you remarry, most of your assets typically pass to your spouse when you die. In a traditional family, that's not a problem, and the family assets typically pass to the children after both parents are gone. With your remarriage, however, you most likely will want to provide for your spouse as well as your children from your previous marriage. Now is the time to take proactive steps to avoid a yours, mine, and ours situation.

Some potential problems include the following:

- When you're dead and your spouse is retired, they may want safer, income-producing investments. Your children, however, may want growth of principal so something is left for them when they inherit.
- Your children may watch every penny that your spouse spends. How will they feel if your surviving spouse wants to buy a new car?

- If your new spouse is quite a few years younger than you, your children may have to wait a long time before they inherit what remains of your estate.

Here are some possible solutions.

- Put together a plan that effectively disconnects the money left for your spouse from the money to be left to your children. You will, of course, want to consult an attorney or estate planning professional to ensure that your plan is structured properly.
- Life insurance can be an effective way of making sure that your children receive money when you die instead of having to wait until both you and your spouse have passed away. Your children can be the primary beneficiaries of your life insurance policies. Another option with life insurance is to have your children take out a life policy on you that makes them the owners and beneficiaries of the policy and you the insured. You can gift them money each year, and they in turn can use the gift money to pay the premiums. Or you can establish an Irrevocable Trust to hold the life insurance for their benefit. This approach can work well if you currently have minor children.

PATRICK VAN NICE, CFP® (West Des Moines, Iowa)

TIP 131 PROVIDING FOR A DISABLED CHILD TAKES PROPER FINANCIAL AND ESTATE PLANNING

Q. Our child is disabled. How can we provide for them after we're gone?

A. You want to have a Trust set up to hold the assets that you'll leave. You want to provide for a successor guardian in the event that your child will require one, and you want to leave a document that describes your child, their condition, and your hopes and expectations so that those you trust to care for your child have some guidance.

Guardianship

If your child requires a guardian as an adult, then you already may have had the court appoint you as guardian. If so, you most likely will not be able to designate an alternate or standby guardian in your Will (as you could for a minor child). Designating an alternate or standby guardian must be done in court, during your lifetime. If you have not already taken steps to name an alternate or standby guardian, you should do so immediately.

Letter of Intent

Although not a legal document, a letter of intent is important because it provides the courts, your child's future caregivers (should they be required), and the Trustee, if any, with valuable information on what you would prefer for your child and what you expect of them. Start writing a letter of intent today, ideally with your child.

Do You Need a Trust?

You need to answer two major questions to determine whether you should set up a Trust for your child. Will they eventually need Social Security disability or Medicaid services? If the answer is yes, then most likely you will want to create a Special Needs Trust.

If the answer is no, then ask the next question: will your child be able to make financial decisions on their own? If yes, then no special planning is necessary. Leave your estate as you would to any other child. If you believe that the disability may reduce your child's earning capability, you may want to leave a greater portion of your estate to the disabled child than to your other children.

If your child will not be able to make financial decisions for themselves, then a standard Trust could be set up. The Trustee would be responsible for making financial decisions for the child.

What is a Special Needs Trust? If your child depends on Medicaid or Social Security disability, or will in the future, a Special Needs Trust can provide for your child without endangering those benefits. A Special Needs Trust does, however, require that the Trustee be someone other than the beneficiary.

A Special Needs Trust specifically limits what the Trust is allowed to pay for in such a way that the beneficiary still qualifies for Medicaid or other government services. The Trust can hold an unlimited amount of funds and can own a house or a car, or other items, which would otherwise disqualify a person from government benefits.

A note of caution, however: The wrong language in the Trust documents can invalidate it. Then the entire fund will have to be used to pay for needed services before the beneficiary will again qualify for covered services. It's critically important to consult a lawyer with specific experience in drafting a Special Needs Trust.

Who should be the trustee? It is important to talk as a family. Parents often believe that their nondisabled children will take care of their disabled sibling after the parents die. Or, conversely, they do not wish to burden their nondisabled children with the care of their disabled sibling. Your children may, however, surprise you.

Once you have talked as a family, consider carefully who should be the Trustee. A corporate Trustee, like a bank trust department, offers certain benefits. The corporation will be long-lived. While bank trust officers may come and go, the bank or its successor carries on. A corporate Trustee often provides professional money management, bookkeeping, and tax preparation. A corporate Trustee also will charge a fee and, more than likely, the bank or trust department's staff will not know your child or your child's unique needs.

A family Trustee, on the other hand, often will work for free and know your child and their needs. Family members may, however, have to pay service providers to handle investments, provide bookkeeping, and file taxes.

Another serious consideration is how having one family member in charge of the purse strings will affect that person's relationship with your child. Will the relationship survive if potentially inappropriate requests are denied? When selecting a Trustee, be sure to think through the personal dynamics.

It's also possible to have both family and corporate Cotrustees. While difficulties may arise if Trustees disagree, the benefits could outweigh the difficulties. It also may be possible to assign individual Trustees designated areas of responsibility in the Trust agreement.

Testamentary or Inter Vivos Trust. A Testamentary Trust is created through the Will after you die. An Inter Vivos Trust is one that functions while you're still living. You fund the Inter Vivos Trust with regular contributions and use its checking account to pay for services or goods for your child.

Inter Vivos Trusts have the following advantages:

- It can own life insurance policies. If an Irrevocable Trust owns life insurance policies, the benefits are excluded from your estate for tax purposes.
- It provides undisputed evidence (check stubs) of the types of expenses that you intend the Trust to cover.
- If the Trust is irrevocable, the assets it contains may be excluded from your assets during needs-based testing. This would allow you to have Medicaid pay for long-term care without having to first deplete the Trust.
- If you are suddenly incapacitated, a designated successor Trustee will take over almost immediately.

How to fund the Trust. While a lawyer will draft a Trust agreement, you will want to use sound financial planning to fund the Trust. Here are some sources of funding.

- *Savings.* Just like your retirement fund, regular savings should be put aside to provide for your child's future.
- *Insurance.* In case you do not live long enough to save enough money, life insurance can ensure that the Trust will have funds to provide for your child. It may be advantageous for the Trust to own the policy and for you to ensure that the Trust has funds to make the payments.
- *Gifts.* Family and friends can be encouraged to contribute funds.
- *Inheritance.* Family can be encouraged to remember your child in their Wills by providing a bequest to the Trust.

PAULINE PRICE (Bronx, New York)

TIP 132 EXECUTORS—HOW TO SETTLE AN ESTATE

Q. I've just been named as executor of an estate. Now what?

A. In general, you need to learn about the probate process and your duties. You will be responsible for settling and distributing the estate of the decedent according to the terms of any valid Will and the Probate Code of the state where the decedent lived as quickly and efficiently as is consistent with the best interests of the estate. The rules do vary some from state to state, and even county to county, so speak with an attorney to determine exactly what may be involved.

Your Title and Duties

First, a quick comment on language: In most jurisdictions, what used to be known as an executor is now referred to as a Personal Representative. We will use the term *Personal Representative* in this discussion. Some use the term *Administrator.* You may have heard of an *Executrix;* this is the female form of *Executor.* Do not worry about the title; the functions are generally the same.

If you are appointed someone's Personal Representative, the friend or family member apparently holds you in high regard and chose you after considering all of the responsibilities you will be undertaking. On the other hand, there is a lot to do. Hopefully, they didn't choose you just because they thought it would be easier and cheaper to settle the estate because you are familiar with it. Most people do not share their total financial situation with friends. Even family members typically are not aware of all the intricacies of an estate. If you are not familiar with legal procedures and deadlines and choose not to work with any attorney, it could take longer to settle the estate, and the estate could incur some unnecessary expenses. However, if a competent attorney is advising you, you should have no problems.

Things to Consider Before You Serve

Not surprisingly, when a family member or friend serves as a Personal Representative, misunderstandings or hard feelings could arise. Certain family members may feel that you did not act impartially and were unfair in your actions. They may not realize that, even if you disagree with the provisions of the Will, you must carry them out anyway.

You also may end up being so involved with your own affairs that you don't have the necessary time and attention to devote to settling an estate, or vice versa. And of course, the possibility exists you may die before your friend or family member does. For these reasons, you may want to suggest that they name an alternate. Alternates can include banks and trust companies. Ideally, you should have had the opportunity to discuss these issues before being named in the Will.

Responsibilities of a Personal Representative

- Locate the Will and other important papers and information. This may require a thorough search of the decedent's home, office, safety deposit boxes, and many other places to find the Will and its codicils (amendments).
- Carry out written instructions of the decedent relating to their body, funeral, and burial arrangements.
- Arrange for the immediate needs of survivors.
- Apply to the court to probate the Will or to terminate joint tenancy and for appointment as Personal Representative, usually no sooner than five days after the death of decedent. Most Wills written in recent years are self-proving. This means that the testator (decedent) and the witnesses signed a sworn affidavit before a notary public or someone else authorized to administer oaths. If the Will is not self-proving, the two (typically) witnesses to the testator's signature must be located, and they must testify to the genuineness of the testator's handwriting.
- Post a bond, if required.
- Apply for Letters Testamentary. These will be used to open an estate account, gather assets, distribute property, file tax returns, etc.
- Select an attorney to handle the estate (if necessary).

- Give legal written notice of your appointment to heirs (no Will) and devisees (by Will). No later than a set number of days (usually 30) after your appointment, you must indicate whether bond has been filed and describe to the court where papers relating to the estate are on file.
- Take possession of estate property, as advisable.
- Notify decedent's life insurance companies.
- Pay expenses for last illness, funeral and burial expenses, and other debts. You must review claims as they come in to determine if they are valid. You may dispute or reject doubtful claims. If you reject a claim, the creditor must sue within (typically) three months of receiving the notice of rejection or forget the claim.
- Some of the estate's assets may need to be sold to pay off debts. Debts are paid in a priority determined by the law. If you pay off someone "lower on the list" first and run out of money before all creditors are paid off, you may be personally liable to some of the creditors. Be very careful in paying off decedent's debts.
- Have real and personal property appraised.
- Prepare and file an inventory of all of decedent's property with inheritance tax section and clerk of court. Complete the application for determination of inheritance tax (if necessary) by filing with the clerk of court. Inheritance tax is a separate issue with the State Department of Revenue and, in many cases now, does not need to be filed.
- Publish a notice to creditors for debts of which you may be unaware.
- Prepare and file federal estate tax returns and state inheritance tax returns, if the estate is subject to estate and inheritance tax.
- Prepare and file state and federal income tax returns for the decedent's last year of life and, if necessary, for the estate.
- Arrange for the heir's ongoing living expenses.
- Determine which estate assets will be needed to pay state inheritance or federal estate taxes (if due), administration expenses, and other costs of settling the estate.
- Satisfy charitable pledges in the decedent's Will.
- Ascertain the values at date of death for all of the decedent's bank accounts. Depending on circumstances, close those accounts and open an estate account.
- Deposit or invest liquid assets of the estate in federally insured, interest-bearing accounts; readily marketable securities; or other prudent investments, if funds are not needed to meet debts and expenses currently payable.
- Distribute assets as required by law of intestate succession (no Will) or by decedent's Will.

These are only a few of the numerous separate and distinct duties for which a Personal Representative can be accountable. The complexity of an estate will determine other responsibilities. In addition to considering your willingness and ability to carry out a list of duties similar to the ones above, consider, too, how your rational abilities might be affected by emotional factors. You may be grieving at the same time that you are expected to carry out a list of important and potentially uncomfortable tasks. If you are in the process of selecting a Personal Representative, you will want to take these same factors into consideration.

COLLEEN MILLER, CPA, JD, CFP® (Windsor, Colorado)

TIP 133 GIFTING STRATEGIES CAN HELP REDUCE ESTATE TAXES

Q. I have enough assets and want to start giving to my children and grandchildren to see them enjoy some of my property. What options are there for making gifts that won't cause me any estate tax problems or use my estate tax exemption?

A. There are many issues to address when considering the welfare of your children and grandchildren. Who will care for them, and how will they be raised if you are unable to do so yourself? Will there be sufficient assets for their education and support? How can you transfer assets to your children and still avoid unnecessary taxes?

Advantages of Gifting

By properly gifting assets while you are alive, you can

- reduce the size of your estate, thus potentially saving your heirs thousands of dollars in estate taxes that would be due on your death.
- see that individuals use your gifts in a manner you deem acceptable.
- know how you are helping the beneficiaries and enjoy their appreciation.

Here are some personal gifting strategies that you may want to consider.

Annual Exclusion

Each year, you can gift up to a certain dollar amount per person ($11,000 in 2004), to as many people as you like, without using your estate tax exemption or incurring a gift tax.

If you're married, your spouse can gift the money too. These annual exclusion amounts, which are indexed for inflation, must be used each year, or they are lost.

In addition, if your spouse is a citizen of the United States, you generally can make unlimited gifts to your spouse without using your estate tax exemption or incurring a gift tax.

Once your gifts exceed the excluded amounts, you will incur gift taxes, which may be eliminated or reduced by your estate tax exemption. You must use your estate tax exemption if any portion of it remains.

Rules of Annual Gifting

Certain rules apply when making a gift intended to qualify for the annual exclusion. It must be a present interest, and it must be a completed gift.

- *Present interest.* The recipient must have a present right to receive the property. This means the recipient will own the property outright or, if held in a Trust, will be able to take the property from the Trust under the Crummey Trust rules.
- *Completed gift.* The property transfers from your name to someone else's name, and you no longer have the power to change the disposition of the property. Whether a gift has been completed is determined by the terms of the gift and the local property transfer laws.

Tax Consequences of Gifted Property

When determining the value of a gift for tax purposes, use its value at the time it's given—not what you paid for it. Let's say that in 2001, you purchased 100 shares of stock for $10. You wish to gift all 100 shares (now worth $45/share) to your grandchild. The gift will be valued at $4,500 for gift tax purposes. Remember, too, that you also are passing an income tax burden to the recipient of the stock. So, if you gave the stock to your grandchild and they sold it, they would have a long-term capital gain of $3,500. Making this gift may save taxes if your grandchild is in a lower tax bracket and can take advantage of the lower capital gains rates upon its sale or lower income tax rates on future dividends.

Gifts to Minors

The rules for gifting to a minor are similar; however, because minors are not of legal age, they cannot deal with their own property. Instead, an adult as custodian or trustee for the minor's benefit must own the property. Here are a few ways to gift to minors.

Gifts to Trusts. A Trust is a contract through which a person deposits and holds money, securities, or other assets for the ultimate benefit of another person. When transferring property to a Trust, it is usually important for the gift to qualify for the annual gift tax exclusion. For a gift to qualify, it must be a gift of a present interest, as discussed previously.

Transfers to a custodian under the Uniform Transfers to Minors Act (UTMA) or the Uniform Gift to Minors Act (UGMA). Establishing either account or transfer is simple. As a donor, you may transfer money, securities, and insurance contracts under the UGMA. Under the UTMA, which has been adopted in many states, you also may transfer real and personal property, partnership interests, and other property interests.

For gifts of cash or securities, banks and brokerage firms have the documents available. You will need to choose a custodian, other than yourself, to manage the property until the minor dies or reaches the age of majority (usually 21, but it depends on your state). At that time, the property must be turned over to the minor or the minor's estate. The assets placed in the account qualify for the annual gift tax exclusion, and the gift is irrevocable at the time of the transfer.

The main advantage to an UGMA account is its simplicity, low cost, and ease of administration. Potential disadvantages include its inflexible distribution requirement at the age of majority, inability to transfer certain assets to such accounts, tax consequences for the child when they withdraw the funds, and your irrevocable loss of control over the assets.

Court-appointed conservatorship. The conservatorship alternative generally isn't an attractive option due to probate costs and accounting requirements.

Types of Gifts

- *Cash.* It must be deposited in the recipient's bank by December 31 to be counted as a current-year gift.
- *Joint tenancy.* Generally, when you transfer property ownership from yourself to you and one or more other people as joint tenants, it's considered a gift. One exception: It's not deemed a gift when a joint bank account is established. A gift, however, can be made indirectly through a joint bank account when a noncontributing joint tenant makes a withdrawal. For example: Mom adds daughter's name to her checking account. Daughter

withdraws $5,000 to purchase a car for herself. Mom has just given daughter a $5,000 gift (indirectly).

Special note of caution: Care should be taken when transferring property into joint tenancy with someone who is not your spouse. Check with an attorney or CPA to determine the gift tax issues related to the specific property you want to transfer.

- *Securities—stocks, bonds, mutual funds.* This entails more paperwork. Your broker or mutual fund company will want your signature on paperwork to initiate the transfer, and the recipient will need to have a brokerage account established to take receipt of the stock.
- *Real estate.* How you transfer real estate depends on a state's laws. Check with an attorney to make sure the deed is correctly done, particularly if you are giving a partial interest in real estate.
- *Insurance policy.* You can transfer ownership of an insurance policy. But be careful when gifting an insurance policy, because it can be added back into your estate for estate tax purposes for three years after you transfer it.
- *Crummey Trust.* You can transfer any type of property into a Crummey Trust. When it's transferred, the Trust beneficiary is notified of the gift and has a short period of time to request that the property be given to the beneficiary directly. This gives the beneficiary a present interest in the property and permits the gift to qualify for the $11,000 annual exclusion. If the property is not withdrawn, the property stays in the Trust, and the beneficiary will have a continuing interest in the Trust. Crummey Trusts frequently hold life insurance policies.
- *Family business.* If you have a family business and would like your children to have some ownership, you can gift to them an interest in the entity. If you are a sole proprietor, you will need to establish an entity (such as a corporation) before you can make gifts. You also will need to have the entity valued by an appraiser before you make the gift. It is best to work with your attorney or CPA on this type of gift, as several issues need to be addressed when transferring ownership of a family business.

Additional Gift Exclusions

Two additional gift exclusions are allowed in the tax code.

1. *Tuition payments.* You may pay tuition expenses directly to a university, college, or a technical school. The exclusion does not include other expenses such as books, supplies, dormitory, or other fees that do not constitute direct tuition costs.

2. *Medical expenses.* Also worth considering are the direct payments of medical expenses (which can be claimed for federal income tax purposes, including medical insurance).

When making these gifts, you get the added benefit of their not counting toward your annual gift amount for the year.

Here is an example. Your oldest grandchild graduates from high school. You plan to pay the tuition, which is $15,000 per year for the private college they will attend. The tuition must be paid directly to the school. You also want to give them a new car for high school graduation. You can do both, as long as the new car does not cost more than $11,000 (in 2004) or if the car costs more than $11,000 but other family members contribute to its cost.

COLLEEN M. MILLER, CFP®, CPA, JD (Windsor, Colorado)

TIP 134 CHARITABLE GIFTING—A WIN-WIN-WIN APPROACH

Q. I would like to leave the world a better place, but I wonder how I could really make a difference. I would like to leave a legacy but am not exactly wealthy. How could I fulfill this dream?

A. First of all, thank you for taking the time to even contemplate how you could use your assets to make a difference. Here are some real stories about people (the names have been changed) just like you who had those same thoughts and desires to make a difference but were not sure how to make it happen.

The Planned Deferred Gift

Several years ago, Lucille purchased a $5,000 single-premium deferred annuity that named her sister as the beneficiary. After her sister died, Lucille simply changed the annuity beneficiary to a scholarship fund at a local seminary. At her death, the annuity proceeds, valued at $8,500, went directly to the scholarship fund. Her estate was able to deduct the value of that gift from the total value of the estate. And, because the seminary is a charitable 503(c) organization, no income taxes on the $3,500 growth in the annuity had to be paid.

Lucille's gift was added to other gifts in the scholarship fund, which now totals $100,000. Each year, in perpetuity, 5.5 percent of the fund's value will be awarded as a scholarship to a seminarian. Lucille's gift has made and will continue to make a difference.

How to do it. In your Will, Living Trust, IRA, life insurance contract, or any investment, name one or more of your favorite charities as beneficiary. While you're alive, you control the asset and have access to it. The plan is put in place now; the gift is deferred to charity until after your death—a simple, effective method that ensures you will have made a difference.

An Immediate, Outright Gift

Nancy is a volunteer with the St. Vincent de Paul Society. She serves on a committee that works with homeless women who are living in a group home/shelter. The goal is to help these women become self-sufficient by training them in basic job skills, teaching them interviewing techniques, and providing them with appropriate clothing for job interviews.

In addition to her volunteer work, Nancy also provides ongoing financial support to the society. When her mother died and left her an inheritance, Nancy established a $25,000 memorial fund in her mother's name, naming the St. Vincent de Paul Society as the recipient.

The $25,000 gift provided Nancy with a very nice charitable tax deduction, and, each year in perpetuity, the society receives a gift of 5.5 percent of the market value of the fund. Nancy plans to continue her current, ongoing financial support and to add more money to her mother's memorial fund.

How to do it. You can make an immediate, outright gift with cash, publicly traded securities (stocks, bonds, and mutual funds), real estate, or closely held stock. The benefits to you include an immediate charitable deduction, and you bypass any capital gains tax on the appreciation of the securities, real estate, or closely held stock owned for more than one year. The charity(s) you named will begin receiving monies immediately and in perpetuity.

The Charitable Remainder Unitrust

Roger is an avid University of California Bear fan. He is active at his church and in environmentalist causes, and he volunteers one day each week at the local National Multiple Sclerosis Society office. He supports each of these organizations financially.

Roger has done an outstanding job of saving, investing, and living within his means. At a meeting with his financial planner, he learned that at his death, his estate will face a significant estate tax consequence. His investment portfolio contained many appreciated stocks that were paying an average dividend of 2.5 percent.

Roger wanted more income but didn't want to pay the capital gains tax he would face by selling this stock. So he decided to gift $250,000 of appreciated stock and established a Charitable Remainder Unitrust in his name, with the following results:

- Because he gifted the appreciated stock to a community foundation, Roger avoided paying capital gains tax.
- The foundation, as a charitable 503(c) organization, escaped capital gains taxes, too.
- Roger got an immediate, very large charitable gift tax deduction that he can carry forward up to five years.
- The Unitrust pays Roger 7.5 percent interest on the value of the Trust assets for the rest of his life. In a Unitrust, if the market value of the fund increases, Roger's income will increase. If the market value of the fund decreases, Roger's income will decrease.

At Roger's death, his church, the University of California Bear Backers for Grants in Aid, the MS Society, a local seminary, and his favorite environmental group will receive annual distributions from the balance of the value of his fund.

A few days after gifting the stock, Roger called and asked his financial planner, "Why do I feel so good after just giving away $250,000?" The answer: Because he is making a difference now and leaving a legacy to benefit future generations.

How to do it. Do you need extra income now? If you analyze your assets, you may discover that you, too, can experience the wonderful joy of giving and have the added benefit of an increased lifetime income as well as a significant, immediate tax break. A Charitable Remainder Unitrust is definitely a win-win-win option.

A Gift Annuity or Charitable Remainder Annuity Trust

At age 90, Wilma is still an educator. After 45 years of public school teaching, she retired to become a full-time volunteer. She has been teaching English as a second language for 20-plus years, is very active in her community, and still assists with printing Braille Bibles.

In addition to giving her time, she is generous with ongoing financial support to a number of organizations. She knows that, after she dies, many of the people touched by her generosity will miss her support. Wilma wants to keep on making a difference.

Like Roger, Wilma has appreciated stock that is not paying dividends that she can use as income. She needs additional income but deplores the idea of paying capital gains if she sells the stock. Unlike Roger, Wilma does not have an estate tax problem.

Age has its benefits. After exploring several options, Wilma decides to establish an endowment fund through the use of a Charitable Remainder Annuity Trust. Because she is 90, the Annuity Trust's guaranteed income is 9.5 percent. Wilma gifts $50,000 of her appreciated stock.

Because this is a Charitable Remainder Annuity Trust, Wilma's annual income from it will always be $4,750. If the market value of the Trust assets increase, her income won't increase. If the market value of the Trust assets decreases, Wilma's income will still be $4,750 a year.

At Wilma's death, the remainder of the assets in her endowment fund will be paid in perpetuity to a local Christian Help Center, the Lutheran Braille Workers, and the Lutheran Bible Translators. Wilma is delighted with the increased, guaranteed income; the tax deduction; and the knowledge that her life dream of leaving the world a better place is, and will continue to be, a reality.

How to do it. Do you need more guaranteed income? Set up a gift annuity with the help of a financial advisor. What organizations do you support with your time, talents, and/or money? Will you be missed if you die prematurely? Explore the concept of giving away assets now so you can actually have more now. Planning is critical and paves the way to win-win-win results.

A Charitable Gift of Life Insurance

Marcy believes in tithing and generously supports several charities. She has a good income but has not accumulated the assets that she knows she will need in retirement. However, she has a passionate desire to improve the world and is concerned about the loss of income at her death to the groups she now supports.

Marcy asked her financial advisor if he had a solution to her dilemma. The answer, Marcy learned, was using life insurance to leverage charitable gifting.

She since has purchased a $150,000 life insurance contract and named a community trust as the owner and beneficiary of the policy. Because the charity is the owner and beneficiary, the life insurance premium is tax deductible.

Marcy can afford the premiums and actually is overfunding the contract (a permanent life insurance policy), so it will be paid up by the time she retires. At her death, the $150,000 will be paid to her endowment fund at the community foundation. Marcy has named five different charities in her fund. Each will be the ongoing recipient of the annual earnings from the invested $150,000. The charitable gift of life insurance is another win-win-win solution.

How to do it. Do you lament the fact that you do not have a sizeable estate or a large income, but you have a generous heart and want to continue contributing to society? The charitable gift of life insurance probably is the perfect solution. A small premium purchases a major gift.

Perhaps you have an existing policy, and the current named beneficiary really could be changed. Name your favorite charity, church, or alma mater.

End Note$

Of course, when there are winners, there must be losers. Who loses? Well, it's poor old Uncle Sam. Only the Internal Revenue Service experiences a loss because of reduced tax revenue. But, even though he loses, Uncle Sam is one smart old gent: He has given his blessing and stamp of approval to these various charitable plans.

MARY ANN SHEETS-HANSON, CFP® (Walnut Creek, California)

MEET THE ALL AMERICAN PLANNER

Sheryl Garrett, CFP®, has been dubbed "The All American Planner" and for good reason. Once a successful wealth manager and full partner in a high-end financial planning and asset management firm, Sheryl eventually decided to shift away from serving "just the affluent"—even though it meant she'd be declining big retainers and steady inquiries from wealthy clients.

"It always bothered me when I had to turn people away simply because they did not meet our firm's minimums and account criteria," says Sheryl. "I began thinking about how I'd like to obtain and purchase financial advice if I were a consumer. It occurred to me that working on an hourly, fee-only basis made the most sense. If attorneys, CPAs, and other professional consultants can deliver quality services to their clientele exclusively on an hourly, as-needed basis, financial planners should be able to do the same."

Sheryl, who has been honing her financial planning skills since 1986, opened her hourly, fee-only financial planning firm in 1998. Instead of offering comprehensive, concierge-level services to the wealthy, she began offering "financial planning and advice to people from all walks of life." Clients had the flexibility to engage Sheryl on a one-time or periodic, as-needed basis—whichever best met their needs. Clients were given written recommendations and the specific steps to implement the advice rendered. Those who desired help with the implementation of the decisions simply paid by the hour (or by the project) for the services rendered. There were no hidden fees or third-party agendas. In addition, people did not have to have a certain income, net worth, or portfolio size to become a client.

By delivering financial advice in a manner very attractive to clients, Sheryl's firm grew to include three other CFPs and approximately 600 clients. Little did she know that she would become the subject of so much media attention by simply following the path of serving clients on the terms *they* selected. In 2000, *Investment Advisor* magazine ran a cover story on Sheryl touting the way she practiced. Financial planners from across the country began to call, saying they'd always wanted to practice in the same way but were afraid they couldn't make a decent living offering services on an as-needed, fee-only basis. Some thought that clients might not be willing to pay for advice by the hour.

Sheryl knew this mode of delivering independent, flexible advice was something consumers did need and want. Never one to shrink from a challenge, she "stuck to her knitting"—serving clients on their terms and proving the naysayers wrong.

THE GARRETT PLANNING NETWORK IS BORN

After much prompting from other planners, Sheryl formed The Garrett Planning Network, Inc. (GPN) (http://www.GarrettPlanningNetwork.com), a nationwide Network of fee-only financial planners dedicated to serving *all Americans*—not just the wealthy. There are no account minimums or long-term contracts to become a client. Nor are there ever any hidden costs or third-party compensation to blur the advisor's recommendations. Services are rendered on an hourly, as-needed basis. "It's a simple way of delivering financial planning services and advice," says Sheryl. "Clients understand the billable hours concept and like paying for just as little or as much help and advice as they need and desire."

A flurry of media coverage has resulted from Garrett's bold move. Jonathan Clements, respected columnist for *The Wall Street Journal,* went public saying "I like hourly fees" and "If you can, find a financial planner who charges just by the hour." On CNBC's *Power Lunch,* Clements told host Bill Griffith that The Garrett Planning Network was the organization he was "really hot on." Jean Chatzky wrote about GPN in *Time* magazine and mentioned GPN on the *Today Show.* Linda Stern heralded the benefits of working with a Garrett planner in two different articles in *Newsweek. Bloomberg Personal Finance* did a multipage story on GPN, and notable publications such as *Money, Smart Money, Kiplinger's Personal Finance,* and many more wrote about this "new breed of planner"—the ones who don't accept commissions or require assets under management but work on a simple hourly, as-needed, fee-only basis.

ABOUT SHERYL GARRETT

A Certified Financial Planner™ professional serving clients since 1986, Sheryl has received numerous awards and recognition for her leadership within the financial planning industry. In 2001 and 2002, she was listed in *Mutual Funds* magazine's "Top 100 Financial Advisors." She was named a "Modern Master" by *Financial Planning* magazine in 2002. In 2003, she was named "one of the top 25 most influential people in financial planning" by the editors at *Investment Advisor* magazine—she's in good company, along side Federal Reserve Board Chairman Alan Greenspan, investment powerhouse Charles Schwab, and industry pioneer John Bogle of Vanguard Funds.

Sheryl has held board member positions with the National Association of Personal Financial Advisors (NAPFA), and the Financial Planning Association's (FPA) predecessor organizations, the International Association for Financial Planning (IAFP), and the Institute for Certified Financial Planners (ICFP). Highlights include being selected to represent the IAFP, ICFP, and NAPFA before Congress regarding proposed changes in investment advisor regulations, and speaking to congressional staff members to raise awareness of the financial planning process at the 2002 "Financial Planning Day on Capital Hill."

She is also the author of *Garrett's Guide to Financial Planning* (National Underwriter Company, November 2002), a book written specifically for financial services professionals about the various options and opportunities available to better serve clients. A frequent speaker at personal finance fairs and within the financial planning community, Sheryl has shared the platform with Suze Orman, Jim Kramer, and numerous leaders within the financial planning community.

JUST GIVE ME THE ANSWER$

This book was written by Sheryl Garrett with Marie Swift, along with 75 other professional financial planners, all of whom are members of The Garrett Planning Network, Inc. The overarching goal is to educate and empower the reader. "Everyone needs and can benefit from professional financial advice at certain times in their life. This book is intended to motivate the greatest number of people possible and inspire them to take a more active role in managing their personal financial affairs. We can all be smarter consumers, no matter how much knowledge we already possess. Whether we do our own research to make our financial decisions or consult with a professional when we need validation or help, we must each work diligently to build the brightest financial futures and ensure the best outcomes. This book will help people make better money decisions," says Sheryl.

ABOUT MARIE SWIFT

Marie Swift, Founder and Principal of Impact Communications, has partnered with Sheryl Garrett since 1999 to raise public awareness regarding the benefits of working with independent financial planning professionals on an hourly, as-needed basis. The results of this multiyear, national campaign can be viewed at http://www.GarrettPlanningNetwork.com.

Under Swift's marketing and public relations direction, the Garrett Story continues to make headlines as prominent news media and personal finance publications (*Time, Newsweek,* CNBC, *Bloomberg Personal Finance, The Wall Street Journal, CBS MarketWatch,* and many more) herald hourly, commission-free advice as "the new choice for smart consumers."

A marketing communications leader for over 20 years, Marie has worked with hundreds of independent financial advisors to strengthen their business identities, improve public communications, and realize their company goals. She's been profiled in *Investment Advisor* magazine and is a regular columnist for MorningstarAdvisor.com. A highly rated speaker, Marie presented her signature "Marketing Muscle Workshop" at Success Forum 2003, the national conference hosted by the Financial Planning Association. In 2004 she again has a full schedule of speeches, workshops, and client business-building projects.

As Sheryl's personal publicist and writing partner, Marie has provided strategic guidance and hands-on assistance to ensure that the Garrett message is both accurate and widely recognized. Her creative writing talent and organizational skills are apparent in this book.

"Working with Marie is empowering. Her ability to see the big picture, manage all the details and work doggedly toward the desired end result makes Marie's partnership a tremendous asset. I valued working with her on *Garrett's Guide to Financial Planning* (National Underwriter Company, November 2002). In addition, her creative writing, editing and research abilities proved vital in completing this book, and I am pleased that she's the person who will be guiding the grassroots nationwide campaign for *Just Give Me the Answer$,*" says Sheryl.

Marie also functions as the marketing communications coach for The Garrett Planning Network's members. She and her business team provide tools, templates, and advice on how to articulate their core business values and unique service offerings. An essential contributor to the network's growing success, she hosts virtual discussions, leads monthly teleconferences, and produces numerous training courses for the nation's premier network of hourly, fee-only planners.

"My relationship with The Garrett Planning Network goes back to 1998 when my husband and I determined that we would benefit from some professional financial advice. We'd been do-it-yourselfers and had done a pretty good job managing on our own, but planning for a 401(k) rollover and a block of stock options concerned us," explains Marie. "We were referred to Sheryl Garrett by a family member, and engaged her services. Even though I'd been working within the financial services industry for a dozen years, we were unaware of the option to receive fee-only, hourly advice. But paying a financial planner a professional hourly fee, just like we did our CPA or our attorney, made perfect sense to us.

"We were extremely pleased when we did the math and compared what we would have paid in commissions and/or asset management fees to another type of financial advisor. Since I've experienced first hand the benefits of working with an independent, objective professional on an as-needed basis, it gives me a real sense of purpose helping Sheryl and the growing Garrett Planning Network spread the word about this cost-effective, valuable service."

Visit http://www.ImpactCommunications.org for more information about Marie Swift, her clients, and her business team.

ABOUT THE CONTRIBUTORS

The following pages provide a thumbnail sketch of the book's contributors. There are 75 financial planners listed. As members of The Garrett Planning Network, Inc., all of these professionals offer their services on an hourly, as-needed basis. Please contact these planners directly should you wish to discuss a possible client/advisor engagement, educational workshop, or media interview.

In addition, there are scores of The Garrett Planning Network members who were unable to contribute to this book. You will find a comprehensive listing of all network members, including individual professional profile pages, on the "Find a Planner Map" at http://www.GarrettPlanningNetwork.com. The site also features educational articles, financial calculators, a recommended reading list, and many other valuable resources. The "Find a Planner" feature is fun and easy to use. You may browse member listings by geographic region and state, read about the advisors, and contact one or more of them if desired.

Larry Ayers, CFP®
Ayers Financial Advisors, LLC
Greenville, SC
www.AyersFeeOnly.com

Thirty plus years of providing sound financial advice to help individuals and families meet their financial goals.

Glenn Bishop, CMA, MBA
GA Bishop and Associates, LLC
Carrollton, TX
www.gabishopandassociates.com

Empowering clients by providing unbiased financial advice and coaching to all, as well as financial analysis for divorcing parties.

Jim Blankenship, ChFC, CCPS
Blankenship Financial Planning, Ltd.
New Berlin, IL
www.BFPonline.com

"The Hometown Advisor." Providing down-to-earth financial advice to the common man.

C. Bradley Bond, CFP®, CFA
C. B. Bond Financial Planning, Inc.
Murrysville, PA
www.cbbondfinancialplanning.com

Independent, objective financial consultation for individuals and families.

Bruce E. Brinkman, CFP®
Brinkman Financial Partners
Rockford, IL
www.brinkmanfinancial.com

Personal financial coaching and investment advice for people from all walks of life who want professional, independent guidance to reach their life goals.

Mary A. Brooks, CFP®
Brooks Financial Planning
Colorado Springs, CO
www.BrooksFinancialPlanning.com

The best way to forecast your financial future is to create it, and while we cannot predict, we can prepare.

Timothy B. Brown, MBA, CFA®
Brown Wealth Management, LLC
Woodbury, MN
www.BrownWealth.com

Your Financial Dreams, Our Solutions. Providing fee-only financial planning and investment advice in the Twin Cities area.

Robert Bubnovich, CFP®
Rio Financial Advisors
Irvine, CA
www.riofinancialadvisors.com

Guiding you through the financial jungle. Helping you make and implement the best financial decisions possible.

Carol Burroughs
Forward Financial Planning
Normal, IL
www.Welookforward.com

Creating financial confidence.

John Carrig, CFP®, CFA®
Gold Coast Financial Planning
Deerfield Beach, FL
www.goldcoastfinancialplanning.com

Helping clients Realize and Preserve the Good Life through independent, fee-only financial advice.

Rich Chambers, CFP®
Investor's Capital Management
Menlo Park, CA
www.feesonly.com

Investor's Capital Management helps clients achieve financial peace of mind with a fee-only program that delivers long-term financial security.

Carolanne M. Chavanne, CFP®
Care Financial Planning
Laguna Niguel, CA
www.CareFinancialPlanning.com

Dedicated to providing our clients with objective, competent financial and goal planning services in a trustworthy and caring environment.

James H. Christie, CFP®
Freedom Financial Planning
Bridgewater, NJ
www.FreedomFinancialPlanning.com

Empowering clients with Financial Freedom through independent and objective personal financial advice.

S. Andy Claybrook, CPA/PFS, CFP®
Fee-Only Financial Solutions, PC
Franklin, TN
saccpa@att.net

Providing fully independent, objective and professional financial planning and investment advisory services to clients in Tennessee and neighboring states.

Bryan D. Clintsman, CFP®
Clintsman Financial Planning
Southlake, TX
www.ClintsmanFinancialPlanning.com

Bryan has over 16 years of experience helping families achieve balance, priorities, and a plan to secure their financial future.

Neil P. Collins, CFP®
Collins Financial Advisors
Melrose, MA
www.CollinsFinancialAdvisors.com

Helping individuals, families and small businesses plan and implement successful financial futures.

Sheri Iannetta Cupo, CFP®
Sage Advisory Group, LLC
Morristown, NJ
www.sageadvisorygroup.com

SAGE is an independent firm that specializes in providing fee-only financial planning services to individuals & small businesses on an hourly, as-needed basis.

Rosemary O. Danielson, CFP®
Balanced Financial Planning
Mission, KS
www.bfplanning.com

Helping our clients develop a financial plan to balance their finances and life style today with meeting their financial goals for the future.

David R. DeLeeuw, MBA, CFS
Chartwell Financial Management, Inc.
Kalamazoo, MI
www.chartwellfm.com

"Working for our clients, not commissions."

Helen T. deLone, Ed.D., CFP®
DeLone Financial Solutions
Burlington, MA
www.delonefinancialsolutions.com

Comprehensive financial planning and/or personalized advice for individuals, families and small businesses on an hourly, as-needed basis.

Kathy Dollard, CFP®, MBA
Nashoba Financial Planning
Boxborough, MA
www.nashobafinancialplanning.com

I help clients make sense of their dollars through objective, comprehensive, cost-effective financial planning and investment advice.

Ken Downer, CFP®, CPA
IHS Financial Planning, Inc.
Prior Lake, MN
www.IHSplanning.com

Helping clients face their financial future with confidence.

Phil Dyer, CFP®
Dyer Financial Advisory
Timonium, MD
www.pdfinancial.com

The vision to guide you to Financial Freedom.

Mahlon Edwards, AAMS
Mahlon R. Edwards Financial Planning & Investment Strategies
Las Vegas, NV
www.myfee-onlyplanner.com

Extraordinary Financial Strategies for Everyday Life.

Rick Epple, CFP®
Epple Financial Advisors
Minnetrista, MN
www.EppleFinancialAdvisors.com

Empowering clients through independent and objective personal financial advice.

Suzanne D. Fails, CPA, CFP®
Roberts & Fails, PC
Stafford, TX
www.RobertsAndFails.com

Building brighter futures with financial planning and tax advice for everyday life.

Eileen S. Freiburger, CFP®
ESF Planning Group, Inc.
El Segundo, CA
www.ESFPlanning.com

Investment Advisor with over 20 years of industry experience who prefers to encourage clients to "do it themselves" by providing objective feedback for self-implementers.

Deidra Fulton, CPCU
Fulton Financial Planning, Inc.
Plano, TX
www.FultonFinancialPlanning.com

Guiding clients along the path to a brighter financial future through professional, independent financial planning and advice.

Randy Gardner, JD, MBA, CPA, CFP®
Gardner Financial Planning, Inc.
Lawrence, KS
rgpfp@aol.com

Teaching individuals to live within their means while accomplishing their financial and personal goals.

Mary Lacey Gibson, CFP®
MLG Financial Planning
San Juan Batista, CA
www.mlgFinancialPlanning.com

Professional financial guidance for the future you deserve. Client centered goals approach to financial planning and education.

John Goddard
Goddard Financial Planning, Inc.
Seattle, WA
www.GoddardFinancialPlanning.com

Dollars and Sense for Everyday life.

Timothy M. Hayes, CCPS
Landmark Financial Advisory Services, LLC
Pittsford (Rochester), NY
www.landmarkfas.com

Helping individuals and families from all walks of life to achieve their most cherished financial objectives.

Sherry Hinrichs
Attain It Financial Planning
Santa Rosa, CA
www.AttainItFP.com

Assisting you to attain your important financial goals.

Bonnie A. Hughes, CFP®
A & H Financial Planning and Education, Inc.
Rome, GA
www.ashbyandhughes.com

A & H utilizes pure financial planning in our Rome office, in our virtual office, or in your home. Tax, planning, and cost analysis since 1981.

Karen R. Keatley, MBA, CFA®, CFP®
K Squared Financial Planning
Charlotte, NC
K_Squared@bellsouth.net

Whether your objective is to achieve financial security or maintain your prosperity, Karen can tailor her services to match your goals and individual situation.

Geleg Kyarsip, CFP®
Kyarsip Financial Advisors
Seattle, WA
www.kyarsipfinancialadvisors.com

Partners in Planning Your Financial Future. No Commissions, No Conflicts, Fee Only.

Theresa Leister, MBA, CFP®, CMFC®, RFC
Financial Advisory Services
New York, NY
FinancialAdvc@aol.com

With vision and planning, possibilities are almost infinite.

Buz Livingston
Livingston Financial Network
Santa Rosa Beach, FL
www.livingstonfinancialnetwork.com

Like a lighthouse to a ship at sea we help our clients reach a secure financial harbor.

Jim Ludwick, CFP®
MainStreet Financial Planning
Odenton, MD
www.MainStreetPlanning.com

Enabling clients to make prudent and thoughtful financial decisions using independent and objective personal financial advice.

Stephen R. Lyddon, CFP®
Opine Financial Advisors
Kansas City, MO
www.OpineFinancialAdvisors.com

Advising families and individuals on their tax and financial affairs since 1992.

Warren F. McIntyre, CFP®
VisionQuest Financial Planning LLC
Troy, MI
www.VisionQuestFinancialPlanning.com

Helping clients achieve their lifestyle goals by providing independent, objective financial advice. Your vision is our mission!

Kristine A. McKinley, CPA, CFP®
Beacon Financial Advisors, LLC
Lee's Summit, MO
www.beacon-advisor.com

Providing professional, personalized financial and tax advice to help you make the best decisions possible.

Martin Mesecke, CFP®
Self Worth Financial Planning
Dallas, TX
www.selfworthfp.com

Enhancing clients personal Self Worth through independent, objective, fee-only personal financial advice.

Colleen M. Miller, CPA, JD, CFP®
Finance by Design, Inc.
Windsor, CO
www.financebydesign.com

Helping clients achieve financial success through independent thinking and objective advice.

Sher S. Miller, CPA
Sher Miller Financial Services
Dallas, TX
www.shermiller.com

Helping our clients achieve a brighter future.

Glenda K. Moehlenpah, CPA, CFP®
Financial Bridges
San Diego, CA
www.FinancialBridges.com

Connecting You to Where You Want to Be.

Jason M. Morley, CPA
Morley Financial Planning
Bohemia, NY
www.MorleyFinancial.com

Providing clients the education and empowerment to make a change today for a better tomorrow.

Connie K. Newby CPA/PFS, CFP®
Newby and Streck, L.L.P.
Greensboro, NC
nscpa@bellsouth.net

Partnering with clients so they find confidence, order and peace of mind in their personal financial world.

Karen Norman, CFP®
Norman Financial Planning, Inc.
Troy, MI
www.NormanFinancial.com

"Guiding your financial future"—providing professional, objective financial advice tailored to your needs.

Bob Nusbaum, MBA
Middle America Planning
New York, NY
www.MiddleAmericaPlanning.com

Providing professional financial advice to everyday Americans through hourly, as-needed financial planning.

James J. Pasztor Jr., CFP®
Pasztor & Associates
Greensboro, NC
www.pasztor.com

Fee-only financial education and planning.

John Pochodylo, CFP®
Dynamic Financial Planning
Phoenix, AZ
www.DynamicFinancialPlanning.net

Fee-only financial planning and advice on an hourly, as-needed basis.

Ed Powell, CFP®
Powell Financial Advisors
Columbia, SC
www.PowellFinancialAdvisors.com

Helping Americans reach their financial goals through independent, objective personal financial advice.

P. Pauline Price
Northdale Financial Planning
Bronx, NY
www.fp.northdalefinancial.com

Northdale Financial Planning is dedicated to helping people manage their finances so that they can achieve their dreams.

Eric Rabbanian, CFP®, JD, MBA
Rabbanian Financial Planning, Inc.
Austin, TX
www.rfpi.net

We educate and help couples and individuals match their fnancial actions and resources with their personal goals, such as providing a top-notch education for their children or enjoying financial independence by a certain age.

Marjorie B. Randles EA, CFP®
The Practical Planner LLC
Argyle, NY
www.ThePracticalPlanner.com

The Financial Farmer—Helps you grow and care for your financial crops through all the seasons of your life.

Ianka T. Rando, CFP®
BG Financial Planning
Plaistow, NH
www.PlanningMadeEasy.com

Helping clients achieve their dreams through affordable and objective professional financial advice.

William L. Rodau, MS, MBA, CFP®
Creative Financial Services, Inc.
Sussex, WI
www.imFeeOnly.com

Providing mature, competent and objective fee-only advice and planning in partnership with my clients, I empower them to fulfill their lifestyle goals.

Alan M. Schapire, CFP®, CPA/PFS
Libra Financial Planning
Media, PA
www.LibraFinancialPlanning.com

"Adding Balance To Your Financial Future" through independent and objective personal financial advice.

Louise A. Schroeder, CFP®
Personal Financial Solutions, Inc.
Stillwater, OK
www.mypersonalfinancialsolutions.com

Providing clients with information and alternatives to help them make informed financial decisions since 1993.

Steven S. Shagrin, JD, CFP®, CRPC, CRC®, CELP
Planning For Life
Youngstown, OH
www.PlanningForLife.info

Helping you explore ways of using your money to "make a life" instead of "your life to make money" through the tools and techniques of Financial Life Planning™.

Mary Ann Sheets-Hanson, CFP®
Planning for Your Life and Legacy
Walnut Creek, CA
masheets@astound.net

Financial counseling through compassionate listening, careful analysis and practical advice.

Todd Shepherd, CPA/PFS, MBA
Shepherd Financial Planning, LLC
Leawood, KS
www.ShepherdFinancialPlanning.com

Providing clients with professional, objective advice to enable them to achieve "peace of mind" in their financial lives.

Brenda L. Sherbine, CPA/PFS
Sherbine Tax & Financial Planning Services
Hamilton, MT
www.sherbineplanning.com

"Building Dreams with Common Sense"

Lee Spadoni, CFP®
Horizon Financial Planning, LLC
Naperville, IL
www.HorizonFP.com

Enabling clients to reach their financial destinations since 1989. What is on your Financial Horizon?

Sherrill J. St. Germain, MBA
New Means Financial Planning
Hollis, NH
www.newmeans.com

Whatever your destination . . . with New Means Financial Planning, you can Plan to Get There.SM

Bob Stowe, CFP®
Stowe Financial Planning, LLC
Plano, TX
www.stowefinancialplanning.com

Serving middle-income and people from all walks of life.

Roger Streit, MBA
Key Financial Solutions, LLC
Montclair, NJ
www.KeyFeeOnly.com

Client-Centered Planning and Advice for Everyday Life.

Jim Taylor, EA, CFP®
A.M.P. Financial Planners, Inc.
Lubbock, TX
www.ampfin@sbcglobal.net

Independent, hourly, as-needed financial planning and advice for the **A**cquisition, **M**anagement and **P**reservation of wealth.

Steve Thalheimer, CFP®
Thalheimer Financial Planning
Silver Spring, MD
www.ThalheimerFinancialPlanning.com

Financial Planning and Advice for Everyday Life™
Hourly, As-Needed, Fee-Only

Bryan M. Totri, CFP®
WellSpring Planning, LLC.
Roswell, GA
www.WellSpringPlanning.com

Providing personal planning solutions since 1989. We can help.

Charles Turner
Turner Financial Planning
Highlands Ranch, CO
www.TurnerFinancialPlanning.com

Helping people achieve financial independence.

Patrick Van Nice, CFP®
Better Life Group
West Des Moines, IA
www.betterlifeplan.com

Life is about change. At Better Life Group we go all-out to help people make successful transitions through those changes.

Timothy A. Vaughn, MBA
LifeSeasons Financial Planning, LLC
Bel Air, MD
www.LifeSeasonsFinancialPlanning.com

Equipping clients to be wise stewards of their resources throughout all seasons of life.

Steven Young, CFP®
Steven Young Financial Planning
Springfield, MO
plannow@direcway.com

Plan for success with independent and objective financial planning.

Index

G

O

P

Q

R

S

X–Y

Share the message!

Bulk discounts
Discounts start at only 10 copies. Save up to 55% off retail price.

Custom publishing
Private label a cover with your organization's name and logo. Or, tailor information to your needs with a custom pamphlet that highlights specific chapters.

Ancillaries
Workshop outlines, videos, and other products are available on select titles.

Dynamic speakers
Engaging authors are available to share their expertise and insight at your event.

Call Dearborn Trade Special Sales at
1-800-245-BOOK (2665)
or e-mail trade@dearborn.com